AWAKE IN ANGELSCAPE

THE SCENIC ROUTE TO THE SACRED SELF

by

Stacie Coller

LSP
DIGITAL

First Edition

Edited by
A.M. Lepri

Formatted and Cover design by:
Linda Daly

ISBN-13: 978-0-9817654-1-9

ISBN-10: 0-9817654-1-6

PUBLISHED BY LSP DIGITAL

www.lspdigital.com

Disclaimer

The suggestions and activities in this book for personal healing and growth are not meant or intended as a substitute for the advice or care of a professional, such as a medical doctor or therapist. The reader is cautioned that the use of the imagination in conjunction with a faith-based spiritual platform can often evoke strong emotions, sensations, or other deep personal experiences. The reader should seek immediate and appropriate care if she or he becomes overwhelmed by the depth of his/her imaginative, emotional, or spiritual experience. The publisher and author expressly disclaim any liability for injury, loss, pain, or suffering resulting from use by the reader of the methods contained within this book.

Do not do these activities while driving, operating heavy machinery, or in any instance where you are required to be fully present and attentive. No claims are made that the activities in this book will diagnose, cure, or prevent disease.

Acknowledgements

To my husband, Richard, for a decade of support in letting me "do my thing", for the loving and fun companionship, and for inviting me to the sacred "Man Room" for NASCAR races on Sunday. I could get mushy and say, "You are my rock and I cherish you", but you hate that stuff, so I'll just skip it (even though it is true). This book would not exist without you.

To my daughter, Becca, for being the best kid I could have possibly imagined. You continue to amaze me every day. No matter what I ever achieve, having *you* is the best contribution I could make to the world. Love and a warm hug and shout out to Dawn and my favorite Canadian Man-Boys (although less like boys every day!).

To my mother, Martha Coller, for creating a family environment where I always knew that I was loved, valued, protected, and respected. The older that I get, the more I realize how rare a gift our family actually was. You and Dad were wonderful parents. Thank you (a million times). A shout out to Oma, my sibs, nieces, and nephews!

To my Focus Group participants, thank you so much for all your valuable feedback and time. You all breathed soul and warmth into the book in a way I could not have imagined. Thank you. A shout out to everyone who did sessions with me on-line or on the phone as part of the early development for *Angelscape* too. Thanks! It all helped to get me to organize my thoughts into a coherent pile.

To Lyn, for your support after my father died, and for many years of productive and synergistic collaboration and friendship. Thank you for all you contributed to my personal healing journey and for helping me to learn how to structure my own divergence. (I never thought I would master the run-on sentence.) We'll always have high-noon in the Valley of Fire. I hope that you like the book--it has your smile.

To Kathy Douglas--I miss you every day. Some of my fondest memories are of doing work with you on my back deck while we got loopy on the energies. You would say, “Why would anyone do drugs when they could do energy work for free?” Indeed! I can sometimes hear your “hee hee” in my mind, along with the curious sounds of can-can dancing. What ARE you doing up there? (Whatever it is, I sure hope you are having a wonderful time.)

To my cousin Eddie and Uncle Philip, for your “atta girl” encouragement and advice. Thanks also to Debby and Art for early support in my decision to write a book.

To my publisher and friend, Linda Daly, for helping to provide me with the sacred space, opportunity, and encouragement to write down this work as a book--and for showing up in perfect time to open a window when everything else looked closed. Thank you Nancy for your editing!

To Sharon, for keeping me company for the whole writing process, working on my wrists and sore you-know-what, sending me cheery gifties to keep my spirits up, for creating the elixirs, *and* for telling Linda that it was time to open the window.

To Pat Hamilton (aka Big Daddy), for walking me down the aisle when my father was too ill to attend my wedding, for being the best Sherpa this side of Tibet, and for being the nittiest nit picker on the block when it came time to proof my manuscript. You’re the best. Thank you.

To Stacie, for drawing the starter images for the first draft of the book, and for the original inspiration to include candles as a dedicated advocacy technique. Also, thank you so much for getting a good author photo out of me--you’re *magic* (and so dewy and fresh). And yes, we have the same name, but we are different people. Honest. We’ve been spotted at the same time and everything.

To all my on-line groups, past and present, and eBay customers around the world for all the learning, growing, exploring, and fun. Thanks to all of you who kept asking me, "When are you going to write a book?" I finally got around to it!

To "Uncle Dick", for my early training in hypnosis and the imagination as a tool, and for the time I spent watching you and my father weave innovation. I guess it all really did make an impression on me. Thank you.

To Stacie (again), Heather (and girls!), Pat (again), Angelique, Jane, and Doug--I am grateful for your friendship, talent, sanity and company. A shout out to Jen and Christi, the Wunderkinds, Bill and Carol, my rock shop buddies, and Terri, Gina, and Angel, part of my cosmic coffee crew. (Maybe I can come off the mountain a little more now that the book is finally done!) A hug and shout out to Cheryl & Crew, and Edna (still hard to say that instead of Mrs. M!).

To Vickie and John, for being the voice of reason when I needed to readjust my own perspective to complete this work. Your advice hit the spot, and I appreciate the back up and support. A howdy shout out to Mrs. B., the kids, the rest of the "Paradise by the Dashboard Lights" crew of Eastern High 1986--Karen, Jenn, Susan, Pam, as well as Janet from Another Planet.

To Natasha Bedingfield, Danielle Brisebois, and Wayne Rodriguez for the song *Unwritten*, which came on the radio/TV at some of the most synchronistic times for me to feel supported and urged forward. *Thanks*. It made a difference when I was scraping bottom.

A personal note from the author . . .

Like most of you, I am no stranger to scouring the internet or store shelves for interesting or helpful books. My methods of selecting have always been largely random and intuitive, but I have often wished that the authors could help make the sorting process a bit easier. Since I am now on the other side of the shelf, I thought it would be dandy to create a simple questionnaire to help you gauge whether or not this book might be helpful to you.

On a Scale of 1-10 (10 being the highest), please answer the following questions:

1. Do you have a strong sense of spiritual faith or a belief in the authenticity of a spiritual reality?
2. Do you believe that your spiritual reality can interact, guide, assist, or intervene in your life if/when that interaction is appropriate?
3. Do you believe that your own free will choices, intention, positive attitude, faith and commitment are critical components of personal success in any area?
4. Do you feel like you have inner work to do for yourself, but feel frustrated in finding a tangible or coherent way to address the process?
5. Are you dreamy, emotionally sensitive, energetically sensitive, or have you been described as "a gentle soul" by others?
6. Are you a person who prays or meditates regularly, or who holds a background conversation with a spiritual reality as part of your inner experience?
7. Do you feel as if you have been positively guided or inspired by your spiritual reality in practical ways in your past?
8. Do you consider yourself artistic, creative, imaginative, right-brained, or eclectic in your thoughts, skills, talents, or abilities?

9. Do you believe that the collective path of humanity improves, even a little, when any individual works for personal and spiritual wholeness?
10. When you ask your inner-guidance whether this book is "for you", is the response you feel strongly positive, such as a sweet tingle, goose bumps, or sense of enthusiasm?

The higher your score is to 100, the more likely that this book will be a valuable tool in your hands. If your score was under 75, I'd recommend that you find another book unless your answer to #10 was between 8-10. I hope this survey has been helpful. Best Wishes.

Love, Light, and Chocolate,

Stacie

Dedication

This book is dedicated to God,
to the memory of my father, Alan Ross Coller,
to the memory of my baby cousin, Joseph Coller,
to the memory of my BFF, "Jammin Janet" Siegfried Beck,
and to the restoration of innocence, optimism, faith, and love
within the heart of the human spirit.

(If you are going to be a dreamer, you might as well dream *big.*)

"I am enough of an artist to draw freely upon my imagination. Imagination is more important than knowledge. Knowledge is limited. Imagination encircles the world."

Albert Einstein

Table of Contents

Preface to a Journey

I had a normal life until about thirteen years ago. Growing up just outside of Philadelphia in an average South Jersey neighborhood, I graduated from East Carolina University at twenty-one with a BA in psychology and a minor in child development and education. I married my college boyfriend and landed a career in day care management. By the time I was twenty-four, I was a director of a child care center with my own child on the way. I stayed home for a couple of years to raise my daughter and then made the career hop to facilitating workshops for day care providers. I certainly thought that I would have a normal suburban life when I grew up. Somehow, I ended up *here* instead. I could probably fill up a whole book on how I ended up from normal to here, but that is for another day. Still, it's probably important to some of you to know more about my journey before you let me take you on yours.

My father was born and raised a nice Jewish boy in New York City. My mother was born a Catholic in Munich, Germany, during World War II. Dad became an educational psychologist and Mom worked in a factory. Despite their widely different cultures and backgrounds, they fell in love and created a family together. My brothers and I were parented under all the warm-fuzzy, self-esteem enhancing child development theories that were all the rage in the early 70's. We had chores, responsibilities, and we were expected to be decent people and to follow the rules of the house. When we didn't follow the rules, we were grounded instead of spanked. They weren't perfect parents and we weren't perfect kids, but as far as families go, I consider myself blessed and lucky to have been born into that one.

My household was not a religious household. My father had a strong Jewish culture surrounding him as he grew up, but for whatever reason, he did not continue that as the head of his own household. The only time we ever attended temple services was when my brother had his Bar Mitzvah ceremony. (My grandfather insisted, under the threat that he did not want to die before seeing it.) We did celebrate some Jewish holidays like Yom Kippur, Hanukah, and Passover; but we also exchanged presents on Christmas Eve, colored Easter eggs, and went trick-or-treating. We *were* the elusive children everyone envied during the holidays.

Other than incidental trips to Friday night service at my friend's Catholic Church (her parents dropped us off at the skating rink after the service), I had very little exposure to organized religion or spirituality. We were, however, a multi-culturally friendly family. It was common for me to see a mixture of religions, cultures, and ideas as part of a normal backdrop of my life. No one talked about angels as far as I remember. No one talked about God unless it was a holiday. Celebrating religious holidays seemed more for tradition than to cultivate spirituality. All that aside, my parents were kind, compassionate, and fair-minded people. They taught those ideals without the mooring of a strong religious background.

I did have a few paranormal experiences as I was growing up. I saw a couple of ghosts and had one or two precognitive dreams--nothing too outrageous. Nevertheless, those brief moments of weirdness did introduce me to the concept of a concurrent spiritual reality just out of normal sight. Even though my experiences scared me, I also found them undeniably riveting. I would have gotten a degree in parapsychology if I had seen any hope that I could do that as a career and actually pay bills after college. Instead, I followed my father's footsteps into psychology and early childhood education. It seemed a more reasonable choice.

I was close with both of my parents, but my father and I were more similar in temperament. My mom was the perfect feisty counterpoint to our general calm. Dad was a very eclectic and out-of-the-box thinker. He had one of those divergently divergent minds (redundancy intended). He saw patterns and relationships between things that others missed and was a dog-with-a-bone researcher. I remember always being interested in what kind of work my father was into and I was often his faithful sidekick.

When I was a teenager, my dad became involved in research and development that dealt with measuring imagination. It was used to predict the probability of a person persisting in tasks related to post-hypnotic suggestions or other assigned work. The better and more vivid the imagination, the more likely someone would persist until the goal was achieved. People with a hazy grasp on their goal often quit trying before they succeeded. Those people needed more encouragement and assistance to endure and persist in the steps necessary to complete their goals.

His research partner was a hypnotherapy instructor and the work was developed using that framework. I was fifteen years old when I completed my beginners' hypnotherapy certification (which made me all sorts of fun at sleep over parties). I was nineteen when I completed my advanced hypnotherapy internship certification (which made me all sorts of fun at college parties). I learned about the use of imagination and altered states of consciousness when most people my age were watching music videos. I chucked what I learned into the "bigger things are going on" file that I already had in my mind and kept on walking. I honestly did not anticipate that there would eventually be a purpose for that growing file.

So what happened? How did I go from facilitating and writing workshops about child development to writing books about cooperative spiritual energy work? Life happened. Well, more specifically, a *fight* for life happened. In 1995, when I was twenty-six years old, my father was diagnosed with cancer. It was a funky kind of cancer that had metastasized from the cartilage in his knee into his lungs. He was given six months to two years to live. The moment before I got that phone call was probably the last normal second of my life.

True to my father's love of research and problem solving, we hit the books like a couple of speed-readers on espresso. I probably have spent enough hours researching and cross-referencing alternative cancer therapies to have gotten a degree somewhere. I was willing to look anywhere I needed to look to find something--anything that might make a difference for him. I stumbled into the realm of energy work during my search to find something helpful. I began with a healing modality called Reiki (ray-key). It is a form of hands-on-healing. I took a session for myself to try it out before taking the classes to become a practitioner. It seemed exciting to me. I could feel the movement of the energy very clearly. It was warm and tingly and it made me feel deeply relaxed. I immediately took the training classes to become a practitioner so that I could work on my father.

The training program for Reiki involved receiving a series of *attunements*. The attunements were used as a way to clear out the energetic channels of a person's system, like a plumber would snake clogged pipes in a house. The energy was described as *Universal* (rei) *Life Force* (ki). This concept is essentially the same as the Chinese concept of *Chi*; such as in the practice of Tai Chi. The main difference is that a Reiki practitioner volunteers to be the plumbing through which the energy flows to get where it is needed. I learned that Reiki could be used to direct universal energy to those who were depleted of it, such as with illness. Bingo. I had a father who was definitely feeling depleted and who wasn't about to get up and do Tai Chi on his own. At least it was something new to bring to the table. There wasn't time to be picky.

Dad took my overtures in Reiki like a trooper, though it was clear that he cast a doubtful eye in its direction. His tossed Reiki into the same category as hypnotherapy; just another tool to convince the brain that something was possible. He called the heat he felt through my hands a "hyperthermogenic hallucination", which of course is not even a real term, and I told him so! Still, to his credit, he let me do my thing. I think he knew that I was in desperate need of not feeling like a helpless observer. He knew his illness was hard on me too, and he was a good papa.

As time passed, he did eventually conclude that the Reiki helped relieve some pain and relaxed him. Other than pain and anxiety relief, I have no idea if the Reiki helped with his longer than expected life span. I can say that the time I spent doing Reiki work for him wasn't wasted. They were moments spent in extreme awareness of the preciousness of life. We didn't have to talk about it; I just had to put my hand where it hurt and let the energies run. It was elegant and simple.

I might have viewed my experiencc with Reiki as a temporary sojourn into alternative healing, but it had an unintended effect that was impossible to ignore. Over the course of a year, it literally blew open my psychic centers and threw me into some kind of rapid consciousness expansion. I can guarantee you that I didn't see that coming! The Reiki attunements apparently cleared my energy channels a little too well! I went through a very uncomfortable time where I felt like I was on a triple dose of cold medicine every waking moment. I went to work one day at the university, after having a strong expansive shift over the weekend--cured two headaches and had contact with two different co-worker's dead relatives. I could barely finish a sentence because of all the movement in the air around me. *Crazy.*

It was simultaneously miraculous and bone chillingly terrifying. I mean, really. I was at *work.* A populated university office building is hardly the place to be having that kind of high strangeness. It was as if the boundaries that normally separated me from everything else had just melted away. The backdrop of the room was no longer a collection of separate individuals and things; it became a larger interplay of brisk action that spilled over into the spaces in-between. I was not on any substances of any kind and I was born too late in the 60's to claim an acid flashback. No one snuck peyote into my oatmeal. Whatever happened to me was generated from within. I just had no idea that the term "in the blink of an eye" was literal. Imagine my surprise.

I might have gone to a psychologist to help cope, but I knew there was no possibility of getting out of there without being labeled as schizophrenic, delusional, or psychotic. (Do you know that there is no category in the diagnostic mental health materials that even *allows for the possibility* of an authentic mystic or spiritual experience?) I had a background in psychology myself and knew there was no history of mental illness in my family. Plus, my experiences mostly involved others who witnessed the phenomena; some who considered me the next best thing to aspirin. I knew it wasn't my imagination, and for better or worse, I felt I needed to learn how to cope with it on my own.

What the heck do you do then? Where do you go? What do you do? I was a newly separated young woman who was juggling a toddler, a career, a dying father, and a flaming case of spiritual expansion that didn't give a flying fig *what* it inconvenienced. It was an extraordinarily difficult time. I muddled through as well as I could and eventually quit my job, got remarried, and moved to Asheville, North Carolina. I reoriented to the expanding perspective by placing myself in contact with others who shared the same or similar strangeness. Normal is relative to the company you keep--and Asheville is dripping with people that are my kind of normal.

My father died March 22, 2000--a solid five-year fight. I was devastated. I thought I would be able to interact with him with my newly opened senses and awareness, but that was *not* the case. I learned the hard lesson that spiritual or clairvoyant gifts do not necessarily manifest in ways that you wish they would, or think they would. They are what they are. You either accept them and move forward, or stamp your feet like a petulant child who wants something better. Dad did manage to "send me an email" months later. My printer spontaneously spit out a happy face and heart symbol one day. It was not exactly Western Union, but you take what you can get.

With my father gone, I refocused the point of my explorations. My online business, which I started once I moved to Asheville, was selling Reiki friendly supplies. It put me into contact with a constant parade of other like-minded people. I made one friend in particular, Lyn, who was a wonderful counterpoint to me. She was organized, structured and well grounded--all the things that I decidedly wasn't. Our process of batting things back and forth, from divergent/intuitive to convergent/logical, was extremely productive for many years. It was through our early collaboration that I developed the skills to create conceptual tools, clarify intention, develop energy work processes, and even to identify what things seemed most important to address in a healing process. I absolutely did not create the work in *Angelscape* in a vacuum. There was a vigorous exchange of innovation and refinement with many people over many years for me to conceive of this book.

The use of tools and spiritual helpers permeates the *Angelscape* work. My own journey with tools and spiritual helpers followed a path of development that reminds me of child development. For example, a child moves through stages of development in little steps of greater understanding through play and practice. S/he manipulates concrete objects before making abstract leaps in thought. Playing with wooden blocks isn't just busy work to a child, it teaches spatial relationships, social skills, problem solving, motor skills, and so on. The pathways created in the brain from playing with those wooden blocks are some of the same pathways that math skills travel upon later. Play and exploration are critical steps to higher functioning because you see what works and what doesn't. You also develop the logic and problem solving skills to make the sort between the two. However, in the same way that playing creates new skills, if a child doesn't eventually move to more complex stimulation that challenges him/her, s/he fails to progress.

Spiritual development, if engaged fresh and without a set religious framework, seems to be a constant progression of resolving a challenge/question that updates what you thought was true, to something *more* true. Sometimes the new replaces the old and sometimes it just expands upon it. My concrete "toys" were my rocks and as many spiritual guides as I could gather. Heck, I even talked to my rocks as if they *were* spiritual guides. The rocks were an effective way to play and explore and gave me something to touch and hold onto while sorting out information. The multitude of spiritual helpers gave me a stage and players to maintain a dialog with my spiritual reality. Eventually, when I realized I was really just playing my way through novel experiences, I moved my focus to purely conceptual tools and a God-specific spiritual framework.

I have to admit, however, I still like my rocks, especially when I need to comfort myself. They are like my father's ratty old vest coat that I wear when I need a hug from him. Sometimes having something solid to touch is important. If you want to hold a rock and it helps you to feel better, hold a rock. We may need help to function in a spiritual or energetic reality, but since we can't know when actual interaction picks up from our own imaginations, it is best to assume that we are *just playing.* We play, however, with practical purpose and--just maybe--the process itself allows for the occasional brush with authenticity. We simply must hold loosely to it like a butterfly that lands unexpectedly upon our hands. Truly blessed and divine moments have a *feel* to them, not a running ticker on the bottom of a screen that explains them. To me, those moments feel like everything finally makes sense, every little detail, every little nuance, and that everything is also *okay*. Of course, the butterfly flies away, and typical human confusion settles back in, but the experience itself can change you for the better if you let it. That is a precious gift.

So, in a nutshell (nut possibly being the operative word), I essentially learned about functioning in a spiritual landscape by playing--and sometimes--by stumbling, fumbling, and falling down. Some of it was fun and some of it was decidedly *not*. Some of it was graceful and inspired, and some of it felt like screaming down a mountainside on a runaway bobsled at midnight. Nevertheless, every baby step led to a new understanding or experience. Everything mattered--the good, the bad, the silly, and *especially* the lessons that left me in an emotional heap. Apparently, emotional crisis is a better accelerant in growth than comfort. I used to joke that someone should have warned me about that little fact in advance of committing to this path. So consider yourself warned: *Comfort is not the goal of a spiritual journey, growth is.* Growth is sometimes a big pain in the rump when it pushes you into another zip code from your typical "feeling groovy" comfort zone. Luckily, there seems to be pauses between the real screamers. And please, whatever you do, do *not* say, "Nothing can surprise me anymore." Just trust me on that one. No matter how high your "weird ceiling" is--you can *always* be thrown right through it.

Sometimes you just have to go loose, ride the bobsled down the mountainside, and have faith that you will still be in one piece when the dust settles. Sometimes, that is all you *can* do. I basically took one-step at a time and decided to have faith that the light at the end of the tunnel was something more like God than a train. *That* is how I got from normal to here. I was an ordinary young woman who was looking for a way to save her father's life. Instead, I found myself deep in the heart of a vast unknown territory without a map or instruction manual. I managed to jot down the discoveries and a rough map for others, just in case it might be helpful. Of course, being lost can often be the best way to learn your way around. If you have a decade to spare, and don't mind extreme mountain sports, you can certainly figure it out on your own. There is nothing special about me except for the decision I made not to run screaming from the building. And like the bumper sticker says, "You don't *have* to be crazy to work here, but it *does* help."

My Country

Thoughts and dust scatter equally as well.
They must be contained and swept together,
Or you have a mess.
My emotions are raw and hungry.
My heart is exposed and looking through glass.
The glass is not rosy, as it was when I was younger.
It is dusty with neglect, refusal, denial--
The space dark and musty.
Wanting, wanting, wanting--*something*.
Knowing without knowing why or what,
Feeling without touching, a sixth sense.
Like a whisper upon waking that you cannot capture,
Or the wind whipping through your hair on a balmy day--
The cloud burst just moments from exploding.
The calm before-- before *what*?
I peer into the glass. I *have* to look.
Into life. Into death. Into myself.
I see all the world from the inside out.
The clouds dump their load--inevitably, the sun shines again,
But the ground stays moist, sloppy, and wet.
Fertile ground--but for *what*?
I didn't used to think in metaphor or speak in riddles,
But I am different today than I was yesterday.
I find aspects of myself that are new and uncharted. Untraveled.
I stand in wait with my telescope to see the edge, that I might fall off of it.
Be here monsters? Or unspoiled country--fresh, wild, and free?
Can you be lost and found, or found and then lost?
My burdens, my lessons, my path--*my country*.
It is time to go inside and wander,
Without a map, compass, or guide--
Deep into the Heather and wild flowers,
And in being lost, I will finally learn my way around.

Stacie Heather Coller, 1996

Part 1: Directions to Angelscape

I
Building a Foundation

Awake in Angelscape uses the Mind/Body/Spirit model of healing and wellness. This model takes the view that the self is a system that is multifaceted and interrelated. The facets of the self may function consciously or unconsciously, physically or non-physically, and may simultaneously exit at higher levels of being, such as the human soul. The theory is that when there is a sense of wholeness, or alignment, there is also wellness. When there is a sense of fracture, or misalignment, there is also disease--or at least the fertile ground for disease. The unseen condition of the internal landscape of the self is viewed as the creational ground and underpinning for conditions that become manifest within physical reality. Holistic healing, therefore, recommends that we address both the seen and unseen realities of the self in order to support sustainable wellness.

The Mind and Body

We know more about the body than any other part of the self because it is solid and physical. We can study the human body as a concrete object, having mostly predictable responses. We know how to take care of the human body to keep it running well. We eat fruits and vegetables (organic, of course); we exercise, drink plenty of water, get plenty of sleep, and try not to live next door to a landfill. However, our mental and emotional states *also* contribute to the state of physical wellness. If we are stressed out, our bodies suffer. If we are depressed, our immune systems are depressed too. If we are happy and calm, our bodies flourish. If we feel good, our bodies feel good. These measurable cause and effect relationships are indisputable. What you think and how you feel affects your health. Knowing this is powerful information.

Fixing the physical and material influence on health is relatively easy; stop doing things that are bad, and begin doing the things that are good for you. For the most part, the "good things" are knowable variables that are easily researched and accessed. Fixing the concealed influences, however, is far more complicated. The concealed influences are, by nature, outside of our awareness--and since they are conceptual and unseen, much harder to address in a practical working format, as we can do with the body.

The mind is complicated; it often takes years of talk therapy to uncover the hidden issues that create misalignment in our systems. When we bury our pain, we bury it deeply. This is a survival mechanism of internal protection that prevents overwhelm to system. The concealment of the pain, however, is not an optimal long-term solution. It creates new problems, such as internal misalignment and the influence of unconscious dysfunctional patterns and distortions. The pain keeps on hurting, but it does so by going underground. It exacts influence in subtle and insidious ways--by a constant internal murmur of negativity, doubt, and criticism. It slowly poisons the internal landscape of the self and undermines the confidence you have in your own value and worth.

Scientists and philosophers are still scratching the surface on the nature of human consciousness, the mind, and human potential. These are intangible aspects of who we are. We cannot pull human consciousness under a microscope, but we believe that the mind defines who we are at this level of being, such as our personality complex. The mind also regulates how we learn, remember, process information, and how we come up with personal and shared realities. Our perceptions, beliefs, and biases have everything to do with how we view our world and ourselves--they define what we consider “real”. As we mature, we become more competent at making the sort of what is true and false. However, many of our perceptions are forged in childhood when we are too young to make a good sort. Sometimes these perceptions have nothing to do with intense pain or trauma. Sometimes a conclusion is made during a time of immature cognitive ability that is simply *wrong*. The conclusion, if accepted as true and real, becomes a belief that continues to color how everything is seen, even into adulthood. A large part of fixing hidden influence within the mind is to correct the distorted perceptions that are limiting and dysfunctional and to replace them with perceptions that are positive and adaptive.

The Spirit

The spiritual aspect of the self is the most mysterious. The body is real, we can touch it. The personality is real, even if the structure of it is not, because we can witness and observe it. The spirit is another matter altogether. Spiritual reality is indefinable, theoretical, and subjective. Many people do report witnessing or experiencing a spiritual reality, but anecdotal evidence will never be considered proof. Embracing a spiritual reality requires *faith*. Faith is the belief in something, even when there is no tangible proof. Spiritual faith, while defined in many different ways in practice, is the conviction that we belong to something larger than ourselves and that some benevolent and intelligent force is at the wheel. Most people call this intelligent force *God*. For purposes of this book, I will also call this intelligent force God.

Spirituality gives us a larger context of belongingness. Those of us who define ourselves as "spiritual" tend to be happier, more adaptive to adversity, and feel as though there is a purpose to living. In short, spiritual people live a more satisfied life. Spirituality helps us to thrive and cope through challenges that we face. It helps us to make sense of things that would be too difficult to grasp. It especially helps us to feel that we are not alone, and that we are loved and valued, even when we find it hard to love and value ourselves. In a spiritual reality, even the most awful of us can find nurturing, forgiveness, and unconditional love. That is a powerful message for someone who is hurting. It is a powerful message for anyone.

The spiritual aspect of reality is where we seek the ways that we plug into larger systems and how those systems plug into us. If there is more to humanity than what we see, something wonderful and glorious, the reality of that potential is seated in the spiritual aspects of who we are, or within our souls. For purposes of this book, I call the untapped highest potential of the self, as held by the soul, the *Sacred Self*. The Sacred Self is the person you could be if you were to consciously express the qualities of your higher soul self--who you authentically are at the spiritual level. Since this goal is elusive, the little steps of progress that we make along the continuum matter the most. There is no destination, because as soon as we move to higher levels of functioning, there are always higher levels to go. The only remotely graspable concept is the journey itself--and it is *definitely scenic*.

II
The Work in Angelscape

Fathoming Faith

This work takes on faith that a spiritual reality is authentic, but it does not attempt to define it. I do use some of my own spiritual beliefs in the context of creating this work, but as few as I could possibly manage. I did my best to create a platform that was as religiously neutral as possible, while still harnessing the potent influence of spirituality and deep faith. If you are not a faith-based or faith-friendly person, this is not the book for you. I am not spending any time trying to convince anyone in the authenticity of a spiritual reality. I am not grabbing references from research or data to sway anyone's opinion. I have neither the wisdom nor authority to define what is true about a spiritual reality to anyone else. I do include a suggested reading list at the back of the book for anyone who would like to do some research on the relationship between spirituality and wellbeing.

What you think and believe, and how you Keep Faith, is between you and God. What I *can say* is that if you believe in the authenticity of a spiritual reality, *Angelscape* can be a very powerful tool in the way you conceptualize assistance from that reality. If you *want* to believe, but are not fully invested with faith, I find that the spiritual reality is more than happy to provide all the encouragement you need if you are willing to get out of the way. Do not be surprised that when you reach up to touch a spiritual reality, that it reaches *back* to touch you. Perhaps all we need is the common ground to do so.

Cooperative Spiritual Energy Work

The work done in *Angelscape* is called *Cooperative Spiritual Energy Work.* It means healing work directed toward the intangible parts of the self in cooperation with spiritual assistance. We do not actively work with the physical body at all in this book. (The Journeyer is encouraged to consider physical health protocols with his/her physician if that seems appropriate.) The *Angelscape* work is directed solely to the intangible parts of the self, under the theory that inner wellness is reflected as outer wellness through the interrelation between the facets. The intangible aspects include the mental, emotional and spiritual parts of the self, which are often described as having a purely energetic substance or fabric. Because they are considered purely energetic in nature, the work directed to bring healing shifts within this fabric is called "energy work". The energy work in *Angelscape* seeks to bring healing and alignment to these parts of the self to improve the condition of the inner landscape. In the Mind/Body/Spirit model of healing, this should theoretically improve the outer landscape as well.

The work is initiated by providing a platform, conceptual tools, and a logical progression of healing activities that can be facilitated within the imagination. *Angelscape* does not rely upon the laws of physical reality in order to function. We can create as many tools as we need in order to conceptualize getting the job done. In addition, because a strong spiritual element is built into the work, the success of the work is not dependant only on ourselves. It does require us to show up and collaborate with a spiritual reality, but it does not require that we understand the unknown without oversight.

Angelscape and Conceptual Tools

Angelscape is a conceptual and working platform that allows us to put things that we cannot see and touch into a concrete format. It is an imaginary landscape that you fill with your favorite spiritual figures, also called Divine Advocates. The Divine Advocates bring you along a progression of activities, which make healing processes more relatable, believable, and experiential. *Everything* in *Angelscape* is some kind of conceptual tool; the helpers, the activities, the tools in the activities, and the processes themselves. Most of the tools have been fashioned after things that are easy to imagine that use skills that are relatively easy to master. The tools and activities lend themselves well to physical props or actual activities to make visualization easier.

Your Imagination

We have a hard time manipulating variables that we cannot see or touch. The only solution is to create strategies in which we can make the variables more solid, even if just in our imagination. The mind does not make a heavy distinction between what is actually experienced and what is imagined. The cascade of effects seems to be the same within the body whether you are sitting on a beach or imagining that you are sitting on a beach. The stress cascade seems to be the same if you are experiencing a stressful situation or just worrying about one. The actual experience seems to have more *intensity*, but the chain of events, or the ripple in the pond, seems to be identical. The more vivid the experience, the more intensity it seems to register.

Your imagination is the key to *Angelscape* because the imagination is the only place where we can stand shoulder-to-shoulder with our spiritual reality while we are still physical beings. It is the only place where we can create tools and conceptual constructs that symbolize healing processes that we cannot access or initiate any other way. If we can create and initiate healing experiences within our imaginations, especially deeply moving ones, we can create the positive cascade of effects that are along the continuum of a real experience. If we can imagine being healed and whole, we toss another pebble into the pond that cascades the message of wellness and wholeness within us.

If we can imagine it, our minds may accept that it is true. If our minds believe something is true, the rest of the system tends to follow. This is like the placebo effect, the phenomena in which the mind believes it is possible that it is getting an actual medicine, and so heals itself under that expectation. The body simply responds to what the mind believes. Instead of controlling *against* the placebo effect, healing work using the imagination *depends* on it--or whatever the process is that governs it. There is significant potential within the human system to be self-healing. Your imagination is the key to unlock that potential.

The work is initiated in *Angelscape* through guided imagery and guided meditation. The visualization for the environments will be developed before you get to the actual activities. Guided imagery and meditation go hand and hand with meditative states of consciousness. There are many terms to describe this level of consciousness, but simply, it is a state of being where the conscious mind is less active and the subconscious mind steps a little closer to the front. It is usually experienced as a peaceful and calm state of being. Receptivity to the experience of healing is most open in this state. Intuition, and the ability to visualize, are also enhanced and opened as your logical conscious mind takes a back seat. In the relaxed state, there is a greater chance of the imagined healing work being accepted as true. Induction, a term used in hypnosis that means transition into the meditative state, is built into the journey as the first activity you do each time you visit *Angelscape*.

The Healing Journey

There are ten activity sections in this book. Each section contains one Direct Route (DR) activity and two Scenic Route (SR) activities. They are set up as a logical progression of events that continue to build and expand upon the activities that precede it. The activities generally fall into one or more of four main categories of healing; cleansing, fortifying, rectifying, and empowering. The Journeyer follows the step-by-step guided meditation instructions, and allows him/herself to experience the scene as vividly as possible. A few basic skills and protocols are used throughout the journey and kept consistent so that the Journeyer has a quick sense of work competency.

Cleansing energetic congestion from the system is seen as one of the largest tasks of the work. The goal of cleansing is to free the system from stagnant energetic and emotional waste. Imagine all of the times that you wanted to cry, but did not. The emotional charge does not go away, but seems rather to be swept under some unseen layer of the self, like a lumpy throw rug we have to ignore. It would be wise to purge the system of this kind of accumulated congestion before we do anything else. The activities in the book that are cleansing specific are used throughout the course of the formatted journey. This is done because each new healing activity can uncover a new layer of congestion that needs to be purged.

The fortifying activities provide system safety, shielding, and buffering to the intangible layers of the self. This includes creating a comfort zone of spiritual oversight and assistance, as well as limiting the impact and flow of inappropriate influence from within or outside of your system. Fortification also means building up the strength and integrity of the fabric of the system, such that your stability is improved, even under situations of distress. It is difficult to make progress if you are wobbling and unable to correct that wobble.

Rectification is the process of correcting misalignments, distortion, and damage from the fabric of the system. Rectification is probably what most people mean when they use the term "healing", although the process of healing is much more involved than just rectifying what has gone amiss. In this book, we use a conceptual vision of the Sacred Self as a template to tag and correct whatever has moved away from that ideal blueprint of the self. You are brought through activities that allow you to visualize the release and rectification of distortions from your Sacred Self patterns, or the pure template of who you are through God.

The empowering based activities are those that seek to usher in higher functioning after cleansing, fortification, and rectification processes have been initiated. The activities may encourage expressing the Sacred Self, identifying special skills and abilities, advocacy work for larger systems, and highlighting a continuing path that supports you to live a better and more fulfilling life. These activities are designed to provide the Journeyer with lasting tools, protocols, and work platforms that cultivate purpose, authentic value, and self-confidence.

All of the activities in the book seek to establish a meaningful interaction between the self and a spiritual reality. As you move forward in the journey, the rapport you cultivate with your selected Divine Advocates will grow and expand. You will learn to listen to inner prompts and guidance, as well as to relax into the experience as it unfolds before you. Each new activity provides an opportunity for you to connect more intensely to your perceived assistance. This allows you to do the work while feeling supported and nurtured. *Angelscape* is like a gigantic toolbox that you can continue to use with spiritual helpers that you can continue to imagine.

The Alignment of Free Will and Divine Will

We seem to be on the verge of a collective insight that perhaps our personal will, also called free will, can influence both our inner and outer realities. What we think and feel may not just be bound up within our own systems, as if we live in a vacuum, but it may spill over into the larger systems of which we are a part. Our free will, or intention, may well be a voice in the communal landscape of unfolding possibilities. Just as there are intangible aspects of the self, perhaps there are also intangible aspects of creation that can be influenced by the shared inner landscape of humanity. In this context, personal healing would not just be a personal triumph--it would pay itself forward. It could be that we discover that "saving the world" has much more to do with "saving ourselves" than placing our attention outside of ourselves to make a difference.

Of course, our personal free will is only part of the equation. If we believe in the reality of a larger intelligent force, or God, than we ought to do our best to bring what we want and desire into alignment with that greater wisdom. Just because we *can* influence our outer reality, does not mean we always *should*, or that we necessarily do it well. Free will means that we are free to be "out of alignment" with Divine Will, if that is what we care to do. The consequences? Probably not so free. Many books about influencing reality with intention (positive thinking, manifestation, and so on) skip the step of bringing one's wishes into alignment with Divine Will. The message seems to be, "So long as it feels good and does not hurt anyone, go ahead and do it." The flaw in that logic is the assumption that we are spiritually mature enough to make the distinction of what is in the highest good or not.

We have only the tiniest view of the larger picture. How can we possibly presume to understand how one event influences another, or if the influence five ripples away may cause more harm than good just because we *think* it is good? A toddler, if allowed to create a life that *he* considered good, might sit in front of cartoons all day, eating nothing but candy and sugar, while covered in his own poo. Toddlers have parents for a reason. They do not have the wisdom or maturity to fully self-govern in the world. They need oversight. In my opinion, no matter how old we become, *the spiritual reality is so unknown to us that we can only ever be children in it.* Knowing that is also powerful information. In *Angelscape*, we request oversight and alignment with Divine Will *voluntarily*. That does not mean that we abandon our personal free will, but we move forward with the self-awareness that we are as if children in the spiritual realm.

About the Cooperative Contract

The overall intentions of the journey through *Angelscape* are detailed in a Cooperative Contract, which we imagine signing over to God. The use of clear intention is highlighted very strongly in this work. Every aspect of *Angelscape* is clearly defined and structured in such a way that God/Divine Will has editing and oversight authority over absolutely everything. The purpose of the Cooperative Contract and the listed intentions is to place the work and ourselves fully into Divine Hands. We are asking to activate our free will through those intentions as responsibly as possible. The listed intentions also provide a clear blueprint of what to expect. The signing of the Cooperative Contract is a powerful way to imagine fully engaging ourselves in a dynamic cooperative journey. It also provides a sense of *accountability* to complete the work in the best way that we can.

The next section of the book is the Cooperative Contract. It includes all intentions listed in every other section of the book. I have kept the specific intentions in the sections where they belong for consistency and easy work reference. Please take some time to glance over the other intention lists in the book before you sign the contract. The contract sets up the structure of the work in *Angelscape*, but it also provides clear permission for spiritual assistance. It is something like a work order, permission slip, and cooperative partnership agreement all rolled into one. Once you have signed over your Cooperative Contract, you may proceed with the next section. *Again, all intentions, goals, and purposes listed throughout the book are understood as part of your Cooperative Contract*. If you feel prompted, you can initial the supporting intentions to reaffirm your agreement with those intentions in addition to signing the contract.

Please do not do the work in this book unless you have signed over your Cooperative Contract.

If you are not ready or prepared to commit to this work using the Cooperative Contract, it is best that you wait until you feel ready. You may safely work with Direct Route Activity #1, the Double Dip, but please do not proceed any further in the activities until the Cooperative Contract is signed over.

"Until one is committed, there is hesitancy, the chance to draw back, always ineffectiveness. Concerning all acts of initiative and creation, there is one elementary truth the ignorance of which kills countless ideas and splendid plans: that the moment one definitely commits oneself, then providence moves too. All sorts of things occur to help one that would never otherwise have occurred. A whole stream of events issues from the decision, raising in ones favor all manner of unforeseen incidents, meetings and material assistance which no man could have dreamed would have come his way. I have learned a deep respect for one of Goethe's couplets: 'Whatever you can do, or dream you can, begin it! Boldness has genius, magic, and power in it."

W.H. Murray
Mountain climber, explorer

III
Cooperative Contract

Goals

- The first goal of the journey through *Angelscape* is to assist the Journeyer to shed what no longer serves the self, what is not authentically a part of the self, or what is seated within the self that is illusion, distortion, or false.
- The second goal of the journey is to correct, heal, and rectify what has been distorted or damaged through life experiences with ease and grace.
- The third goal of the journey is to strengthen, empower, expand, and integrate the healing shifts and wholeness initiated through cleansing and rectification work, such that they sustain and continue to provide growth, evolution, competency, and a sense of worth, spiritual connectivity, and self-efficacy.
- The fourth goal of the journey is to bring into conscious awareness what is authentic, sacred, and holy about the self, to cultivate the commitment to embody the Sacred Self, and to find ways to apply those sacred qualities toward the improvement and goodness of everyday life.
- The fifth goal of the journey is to cultivate a sense of purpose within the individual to apply his/her Sacred Self qualities and resources, when possible and appropriate, toward the improvement and goodness of the larger world.

Intentions Supporting the Goals

- The entire creation, function, adaptation, and maintenance of *Angelscape*, all tools, activities, and all helpers directly under the authority and oversight of God/Divine Will.
- The nature of *Angelscape* and all contributing facets to be authentic assistance, holy, sacred, incorruptible, inviolable, and sealed in perfection under the authority and oversight of God/Divine Will.
- All assistance, healing, intentions, work, and benefit to be applied across all layers, levels, and aspects of the Whole Self, and any other relevant networks of connectivity, as

appropriate, such as, soul self, family/ancestral network, and so on.

- All work applied to be corrected in perfection, integrated in perfection, and sealed in perfection, such that the work provides authentic assistance, healing, and growth that is sustainable and that results in higher levels of functioning and an improving quality of life.
- Immediate application of oversight, safety, protection, guidance, care, and nurturing within Divine Will for the Journeyer and relevant networks of connectivity.
- All visits to *Angelscape*, or complementary work and activities, to be fully protected and guided. Shifts to optimal states of consciousness to be automatically adjusted and secured upon entrance or exit from *Angelscape* environment.
- The Journeyer understands and agrees that his/her free will is placed in synergy, cooperation, and voluntary alignment under Divine Will for maximum possible spiritual intervention and care.
- Support provided to cultivate wisdom and humility to wield personal will and power in appropriate alignment with Divine Will. All advocacy work applied by the Journeyer on behalf of others to be in Divine Alignment and with respect to the sanctity of human free will.
- The Journeyer understands that engaging the work in this book may initiate emotional surging or release. The Journeyer understands and agrees to initiate self-care, maintenance, and to take proactive steps to manage and alleviate any healing crisis or overwhelm resulting from the activities in this book. This includes, using the tools provided in the book, seeking support from loving friends, or seeking the help of qualified real world professionals, such as, crisis counselors, medical assistance, therapy, and so on.
- The Journeyer agrees to take personal responsibility for his/her outcomes and actions and to hold all other parties harmless for any consequences of doing the work activities in this book, including the author, publisher, and any third parties guiding the Journeyer through the activities, such as a therapist or friend.

- The Journeyer agrees to treat him/herself with respect, value, and good faith and to take responsibility for taking care of him/herself in the best way possible and to place the well being and care of the self as a priority in his/her life.
- The Journeyer agrees to place him/herself accountable for sabotaging, avoiding, or distracting him/herself from engaging in personal healing and wellness activities, including the engagement of the activities in this book, or any other healing process the Journeyer is prompted to use to advocate for personal health and wellbeing.
- Support provided to bring awareness to the Journeyer when s/he is engaging in self-limiting behaviors and support provided to overcome and triumph over limiting or suppressive internal or external influences.
- The Journeyer understands and agrees that s/he alone must take responsibility for personal or spiritual beliefs, understandings, and agreements held with God. S/he understands and agrees not to abdicate that responsibility to any other, nor to be inappropriately influenced by any other. The Journeyer agrees to Keep Faith with God in whatever ways are deemed important, as defined by the Journeyer.
- Support to help the Journeyer to be the best person s/he can be at his/her functioning level of development.
- Support provided for the Journeyer to maintain or acquire real world integrity, appropriate prosperity, and opportunity for social support, companionship, and safe harbor.
- Support provided for the Journeyer to identify, cultivate, honor, and develop God-given talents, skills, passions, and natural abilities, such that an empowered personal Path of Light can be found and followed.
- Support provided to assist the Journeyer to succeed in meeting or exceeding personal challenges, tests, trials, and hardships with as much ease and grace as possible. The Journeyer to be fortified and supported with increased integrity, strength, and resiliency when personal integrity requires augmentation to meet and succeed challenges. Journeyer supported to achieve increasing levels of coping, competency, and ability to use learned tools and techniques to address new challenges with confidence and wisdom.

- Support provided for the cultivation of the belief and faith necessary to facilitate spontaneous miraculous healing, as well as the belief and faith necessary to have the patience, positive long-term outlook, and surrender to gracefully endure longer healing processes. Support provided to release expected outcomes and to allow the process to "be what it is".
- The Journeyer understands and agrees that all supporting intentions and goals listed in their individual sections of the book are a part of the Cooperative Contract, and as such, the Journeyer will read those intentions before signing over the Cooperative Contract.
- *Angelscape* environments are to provide intended functions to meet goals, as stated in environment and activity descriptions. All listed goals, descriptions, and intentions understood to be corrected in perfection and improved in whatever way is most beneficial and supportive to meet the functions of the environment and needs of the Journeyer.
- Every function and facet of *Angelscape* to be customized and individualized to the specific needs, beliefs, and spiritual traditions of each Journeyer. Support provided for the creation of new spaces or activities to meet emerging needs of the Journeyer, or to provide an alternative activity that is aligned with the Journeyer's personal spiritual beliefs.
- *Angelscape* activities, action statements, and equated alternative complementary activities to provide work, healing, and advocacy, as intended, with all intentions and consequence of activities to be corrected in perfection, customized to the individual, paced for ease and grace, and fully sealed under the authority of God/Divine Will.
- The Journeyer understands and agrees that whatever work is not appropriate to initiate, for whatever reason, is to be vacated, delayed, or nullified according to the Journeyer's highest and best good. Support for Journeyer to replace vacated activity with one that is appropriate.
- The Cooperative Contract considered valid and secured into God's Hands as soon as it is signed, either by intention and imagination, or by a physical signing of the book. A ceremonial handing over of the Cooperative Contract is arranged later in the journey within the Chamber of Light.

Cooperative Contract

"I request for, and give unlimited permission to God (Highest Divine Power or Consciousness), to initiate and complete, at His discretion, any and all activities related to the fulfillment of the goals and intentions described in the Cooperative Contract and all corresponding Angelscape *environments and activities. I further request and give permission for God to correct, improve, or include any other intentions that have not been listed, but which are favorable to meet all of the stated or related goals. I ask that this work be blessed and eternally applied as directed by God. I ask that it unfold for All of Me, in the most appropriate way, across all relevant dimensions or aspects of my Whole Self. I ask that all work manifests in perfection with Grace, Ease, Mercy, Compassion, and Love. Amen and Thank You."*

*X*______________________________________

*Date:*__________________________

A scroll in the hand of a statue.

Photograph 103654
by morguefile.com
user: Darnok

IV
How to Use this Book

What You Bring to the Table

This is a book that you *do*, not a book that you just read. You are not required to have special skills, but you are required to engage the activities to the best of your ability. The following list details some of the things that you are expected to bring to the table to advocate for yourself. It may not be an exhaustive listing, but it does detail the things that are the most important.

- A willingness to take the journey with an open heart and mind.
- A willingness to use your imagination as a tool, at whatever level you can.
- A willingness to surrender the experience to be what it is, not what you expect.
- An understanding that *Angelscape*, and everything in it, is intended as a *conceptual aid* for practical application of a Mind/Body/Spirit model of healing and wellness.
- Your own faith and belief in the existence of a spiritual reality that is dynamic and interactive.
- Self-compassion, love, acceptance, personal responsibility, and the willingness to be your own best advocate, regardless of, and in coordination with, any other assistance you seek.
- A genuine desire to be the change you wish to see in the world.
- Vigilance, courage, honesty, and a tolerance for out of the ordinary experiences.
- Persistence, tenacity, and the willingness to surge through limitations, fear, and resistance.
- Commitment to be the best person you can be, always reaching for higher functioning.
- A sense of playful exploration that allows for fresh and unexpected outcomes.

Honoring Your Religious Perspective with Divine Advocates

This is a spiritual book in many ways, but it is as religiously neutral as possible. You are welcomed and encouraged to add in the details that matter to you and edit out the details that are not consistent with your own beliefs. This book provides a framework for functioning, not a religious base. You can easily adapt the work to reflect your religious background by adding Divine Advocates that you know and love already. For example, my Catholic friend chose Christ as her dedicated Divine Advocate to guide her entire journey. My Jewish friend enjoyed working with the four main archangels and the Divine Presence of God, which she called the Shekinah. People see and experience things on their journey that are *consistent with what they know and love*. That is fine. In fact, that is perfect. Honor and keep your faith. You are being asked to make room in your heart for something more, not something different. *Angelscape* just sets the stage; it does not cast the players. You cast your own players. How you view your spiritual reality is between you and God.

Discretion Using Divine Advocates and Spiritual Helpers

I believe there is a good reason behind the phrase, "The messenger is not important." It is common for people to develop rapport with particular Divine Advocates, but please do not make the Divine Advocates, or any of your spiritual helpers, the focus of your work or attention. I do not think we can help wanting to deeply relate to a more humanized version of spiritual consciousness. Nevertheless, I think it is important to understand that we may create a few imaginary friends in order to wade through our own limitations in perceiving authentic spiritual assistance.

It is my understanding that the conceptual helpers you use in *Angelscape* should be "as nothing" between you and God--meaning they are transparent and allow the nature of God to shine through without obstruction. If they are "as something" between you and God, then they also can cast a shadow. I personally view spiritual helpers as if they are like marionettes that God uses so that we can function within a spiritual reality without becoming overwhelmed. The real power and presence is far above, pulling all the strings. In my opinion, the helpers are characters that God springs to life because our limitations require us to work with what is more familiar. It makes sense for us to work within our limitations, but also to be mindful that our affection and sense of connection should be seated with God/He Who Pulls the Strings, not the marionettes.

Terminology and Language

I often use special language throughout the book to meet the distinctive style of the work. I do my best to define new terms within the intention listings that are part of the Cooperative Contract so that you know what they are. I use religious terms, when appropriate, because they are the most *precise*. We all know that God means *God*; the head honcho, the top of the ladder, the Prime Creator, All That Is, and so on. The term "Higher Power", while a more comfortable term to many, is not specific enough. We have no idea how many layers of consciousness exist between God and ourselves. A "High*er* Power" could be a dolphin in the South Pacific named Ralph. You do not really mean to stop at some rung of consciousness on the ladder along the way to the top.

If you find yourself unable to move past the God reference terms, replace them with the notion of "High*est* Power" or "High*est* Spiritual Consciousness". In the book, I use the symbolism of an eternal flame to convey the *Divine Presence of God*. I call it the *Eternal Flame of God's Grace and Love* to clearly define it as a symbolic reference to the *outpouring of love* from God/Highest Power, *not* that the fire itself is supposed to be seen "as God", which would be inappropriate. I use the terms *Breath of God*, *Healing Light*, and so on, which all convey a relationship back to the idea of an active God principle, energy, or force. Also, I use the more accepted "His" or "He" when referencing God in some places, but I do not actually mean to convey a supposed gender.

I do my best to use language that is the most universally understood and most precise. I do realize that when addressing a wide range of different spiritual backgrounds, that it is impossible to use terminology that is completely acceptable across the board. Please forgive me in advance for any failing on my part to come up with completely neutral language, because I found it impossible. Give yourself permission to use different terms to describe spiritual concepts if you find yourself distracted or uncomfortable with the ones that I have settled on for this body of work.

Imagination and Your Experience

You will be using your intuitive mind for this work, which is not analytical or logical. The intuitive mind and rational mind are like two different trains that travel in different directions. You cannot ride both at the same time. If you try to "jump trains" in the middle of receiving intuitive information, you will lose your place and interrupt the process. Please allow yourself to enjoy the events as they unfold with a sense of adventure and possibility. Do not scrutinize or doubt yourself during your journey. Let it be what it is. Any time you find yourself starting to "jump trains" during your journey, remember this phrase: "Experience first. Analyze later." No one is asking you to abandon your reason, just use restraint and patience when applying it.

All of us have some capacity to imagine or visualize nonphysical events. You do it every time you have a memory, read a book, or daydream. A keen imagination is a fabulous tool to access for this work, but you are not required to be very good at it in order to receive benefit. Everyone is different, and some people will have more or less intensity within their perceptions and experiences. Some people will do better feeling, hearing, smelling, or using other senses to imagine. All of that is perfectly fine. There is no right way; there is only the way that works for you. We will discuss the use of props as a way to expand and strengthen your visualization skills in a later section.

I used my own imagination and the feedback of others to paint the broad strokes of *Angelscape*. You may change, modify, or adjust any environment or detail that does not work for you. The landscape should make sense and should be as easy for you to conceptualize as possible. Even the activities can be modified according to what makes sense to you, so long as the main points are covered.

Working Alone or with Others

You can work through this book alone, with a partner, or in a small group. There are pros and cons to each choice. Most people will go through the book alone because they can proceed at their own pace and schedule. Some people prefer silence and privacy to do meditative activities. The only challenge to a solitary trip is that you have to keep a foot of awareness in a regular state of consciousness. You are responsible for properly moving yourself through the activities and for taking adequate notes. If you easily fall asleep from a relaxed state, you may have to schedule your journeys during a time when you are normally perky and well rested.

If possible, doing the book with a partner or a small group can be an exciting and rewarding option. One of the best things about it is having the opportunity of taking turns "going in" while someone directs the activities and takes notes. Another fun thing about doing the book with others is that you can share each other's visualization strengths and build a composite scene with the pieces that everyone shares. It is also helpful to have working friends to stay on track, to enjoy social support, and to have some additional sense of accountability.

Taping Your Activity Sessions

If you are doing the work in the book by yourself, you may find it useful to tape the guided meditation activities so that you can keep your eyes closed and follow along to the sound of your own voice. If you do it this way, be sure to leave some pauses between each step so that you have time to develop the scene fully. The instructions are given in little step-by-step chunks, which gives you the proper pause between newly developing scenes within the meditation. You might also enjoy taping your reactions to your sessions after you have completed them to capture as much of the experience as you can. You can use the tape as a way to jot down notes later.

Taking Good Notes

Take good notes during your journey. The recollection of events while you are on the "intuitive train" is often hazy and dream-like. Details do tend to fade away. You may receive conceptual gifts, tools, or resources that you will want to remember after the journey is over, so take the time to jot it down so you can recall them again. Many things that happen on your journey will require additional follow-up work at some point in the future. Sometimes, just like in dreams, symbols and objects you see on your journey may have a deeper meaning. These symbolic inner messages can help give you insight if you take the time to write them down so you can look them up later. I recommend that you go to a used bookstore and browse around for several dream dictionaries that have solid symbolism interpretation. They may come in handy as you move through the activities in the book and begin to notice these subtle inner messages. I always use more than one reference book to look up the same concept to get a broader range of what it might mean; some interpretations are better than others.

Pay attention to colors, objects, flowers, tools, gifts, or anything that seems unique and special along your way. If you are deep into the meditation activity, you can just jot down one or two word phrases that will help you to recall the entire event later. I also strongly recommend that you get yourself a dedicated notebook for this work. You may want to follow up your sessions with journaling, drawing, or some other creative expression, like poetry. It will be nice for you to have a place to express yourself and keep your thoughts and feelings together. The time you spend sitting with and sorting out your experience is an important part of proactive follow-up and integration.

Choosing the Right Pace

There is a lot of work in this book. The activities are set up in a sequence that makes the most sense. Some activities build upon previous activities, so you should go through them in the order provided to maintain that continuity. Every section has three activities, one Direct Route (DR), and two supporting Scenic Route (SR) activities. *I do not recommend going any faster than one section per week.* You can, however, go *slower* if you feel you should. Some of the sections will require you to spend more time processing and purging, depending on how much congestion you need to release. Do not push yourself beyond your ability to comfortably manage. Some things will just need more time.

Resistance and Keeping at It

There may be times when you just are not in the mood or space to do the activity you want to do that day. Perhaps you encounter some internal resistance and negative backtalk about it and need some time to work through that resistance. If you encounter resistance, ask for help from your spiritual assistance. Tag the resistance and observe, without judgment, what the voice sounds like and how it is undermining your efforts. Tag how the voice of resistance and fear is different in quality from the voice of higher guidance. Give yourself permission to move forward, even if you feel resistance from negative inner dialog.

The desire to *rest* is different from internal fear and interference. If you need to rest, rest. If it is time to move forward, move forward. Sometimes an activity will not fully run to completion for whatever reason. That is okay. Re-engage that activity when you feel you are ready before moving on. You may use the Double Dip activity as an "in the meantime" activity to encourage readiness and to keep yourself warmed up for continuing work. Persistence and momentum are important. Keep at it. If you are working with others, you can help each other to move beyond internal resistance and to engage reasonable follow up when needed.

Normal Sensations of Cooperative Spiritual Energy Work

Some of the normal sensations you might experience in *Angelscape* include; euphoria, dizziness, lightheadedness, muscle twitches, body buzzing, emotional surges, color or pattern play when you close your eyes, body pings and pangs, difficulty concentrating, feeling tipsy or intoxicated, feeling disconnected from your physical body, a heaviness or lightness, temperature changes, and so on. These sensations are normal side effects of energy work and deep meditative states. It may be especially pronounced for those of us who are more sensitive to subtle energies. The intensity of the sensations can vary depending on how much work you have done and how long it takes to integrate it. It usually feels nice, but the challenge is that some people have difficulty reorienting to regular functioning from the meditative state of consciousness. It is called being *ungrounded.* It essentially means you are not fully back in your physical reality. This can create a temporary impairment to regular world functioning, similar to being intoxicated or on cold medicine.

You should *not* do this kind of work before you drive a car, operate heavy machinery, or do anything else that requires you to be "all there". If it takes you a long time to reorient, you can intentionally schedule your work sessions when you have the luxury to be ungrounded for a while. Scheduling near bedtime is a good option because you can enjoy floating around until you fall asleep. The end of every session has a transition activity built into it to assist you to reground and move back into a normal waking state of consciousness, but everyone is different. You may need more or less time to refocus your awareness. It takes as long as it takes. Do not go about your regular activities until you feel able to do so.

You might feel *absolutely nothing* during or after your journey. That is fine too. The range of sensations indicates your own sensitivities. It is like eyesight; some people are blind, but that does not mean that the room they are in does not exist. Some people need glasses to see, others can see with extreme clarity. Sight does not qualify the reality it observes any more than your sensations qualify the benefits of the work you receive. Seeing and feeling are nice, but they are not the point of the work. It is not a requirement in the success of the process.

Overwhelm, Crying, and Recovery

Energy work can have a tangible impact upon your system, so please be aware of the signs that are telling you to slow down. Some of these signs include; muscle twitches, fatigue, mental fogginess, diarrhea, flu-like symptoms, feeling weepy or emotional, and so on. This generally means that the amount of energetic congestion being purged is not able to exit as swiftly as it is bubbling up. Think of it as an energetic detox process that sometimes can be uncomfortable if moved through too rapidly. If you feel overwhelmed, stop all work and let your system catch up with the congestion being released.

You may need time and space to physically "cry it out" and to give yourself the needed release of emotional stagnation. If you need help initiating a good cleansing cry, you can set up a sad movie marathon during the weekend when you have time to release and recover before going back to normal life. That will help drain the emotional surge for you in a non-confrontational way. Being weepy during rapid shifts is not uncommon, but if you find yourself feeling despondent, depressed, or with severely impaired thoughts, such as wanting to harm yourself--stop all work and immediately contact a professional therapist. Sorting through deep emotional debris that makes you feel a *little* lost is different from feeling despondent or suicidal. If you have a history of major depression or significant trauma, please do not do the activities in this book without professional assistance if you begin to feel overwhelmed in any way.

After doing energy work, it is important that you help your system to recover and rest. The guided meditation activities use the same exit strategy each time that includes recovery care and integration assistance into the normal flow of events. You can also use many concrete tools and practices that are useful in assisting a system in rapid flux to remain as stabilized and as comfortable as possible.

Integration Tips and Strategies for After Activity Recovery

- *Pace yourself gently.* More is not better if you move too fast for your congestion to gracefully purge. The work needs to be introduced, congestion purged, and then the healing shifts need to settle in so that they become permanent. Healing takes time. Be good to yourself in the process. The point is to heal, not to re-traumatize or aggravate your delicate system.
- *Use Your Tools.* The book has many strategies for coping with overwhelm or congestion that are very efficient and useful. Always use your tools instead of flopping around without direction. Take action when you feel uncomfortable. Do not wait for your feelings of discomfort to surge into something overwhelming. Be proactive about your care and upkeep. The *Double Dip*, which is the Direct Route Activity #1, is a superior way to keep ahead of the congestion purge. Use it as often as you need, such as daily, or even several times a day, to maintain comfort when you hit a new layer of congestion.
- *Three Cheers for Crying.* Crying is good. It is the quickest exit for emotional and energetic congestion that we can use. If you have spent your whole life "swallowing your tears" you can expect that a few finally want to be shed. Watch sad movies to help you "dump the bucket" when you want to

purge in a controlled setting. Keep a cold pack in the freezer and cucumbers in the fridge to take care of swollen hot eyes.

- *Three Cheers for Laughing.* If crying is a good emotional release, you have to believe that laughing is too. Laughter is good medicine and always has been. If you begin to feel too heavy and serious through the work, give yourself a laugh break. Watch a funny movie marathon or throw a funny movie in between your sad movies to provide you with some balance. Go to a comedy club, do something silly, or do something fun and playful.
- *Sea Salt Baths.* Sea Salt is one of the best ways of leaching out energetic congestion, as well as being good for physical detox. Often one long soak will make you feel worlds better. Add 1-2 cups of sea salt (any kind) to a comfortably warm bath and imagine going through the Double Dip activity. Medicinal clay or herbal baths are also nice. You can integrate other appropriate medicinal bath elements with the sea salt as you wish.
- *Flower Essences.* Look for flower essence blends that deal with "rescue" and stability, stress relief, and major healing transitions. You can take flower essences under the tongue, in water, or in your bathtub. I will have resources for *Angelscape* flower essence blends on my website, but store bought brands that address energetic stabilization would be fine too. I like them all.
- *Homeopathic Remedies.* Look for remedies that deal with calming the system, helping recover from exhaustion or tension and stress relievers. Consult your doctor and take as directed.
- *Herbal Teas.* Herbal teas are a wonderful complement to energy work. The calming herbal blends for sleepy time, or taming tension are nice. Use whatever you enjoy.
- *Talk it Out.* You may need to have time to talk out your experience, your feelings, or use verbal forms of purging congestion (shouting or singing works). If you are doing the work with a friend or in a group, you already have a dedicated group of people who will be able to offer that support.

- *Write it Out.* Writing is an excellent medium to explore and release pent up emotional and energetic congestion. You can journal, blog, write long emails, or write poetry. Sometimes poetry is the best way to purge and process, so I highly recommend that if you enjoy writing poetry.
- *Draw it Out.* Artwork, or any kind of creative endeavor, is a fabulous tool for expressing what cannot be expressed through verbal or written avenues. Have plenty of art materials in your house when you are doing this work, even if you never had an interest in art before. A drawing tablet, colored pencils, watercolors, and markers should be plenty with which to start. If you are inspired to create something at any time during your process, please do not ignore those prompts.
- *Move it Out.* Physical movement is another good way to help shake out congestion from energy work. Dance, dance, dance. Exercise. Jump. Run. Sometimes a solid round with a punching bag can do wonders if you have old anger to release. Physical expression is powerful and can improve your wellness in physical ways too.
- *Breathe it Out.* Deep breathing exercises are a part of the Double Dip activity, which you should be doing to mitigate overwhelm, but you can also increase the times in a day that you focus your attention on your breath without imagery. Breathe deeply for several minutes, go outside if you can, and use that time to recenter yourself in a more relaxed and loose state.
- *Rest it Out.* You may find that the activities leave you feeling as if you are tired, or even exhausted. Add more sleep into your schedule, when possible, or catch up on rest during the weekend. It takes a lot of energy to heal the fabric of the intangible parts of the self. If your system is responding to the work by feeling tired, you *need* to sleep. You may need more alone or quiet time during some of the activities. You might want to have some light busy work available, such as crossword puzzles, knitting, light reading, or any other peaceful activity that keeps you just partially engaged to give your mind a chance to refocus and rest.

- *Flush it Out.* Water is the universal solvent, even with energetic congestion. Please consider increasing your daily fresh water intake to the recommended eight glasses a day to assist flushing your congestion. Some people like to add liquid minerals or electrolytes to their water to support the free movement of energy through the body. You can find liquid mineral supplements or electrolytes at any health food store. Please consult your doctor and take all products as directed.
- *Mood Music.* You can wash your senses in soothing music, such as classical or new age. You may also wish to work with singing bowls, bells, or toning to help release congestion. You can keep it simple and hum or sing the musical scales.
- *Mood Colors.* Colors can be helpful in the support of specific mood states. If you find yourself being attracted to a particular color any time throughout the course of the work in the book, try to wear it more often in clothing or jewelry, or place it around you more often such as art, flowers, sheets or pillows.
- *Follow Your Prompts.* Listen to your own inner guidance and prompts to respond to your healing and recovery needs. There may be something useful and unique that you should consider as part of your care. For example, you may have the urge to go to a Reiki practitioner, acupuncturist, massage therapist, or perhaps schedule a confession, go to church, write a letter to a dead relative, read a book, work with crystals, take a trip, or whatever. If you have a strong desire or urge to do something related to your wellness, recovery, or process, please do it.
- *Ask for Spiritual Assistance.* Part of receiving assistance from a spiritual reality is in requesting it in a clear way. Have an ongoing dialog with God/your spiritual helpers. Report on your status and any challenges you have. Remember to ask. If you do not ask, you do not get. If you follow a particular religion, ask for assistance in the manner that you are most familiar and which supports your belief system. Go to church regularly if that is a part of your spiritual practice in communing with and receiving spiritual assistance.
- *Go to a Professional Therapist.* If you had a harder than usual life and had harder than usual experiences, it would follow that healing and recovery may be harder than usual as well.

Sometimes self-help is not the best way to go. You can take out a splinter on your own, but you cannot do major surgery on your own. Get help when and if you need help. If you already have a therapist, that makes it easier, try the activities *there* first. The activities in this book are guided imagery activities. Any competent therapist with an open mind should be able to talk you through the activities right in the office. That will let them help you with any immediate purging or issues you may need to sort out. The use of guided imagery, even spiritual imagery, is a perfectly acceptable therapeutic tool.

Using the Activity Sections

The activities are the bulk and heart of the book. They are structured in a way to make them as easy to navigate as possible. Again, there are ten sections overall with one Direct Route activity and two complementary Scenic Route activities per section. The Direct Route activities are the main activities in each section that complete the broadest task associated with the work of the section. The Scenic Route activities are complements to the Direct Route, but often are important in their own right as well. There are thirty activities involved with the formatted journey through *Angelscape*, not including the environment set up and preparations. You will like some activities more than you like others. You do not have to spend a lot of time on the activities that do not excite you, but some of them teach skills that will be helpful later on--*so please move through them at least once*, even if you do them rapidly.

Summary of Activity Subsections

- *Introduction to Section Activities*: Each section starts with an introduction that briefly explains the overall tone, foundation, or new concepts of the work in the activities.
- *Direct or Scenic Route*: Each activity is clearly marked whether it is a Direct Route, the main activity, or Scenic Route, the complementary activities. In the DR activity, the complementary SR activities are listed.
- *Environment Setting*: The environment in which the activity is set is clearly listed. You set up the visuals to the environments before you start your activities so you do not have to spend time creating a new visualization before going to work

- *Purpose*: The goal and purpose of each activity is clearly summarized in a type of mission statement that is understood as being supported in the Cooperative Contract.
- *Usage Suggestion*: Some activities are useful for maintenance, continuing support, or occasional use. Some activities are ceremonial and do not need to be done again. The usage section makes recommendations for continuing use.
- *Activity Props*: In this subsection, I make recommendations for possible props or activities that you can use to help get into the visualization of the activity. Props can be physical objects, pictures, media, or physical activities you can use to anchor your concentration on the imagery corresponding to the activity.
- *Summary*: This is a summary of the guided meditation in simple paragraph form. It is recommended that you read the summary and the step-by-step directions before you begin the work so that you know what to expect before you go into a meditative state, especially if you are reading through the session.
- *Helpers*: This gives you an idea of what kind of Divine Advocates or spiritual helpers show up to assist in the work. Often, it is up to you, but if there are particular jobs or tasks that are designated to particular helpers, it will help you set up your visualization ahead of the work.
- *New Concepts*: There are many conceptual tools and concepts introduced throughout the book. New concepts are clearly marked so that you know that something novel is going to be introduced in the activity. The new concepts are detailed and defined in the "Intentions Supporting Activities" section to include them in the Cooperative Contract.
- *Intentions Supporting Activity*: These clearly describe all of the intended pieces of supporting work or goals related to the activity, the assistance requested, and the inclusion of these into the Cooperative Contract.
- *Action Statements*: The Action Statements are a way to initiate energy work. They are also found in sections when command functions are relevant to follow up tasks. The use of Action Statements is an energy work technique that is not *Angelscape* specific.

- *Step-by-Step Instructions*: These are the instructions for the guided meditation in easy chunks of action. Each activity starts at the Lotus Pool for cleansing and transition to a meditative state and ends with the TLC Bath and integration activities for transition back to a normal state.
- *Continuing Thoughts*: These are brief follow up thoughts that do not make much sense until after you have completed the activity. They are sometimes suggestions for integrating new concepts into daily life or other tips.
- *End of Section Summary and Wrap Up*: At the end of each section, there is a wrap up with Complementary Activities, Project Ideas, Reflection Questions, and Focus Group Feedback.
- *Complementary Activities*: I recommend some other activities that are in alignment with the focus and goals of the work from the sections activities. You are welcome to follow up and engage these activities, or not, as you see fit. These suggestions are in addition to all of the other integration tips previously listed.
- *Project Ideas*: Occasionally, there are little projects, crafty or otherwise, that you can do to support the activities of the section. These are optional and are provided to give additional integration, practical application or prop suggestions.
- *Reflection Questions*: It is necessary for the Journeyer to reflect upon his/her experiences throughout the book. The Reflection Questions are a series of open-ended questions that you can use to help reflect upon your experiences. If you journal and take notes, some of the answers to the questions will be helpful later in the book.
- *Focus Group Feedback*: Real people worked through the activities while I was writing, revising, and refining this book. *I recommend that you wait until you have your own experience before you read the Focus Group comments.* There are fewer comments in the later activities because some Focus Group members needed to pace out their journey longer than my writing schedule. Thanks again to the Focus Group participants!

One More Thing Before We Start the Journey

In the next section, you will be asked to set up the imagery for the various *Angelscape* environments. There is no actual work done in these introductory guided meditations (or very little), so you can do as many set ups as you wish in one working session. It would be good for you to have some art material or a notebook to sketch or take notes about some of the details you experience. Have fun with it and make your *Angelscape* something enjoyable and full of love and support. The more fully you construct it, the better your results.

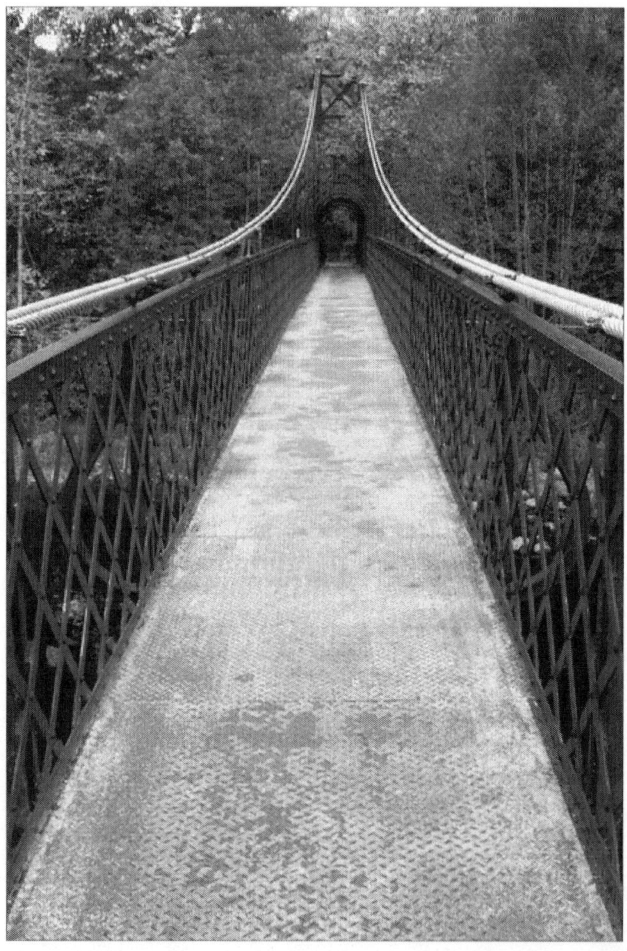

In order to enter Angelscape, you have to allow yourself to cross a threshold from the ordinary to the extraordinary.

It is a leap of faith.

Photograph 185932 by morguefile.com user: hotblack

V
Angelscape Environments

Overview

The title *Awake in Angelscape* means a spiritual dreamscape setting within which you can work and function in a lucid and intentional way. The landscape used to represent *Angelscape* is full of different buildings, structures, and natural settings. It is set up like a little imaginary kingdom. The architecture that people tend to see the most is similar to ancient Greek or Roman styles, such as white carved stone, rounded rooms, domes, and pillars. You may express a different style according to your own interest. Your vision/version of *Angelscape* should be crafted to be as deeply stirring to your emotions and senses as possible.

Angelscape has three categories of environments: work, continuing support, and natural. The work environments are primary and secondary activity environments used during the formatted journey. The Chamber of Light, the *Angelscape* Spa, and the Garden of the Little Ones are utilized the most in the formatted journey as settings for both Direct Route and Scenic Route activities. Continuing support environments include those whose practical use will continue even after the formatted journey is completed, such as the Dream Room and the *Angelscape* Elixir Café. The natural settings are mostly incidental and fill in the blank spaces of the countryside, but some natural settings, particularly the beach, are used for some activities.

Natural settings are easier to visualize, so they do not need dedicated preparation before you begin those activities. For example, everyone knows what a beach looks like or can get a picture of one without trouble. You may explore the natural settings to expand your personal horizons. The landscape represents the limitless opportunities for exploration of deeper parts of a spiritual reality and ourselves. You may be led to discover something new and unique or something that is a blessing just for you in any of the natural areas. Not everyone sees the same exact landscape and you should not assume that the map I have drawn is complete. There may be many paths not yet taken in *Angelscape* that await discovery.

Environment Set Up and Capturing the Scene

Before you begin your work in *Angelscape,* you are asked to construct and familiarize yourself with the environments you will be visualizing to initiate the activities. The work and continuing support environments have description write ups that include the purpose of the environment, recommended props, intentions supporting the environment, and an introductory guided meditation. The guided meditations for the environment set ups are not *work* meditations, but simply expose you to the settings and allow you some time to "get a feel" for the landscape. At the end of each environment set up section you are asked to "capture the scene", or to modify and adjust the imagery to your liking. It is recommended that you create collages or a scrapbook for these settings, such as pictures that remind you of the setting, once you have had some basic exposure to them through the set up meditations. In the resource listing at the end of the book, you will find websites that have public domain and royalty free images. I used photos from morguefile.com throughout this book. You can go to the website to download the photos in full color for your own collages, if you wish. Thanks to all of the talented photographers whose pictures appear in this book.

If you have a tougher time visualizing the settings, please do spend some time looking for pictures that will help you set the scene. In this instance, it is perfectly okay to create a "cheat sheet" for yourself. You can use memories of similar environments to construct your *Angelscape* settings. For example, the Garden of the Little Ones can be a playground setting that you loved as a child or a scene of an English garden from a movie, like *The Secret Garden*. The Spa, which is set in a cavern, can be set in a cavern you have seen in real life or on TV. Take pieces of your own life experiences to patch together a visual landscape that you can readily recall. You can always adjust and modify the setting as you go along. Most people find that the more they visit, the more details become visible, the more real it seems. Just do your best, use pictures and props, and allow it to be what it is. The visual does not have to be vivid and lifelike to work well, but it should be as developed as possible according to your own abilities.

Quick Summary of the Angelscape Environments

Work Environments

- *Transition Platform, Lotus Pool & TLC Bath*: The Transition Stations include the Lotus Pool and the TLC Bath. Both are small, Roman-style like baths that are situated near each other on a hilltop pavilion overlooking a lake. This area is the dedicated entrance and exit platform for *Angelscape*.
- *Chamber of Light*: The Chamber of Light is like a Temple *within,* and is used for sacred work where the active *Presence of God* is

visualized. At the center of the Chamber of Light is the *Eternal Flame of God's Grace and Love*. The ceiling of the chamber has a circular domed opening that allows in sunlight, which softly illuminates the central Eternal Flame.

- *The Garden of the Little Ones*: The gardens contain a playground, baby pools, an outdoor amphitheater, wishing well, and other child-friendly spaces. It will be full of laughter, rainbows, butterflies, and fun.
- *Angelscape Spa*: The spa is a dedicated healing environment, set up like an actual spa with mud baths and healing rooms, which is located within a large cavern or cave. That may appeal to some of you and not others. You may set up your spa in whatever way that makes sense to you if you do not like caves.

Continuing Support Environments

- *Dream Room*: The Dream Room is for you to cultivate a sense of permanent place in *Angelscape.* At the summary section of the book, it is used as the platform for continuing care and maintenance. Your Dream Room is to be a visual of the most comfortable and personal space you can imagine creating. It can be modified and updated as desired, so you may start simple and get more complex as you go. It can be located anywhere in the *Angelscape* countryside. You will create it before you begin the formatted journey though we will not discuss it again until the end of the book.
- *Angelscape Elixir Café*: The café is a fun, social space to visualize using the elixir energy drinks. You will set up the visual to be your favorite pub, café, restaurant, or your ideal vision of what a perfect café would look like. The last activity of the book unfolds in the *Angelscape* Elixir Café.

Natural Settings

- *Waterfall*: The entrance to the *Angelscape* Spa is seen as a waterfall that is in front of an opening in the rocks. There is a swimming hole here and a place for you to relax. Some people see the waterfall as being immediately next door to the Garden of the Little Ones.
- *Cliffs over the Ocean*: The Cliffs overlook a beach and beautiful ocean. There are woods that grow almost to the sides of the cliff. It is a tall and rocky cliff, but there are stairs hewn into the rock that lead down to the beach. The beach is used to visualize large

gatherings. Some people imagine that the Garden of the Little Ones is found not far from the top of the stairs from the beach.

- *Mountain Lake w/ Meadows*: The lake is large and is surrounded by rounded green mountains or dramatic tall ones, depending on your preference. The lake features predominantly in my vision of *Angelscape.* It is the view from my Dream Room and I find it particularly soothing. The meadow, which also overlooks the lake, is a breezy flower- filled natural setting where people can go to clear there minds and be refreshed.
- *The Forest*: The forest is a deep primeval forest with a rich green and earthy smell. This environment is misty and without definition. A small clear stream has been described within the forest. Many people describe walking from one place to another on paths that often go through the forest.

This is a good size representation for the baths. Imagine it outside overlooking a mountain lake.

Photograph 205390
by morguefile.com
user: Alvimann

Environment: Transition Platform, Lotus Pool and TLC Bath

Purpose: The Transition Platform, including the Lotus Pool and TLC Bath and corresponding activities, tools, and helpers, is designed to provide optimal transition into and out of *Angelscape*. Its purpose is to provide comfort, soothing, cleansing and purification, stress reduction and management, pre-work preparation, and after-work recovery. The *Double Dip* activity, using the Lotus Pool and TLC Bath, can serve as an independent cleansing, comfort and resiliency meditation that can be initiated without additional *Angelscape* related visualizations.

Suggested Environment Props: You may do your Transition Platform work in an actual bathtub, whirlpool tub, swimming pool, hot tub, or your favorite natural water setting. Fizzy bath bombs would help you to recreate the effervescent quality of the Lotus Pool water for a little while. Milk and honey or some similar bath addition may be helpful for the TLC Bath. You may use actual flowers, potpourri, essential oils, or flower essences to capture the essence of the lotus flowers. You can use a honey sweetened floral tea to recreate the nectar sipping activity. A nature sounds CD that includes a 'babbling brook' audio may be very helpful. You can use a fuzzy bathrobe to stand in for any of the wraps used in the environment.

Intentions Supporting Environment

- Journeyer to create the environment setting according to personal taste and to adjust provided imagery as s/he sees fit.
- Platform for transition to optimal meditative state.
- Platform for return to optimal waking state.
- Transition Platform to support the Double Dip activity independent of other *Angelscape* related work, activities, or visualization development.
- Lotus Pool meets all needs for Whole Self cleansing and purification.
- Lotus Pool prepares Journeyer for productive, beneficial work session.
- TLC Bath meets all needs for relaxation, soothing, and recovery.
- TLC Bath assists in recovery and integration after work session.

- Fluid in Lotus Pool and TLC Bath as Holy Water, incorruptible, self-purifying, and healing.
- Spiritual helpers to meet all needs for support in all relevant activities.
- Tools to meet all needs for support in all relevant activities.
- Functions and skills used to be integrated into other environments and protocols, as appropriate.

Starter Imagery to the Transition Platform

The Lotus Pool and TLC Bath are small stone pools that look like Roman-style baths. The Lotus Pool and TLC Bath are located on opposite sides of a stone pavilion, flanked by four solid columns, but open to the sky. The pavilion is found on the top of a hill that overlooks a mountain lake. Trees and flowers grow around the outside of the pavilion. You can smell the honeysuckles that are growing over a nearby bush. A gentle breeze rustles the leaves and tickles your cheek with a tendril of your hair. Several cheerful birds greet you with song before gracefully flying away.

Walk to the side of the Lotus Pool. It is distinct from the TLC Bath by the floating lotus flowers on the surface of the water. The water in the Lotus Pool is gurgling, warm, and fizzy. It seems to be faintly glowing, as if lit from within. You step down the wide stone stairs and into the pool. The water feels silky and warm. It tingles your skin like the caress of a million little massaging bubbles. You bring your attention to the lotus flowers floating on the surface of the water. You close your eyes to bring the fragrance deeply into your lungs, filling your whole body with a sense of deep contentment.

Helpers assigned to this area approach from stone stairs that lead down the hill and toward the lake. They have kind faces and knowing smiles that radiate wisdom and welcoming. One of the helpers reaches into the Lotus Pool and retrieves a lotus flower, tipping it up like a cup to drink the nectar. You are gestured to do the same. You reach down and pick up one of the flowers with velvety petals and a thick lingering perfume. You follow the prompting of the helper and tip the flower to your lips, allowing a small amount of precious sweet fluid to drizzle into your mouth.

The nectar acts upon your body and mind like a perfect divine tranquilizer, spreading a soothing wave of warmth and relaxation all over your body. Imagine that you feel perfectly at peace.

The helper gestures you to come out of the Lotus Pool and to try out the TLC Bath next. You walk up the stone stairs on the other side of the Lotus Pool and are wrapped in a spa-style robe. This robe is a work support robe that you will wear when you come for your activity sessions. It helps you to be receptive and prepared for work. You walk around the pavilion with your work robe for a moment to get a feel for it. You gaze out onto the mountain lake and the beautiful natural setting surrounding the pavilion. When you are ready, you take off the work robe and approach the TLC Bath.

The TLC Bath water is thicker than the Lotus Pool water. It is comfortably warm and velvety, like a perfect emollient lotion. You notice that the water has an iridescent shine, and little glitter sparkles, that are in soothing pastel shades. You walk into the bath and sit down on the stone step so that your body is submerged to your neck. The water coats your system like a sweet layer of comfort and soothing. You have a sense of deep relief, as discomfort seems to melt away. The water seems to go through a progression of pastel colors and sparkles that allow you to feel more centered in your awareness. Your helper gestures for you to come out, places a pastel rainbow towel around you, and claps three times to move you back to your normal waking state.

When you are ready, open your eyes.

Capturing the Scene

Write down a summary of your experience as soon as you have opened your eyes from the introductory visit. Describe as much as you can, especially details not discussed in the imagery. Describe the setting using all of your senses, your emotions, and your intuition. What do you want to adjust or change so that it is more suited to your personal taste? Go ahead and make those changes as you imagine the setting with the updates and edits.

Create a collage using images from photos, old magazines, the web, scrapbooking supplies, or personal drawings. Capture the elements of the setting that you experience most vividly and expand upon elements that you experience less vividly.

"To unpathed waters, undreamed shores."

William Shakespeare

Environment: Chamber of Light

Purpose: The Chamber of Light is a platform for prayer, advocacy, and the conceptual connection to the Divine Presence of God, spiritual helpers, and to all creation. The Chamber of Light serves as a symbolic temple within, which contains an outpouring of love and support from God through the Eternal Flame of God's Grace and Love.

Suggested Environment Props: You may attend an actual church or temple when meditating or initiating the work that unfolds in the activity, if you have the privacy to do so. You may light actual candles in a church or temple when lighting the candles in the Chamber of Light. You may light actual candles in your own space as a way to connect to the Chamber of Light.

Intentions Supporting Environment

- Journeyer to create the environment setting according to personal taste and to adjust provided imagery as s/he sees fit.
- Platform for tangible connection to God and All that is Holy, Divine, and Sacred.
- Platform for prayer, advocacy, and requests for spiritual assistance within Divine Will.
- Platform for candle lighting visualization as symbolic prayer request for all appropriate assistance within Divine Will.
- Platform for harmonization, balance, and unity within, among, and between All Creation.
- Chamber of Light symbolic of "temple of the soul" or "temple within".
- Eternal Flame of God's Grace and Love symbolic of outpouring of grace, love, and support from an authentic spiritual reality.
- Eternal Flame as receptacle of anything that is placed "in the Hands of God", such as the Cooperative Contract, scripts to release, affirmations to empower, and the Journeyer.
- Platform for non-physical spiritual community and gathering place.
- Platform for cultivation of responsible, cooperative, faithful, and compassionate worldview.

- Functions and skills used to be integrated into other environments and protocols, as appropriate.

Starter Imagery to the Chamber of Light

The Chamber of Light is known as "the temple within", which contains the Eternal Flame of God's Grace and Love acting as a conceptual platform for our interaction with God. The Eternal Flame of God's Grace and Love is like a large campfire or bonfire that is centrally located in the building. The domed roof of the chamber is open to the bright blue sky and sunlight streams around the flames in a wide radius. You may see people kneeling and praying by the Eternal Flame while lighting candles. There are many candles burning brightly around the perimeter of the chamber. You may see and smell flowers as well. The candles are used as vehicles for advocacy and compassion, lit as living prayers that request support and blessings in alignment with Divine Will.

Enter fully into the Chamber of Light. Notice the perfect reverberation of sound, such that every whisper sounds like music, and every prayer like a precious song. Kneel or sit meditatively in front of the Eternal Flame of God's Grace and Love. Offer up your favorite prayer aloud in the chamber. Notice the flames dancing and moving to the rhythm of your voice, responding and radiating a connection directly into your heart.

Imagine the Cooperative Contract you signed earlier in the book, as if it were a scroll in your hands. Sign the scroll, if you have not done that already, roll it up and secure it with a ribbon. Take a deep breath and toss it into the Eternal Flame of God's Grace and Love in order to "place it in God's Hands". Notice any immediate changes or sensations within you that seem to be in response to placing your Cooperative Contract in God's Hands. Allow those sensations to run to completion with faith and trust in the process.

A young spiritual helper approaches you with a basket of white candles. Select a candle from the basket and light it while requesting for your journey in *Angelscape* to be blessed by God's Grace and Love. Hand the lit candle to the spiritual helper to place in the perimeter of the chamber. Sit and meditate in front of the Eternal Flame, pray, or light additional candles as you are prompted.

When you are ready, offer your gratitude and exit the Chamber of Light.

Capturing the Scene

Write down a summary of your experience as soon as you have opened your eyes from the introductory visit. Describe as much as you can, especially details not discussed in the imagery. Describe the setting using all of your senses, your emotions, and your intuition. What do you want to adjust or change so that it is more suited to your personal taste? Go ahead and make those changes as you imagine the setting with the updates and edits.

Create a collage using images from photos, old magazines, the web, scrapbooking supplies, or personal drawings. Capture the elements of the setting that you experience most vividly and expand upon elements that you experience less vividly.

The Chamber of Light is a dedicated place of prayer, using candles to symbolize the accumulating energy behind each prayer.

Photograph 159593 by morguefile.com user: hurley_gurlie182

Environment: Garden of the Little Ones
Including the Amphitheater, Baby Baths, and Wishing Well

Purpose: The Garden of the Little Ones is a platform for identifying and releasing distorted perceptions created in the past, also for nurturing and healing of inner children, reconnection with innocence and joy, a safe haven for traumatized parts of self, a sacred space of play, creativity, spontaneity, and a connection to positive and revitalizing energies of youth.

Environment Props: The Garden of the Little Ones is a child-friendly outdoor space. You may go to an actual playground to do the meditation. You may also enjoy a bubble bath or blowing bubbles for this meditation since bubbles and suds feature predominantly in the area. Since the Garden of the Little Ones is a child-specific area, you may integrate pictures of yourself as a child into your collage or have a picture album handy while you do the activities. You might enjoy having art supplies handy for the Garden of the Little One activities.

Intentions Supporting Environment

- Journeyer to create the environment setting according to personal taste and to adjust provided imagery as s/he sees fit.
- Platform for connection to childhood, childhood issues, hidden issues, inner children, and innocence.
- Safe haven and gathering place for all dissociated parts of self needing care and nurturing.
- Platform for graceful processing, cleansing, releasing, and healing past pain, trauma, and suffering without the need to re-experience it.
- Platform for identifying, tagging, refusing, and rescripting distortion from the system.
- Connection point for inner strength, beauty, creativity, joy, resiliency, and hope.
- Spiritual helpers to be exactly what is needed to re-nurture, re-parent, and comfort inner children.
- Garden of the Little Ones as a place of play, joy, discovery, and expansive child-like dreaming.
- Platform to reflect upon personal behavior, motivation, and interactive drama.
- Platform for all necessary preparations for healing and re-integration of inner children with Whole Self/Sacred Self.
- Functions and skills used to be integrated into other environments and protocols, as appropriate.

Starter Imagery to the Garden of the Little Ones

The Garden of the Little Ones is a large child-centered enclave situated within a larger garden complex. It is surrounded by very tall lush green hedges that create the sensation of stepping into a secret area that is completely protected from the outside world. You can hear the sounds of children playing and laughing and see them running around the gardens having fun. Some of them look up to see you before turning back to play. You look around the garden and notice a large playground area, a baby pool with a small waterfall like play shower, fine mist sprinklers, a small outdoor amphitheater, and a beautiful wishing fountain built into a stone wall.

The sun is shining brightly, throwing rainbows through the droplets of water from the fine mist sprinklers. There are flowers of every color spread out through the garden. Butterflies and ladybugs buzz from bloom to bloom. Some of the children are jumping happily in little mud puddles. You notice there are adult attendants in the garden. They are the personification of kind and sweet motherly and grandmotherly type figures. They may even look like adults from your past that you loved and trusted most and who loved you the very best. You may hug them and say hello if you wish.

Go over to the playground and sit in one of the swings. Smile at the children around you and begin to swing yourself back and forth, feeling the fragrant wind on your face and the sensation of your hair swinging in the breeze. Take a deep breath, close your eyes, and swing until you feel like you are finished. When you are finished, you may jump off the swing or stop it and get off. Make your way to the baby pool area.

Peel off your shoes and socks and wade into the baby pool. You notice that it is a mini version of the Lotus Pool. There is another one that is a mini version of the TLC Bath. One of the adult attendants smiles at you and pours a thick liquid into the pool. Sudsy iridescent bubbles begin to froth and form in the little pool. The bubbles tickle your feet and make you feel like giggling. Several children come dashing from other parts of the garden to play in the baby pool with you. They like the bubbles. It is one of their favorite things. Pick up a handful of bubbles and blow them at the children. You might get splashed. Play in the pool until you feel you are finished.

When you step out of the baby pool, go over to one of the fine mist sprinklers nearby. They seem to be everywhere in the garden. Jump through the fine spray mist. If you want, you can do a conga-dance through the sprinkler with any of the children who feel like dancing with you. When you are finished, an adult attendant will bring you a towel.

After you are dried off, one of the children takes your hand and walks you over to the outdoor amphitheater. Several children are playing "make believe" and have dressed up in costumes with all the stage prop trimmings. Some children are coloring and making art at tables near the stage. Sit down and watch them play. Perhaps one of the little actors will come into the audience and offer you a costume to wear and a role to play. If you feel like playing make-believe with them, you may. One of the children may show you a picture and offer you some paper and a crayon. If you want to color, you may. When you are finished, clap and cheer loudly and tell the children you will see them later.

One of the children takes your hand again and leads you from the amphitheater to the far corner of the garden where there is a long stone wall. At the center of the wall is a large carved lion's head. There is a stream of water flowing from the lion's open mouth into a wishing fountain. The child hands you a coin and motions you to toss it into the fountain. Close your eyes, make a wish, and toss the coin into the fountain.

When you are finished at the fountain, you may linger and play in the garden, or you may exit.

Capturing the Scene

Write down a summary of your experience as soon as you have opened your eyes from the introductory visit. Describe as much as you can, especially details not discussed in the imagery. Describe the setting using all of your senses, your emotions, and your intuition. What do you want to adjust or change so that it is more suited to your personal taste? Go ahead and make those changes as you imagine the setting with the updates and edits.

Create a collage using images from photos, old magazines, the web, scrapbooking supplies, or personal drawings. Capture the elements of the setting that you experience most vividly and expand upon elements that you experience less vividly.

This is close to what I imagine. Visualize bubbles, toys, and kids playing in the fountain.

Photograph 202464 by morguefile.com user: clconroy

Environment: Angelscape Spa
Including the Lobby, Mud Bath, Mineral Bath, Diagnostic and Healing Rooms

Purpose: The *Angelscape* Spa is a platform for healing and rectification of any departure the self has made from the Sacred Self Template, or as God intended you to be without distortion. The spa is a conceptual connection to healing processes, a healing team, and ongoing healing support.

Environment Props: You can do the activities in this environment in your bed, in the shower, during bodywork sessions, or while you are in the sauna of your local gym. If you are lucky enough to visit an actual spa on a consistent basis, you can do the imagery activities while you are engaging in a similar real activity.

Intentions Supporting Environment

- Journeyer to create the environment setting according to personal taste and to adjust provided imagery as s/he sees fit.
- Platform for conceptual healing of Whole Self, such as the mental, emotional, physical, and spiritual bodies, in any way needed.
- Platform for identifying and rectifying distortions from Sacred Self Template.
- Platform for conceptualizing active or passive healing sessions of any kind.
- Platform to conceptualize practical health care and assistance provided through a spiritual reality.
- Platform to support the Journeyer to feel proactive, optimistic, and empowered in the care and tending of his/her own healing needs.
- Support for Journeyer to explore various healing modalities through the imagination, and to create personalized healing routines out of the integration of a variety of modalities.
- Functions and skills used to be integrated into other environments and protocols, as appropriate.

Starter Imagery to the *Angelscape* Spa

The *Angelscape* Spa is found within a mountain. It is a large cavern of different healing rooms and spa-like spaces. The entrance of the spa is found behind a small waterfall, not far from the Garden of the Little Ones. The spa is located within the earth to symbolize that our physical bodies are made of the same elements that are found in the earth, and that our mending requires the introduction of the natural raw materials from which we were fashioned.

Walk behind the waterfall and into the spa. A spiritual helper greets you with a big smile. The cave is dimly lit, warm, and moist. You can smell earth, different herbs, and the aroma of hot mineral springs.

You enter deeply into the cave opening and down a long hall. You emerge into a large central gallery in the cavern. The ceiling is high and made of stalagmites. The floor is lit with colored lights and has pathways, pools of water, potted ferns, and places to sit and rest between treatments. It reminds you somewhat of a 5-star hotel lobby set inside a cavern. There are hallways to other parts of the cavern and spa workers are busily going about their business. A large fireplace is built into the wall of this gallery and you see people in spa robes resting and sipping healthy drinks, reading books, napping, or chatting lightly with one another. An attendant approaches you and hands you a drink. It is a healing drink of some kind. Imagine sipping it. Place your awareness within your body and notice where the drink seems to be causing a response. Please make a note of what the drink tasted like, felt like, or what actual substances it seemed to reflect. When you are finished with your drink, your helper leads you from the main gallery down one of the many hallways branching off of it.

You walk into a multi-chamber area. It is steamy and warmer in this area than the other parts of the cavern. There are two small cozy chambers, among others, that your helper shows you; a mud bath, and a hot mineral spring. They each have their own separate area, though they share a common nook and sitting area in the cavern. You are encouraged to stick your hand into the different types of baths, to feel the textures and sensations. You will get to bathe in them later. When you have looked around the medicinal bath area, your helper ushers you back out into the main gallery to walk down another hall of the cavern.

Your helper brings you down another hall from the gallery. This area looks brightly lit compared to the ambient colored lighting of the other areas. It does not feel damp, like the other places, but it is still warm and welcoming. You walk further down the hallway. It begins to remind you of a very cozy doctor's office. There are many different rooms. The commonality between the rooms is that there is a table in the center of all of them for different kinds of healing work. The room that you are guided to enter looks more like a real room, not like a cave. There are objects that look like computers, scanning equipment, and a comfortable doctor's examining table.

Spiritual helpers enter the room wearing doctor's lab coats. One of them is carrying a file that has your name on it. It contains your *Sacred Self Template*, which is the pure design of you, without distortion, disease, or damage. It is the you that God originally intended you to be. In this room, called the *Healing Room*, your *Healing Team* will assess where you have moved away from this original template and work to rectify and heal whatever issues you have that stray from the creational blueprint of your Sacred Self Template. They use the template as a kind of tuning fork to bring your system back to its original state. Your helper gently takes your hand and places it on top of the file with your name on it. What do you experience? When you are ready, your helper will lead you back out of the Healing Room area and into the gallery again.

Your helper sits you down on a cozy seat in the main gallery. There are more areas in the spa, but you have seen the main areas that you will be using in the Direct Route and Scenic Route activities. You may explore the rest of the spa, as you wish, and create spaces that appeal to you and your healing needs. You may even create spaces outside of the spa cavern if you desire. You may curl up and take a nap, order another healing drink, or stick your feet into one of the small bubbling hot springs next to your seat.

When you are ready, offer your gratitude and exit the spa.

Capturing the Scene

Write down a summary of your experience as soon as you have opened your eyes from the introductory visit. Describe as much as you can, especially details not discussed in the imagery. Describe the setting using all of your senses, your emotions, and your intuition. What do you want to adjust or change so that it is more suited to your personal taste? Go ahead and make those changes as you imagine the setting with the updates and edits.

Create a collage using images from photos, old magazines, the web, scrapbooking supplies, or personal drawings. Capture the elements of the setting that you experience most vividly and expand upon elements that you experience less vividly.

Note: *Try as I might, I could not imagine the spa in any other setting. However, some people do not like caves or caverns. If you do not respond to the cavern images for the spa, please create one above ground with all of the specific healing spaces that were introduced in the imagery exercise.*

The spa is inside a cavern, this will help you to visualize those kind of features.

Photograph 144029
by morguefile.com
user: Carmem L. Vilanova

Environment: Dream Room

Purpose: The Dream Room serves as a dedicated personal "place" within *Angelscape* for the Journeyer before and after the formatted journey is completed. Many of the useful maintenance and ongoing care protocols are built into the functioning of the Dream Room for continuity, as well as to establish a lifestyle of supported care and competent functioning within a cooperative spiritual common ground on a continuing basis.

Suggested Environment Props: The best prop is for the Journeyer to actually create a supported space within his/her home that contains as many of the elements as possible of the Dream Room. If that is not possible, the Journeyer is encouraged to draw or create a collage of his/her

Dream Room. S/he is also encouraged to decorate his/her Dream Room and actual room with matching or similar accessories, such as pillows, knick-knacks, colors, artwork, and so on.

Intentions Supporting Environment

- Journeyer to create the environment setting according to personal taste and to adjust provided elements as s/he sees fit.
- Platform for continuing personal "place" within *Angelscape.*
- Platform for ongoing maintenance and care, translated from the formatted journey to a graceful lifestyle routine facilitated through functions of the Dream Room.
- Platform for privacy, personal gestation, healing, centering, and safety, as needed during formatted journey, and after, as a safe haven during times of stress.
- Functions of the room to be in alignment with functions of *Angelscape* environments, tools, and protocols.
- Dream Room to provide Journeyer with a sense of deep personal safety, uniqueness, expression, creativity, and ownership of personal boundaries and space.
- Dream Room as a continuing connection point for Journeyer and spiritual guidance, assistance, and interaction, as appropriate and beneficial.
- Dream Room as dedicated protected space during altered states of any kind, such as spiritual working space, sleeping, or meditation.
- Functions and skills of other areas to be integrated into the Dream Room, as appropriate.

Constructing Your Dream Room

Your Dream Room is constructed *entirely* out of your own idea of a "perfect room", or a space that is absolutely just right for you. Since this is an imaginary space, you can be extravagant and lavish, if that is what you want. The Dream Room can be a simple dorm style room or can be an apartment, a house, or whatever appeals to you as a safe, private space. It can be placed anywhere in *Angelscape,* on the ocean, in the forest, and so on. The scenery out of your window should be something beautiful and peaceful to you. The space should feel sacred, personal, private, and totally "you".

You may use graph paper to draw your Dream Room out, or just construct it in your imagination. You may cut out decorations from magazines that show items that match your style, use paint swatches from the hardware store, or gather any other "inspiring" ideas, as if you were actually creating a personal room/space of your dreams. The more real you can make it, the more useful it will be to you.

There are elements within the Dream Room that you need to include when you create it:

- A bed with blankets.
- Nightstand.
- Desk with a computer.
- Window with a view.
- Bathroom with a tub, shower, sink, and medicine cabinet.
- Closet.
- Globe of the earth, or a large map of the earth on the wall.
- Prayer shelf of candles.
- Fireplace.
- A water fountain.
- Potted plant or patio garden.

In the Meantime

The Dream Room is not discussed until the end of the book. You may, however, hang out within it at any time during your formatted journey if it makes you feel at ease. You may go to sleep in your Dream Room when you go to sleep "for real" at night, to imagine sleeping in supported, sacred space. Make it as comfortable as you can as a place you would dearly love to spend time within in order to recharge and regroup.

The Dream Room should be cozy, beautiful, and the most personal sacred space you can imagine.

Photograph 19056 by morguefile.com user: clarita

Environment: Angelscape Elixir Café

Purpose: The *Angelscape* Elixir Café is a platform for a social "place" within *Angelscape* and as a dedicated environment for the distribution of elixir energy drinks. The café is also designed to support a sense of playfulness, lightness, and fun, which are critical to the supported exploration of new concepts and functions.

Suggested Environment Props: The *Angelscape* Elixir Café uses elixir drinks as its main imagery, so using actual fluid for drinking can be an excellent prop. You can also use pictures, ideas, or your actual favorite café, restaurant, or bistro to help you develop the scene.

Intentions Supporting Environment

- Journeyer to create the environment setting according to personal taste and to adjust provided elements as s/he sees fit.
- Platform for continuing social place within *Angelscape.*
- Platform for the delivery of specific, goal oriented, supportive energy downloads in the form of energy elixir drinks.
- Angelic Barista to be "divine mixologist" for appropriate energetic support and download streaming.
- Support for the use of vibrational elixir drinks as a physical tool.
- Support to request specific support and assistance from spiritual helpers through the Angel Surprise Elixir.
- All elixirs to successfully relate, address, or support, described definition.
- Platform to receive any energy elixir drink available within the formatted journey, or through the elixir drink menu.
- Support for non-confrontational, casual, and "as part of life" communication with spiritual helpers, deceased loved ones, and Sacred Self.
- Functions and skills of other areas to be integrated into the Dream Room, as appropriate.

Constructing Your Angelscape Elixir Café

The *Angelscape* Elixir Café is constructed entirely of your own perfect image of a café, restaurant, lounge, or bistro. It should be an environment that is exactly as you would want it to be for relaxing and hanging out with your friends. It is meant to be a place of fun, adventure, comfort, and joy. You will need to place an angelic style "Barista" at a counter to create your elixir energy drinks, but otherwise, you have complete authority to create a space that is totally appealing to you.

In the Meantime

The *Angelscape* Elixir Café is not discussed until the very last Scenic Route activity. It is used as a continuing care space that is introduced to you as you are finished with your formatted journey. You may, however, visit the café any time you care to in order to request any of the elixir energy drinks used liberally throughout the formatted journey. You can also just request the "Angel Surprise", which is whatever you might need at that very moment.

Onto the Healing Journey

You are now ready to begin your formatted journey through *Angelscape*. It is okay for you to update your visualizations as you move through the various activities. Please make sure you have all your support tools and accessories available to you before you need them (such as described in the Integration Tips section). Please do the Double Dip activity as often as you feel you need to if you have a lot of congestion to purge. You signed a Cooperative Contract to *God* that you would take care of yourself, so I am holding you to that agreement. If you need help, get help--otherwise it is best to expect the unexpected. The activities have been created to help you use your imagination as a powerful tool of transformation in cooperation with your spiritual reality. Between you and me, I would recommend a good old-fashioned seat belt and a hearty sense of humor as you move your way through unknown territory. It will be okay. Just keep breathing, keep moving, and keep believing. Have faith that God knows what He is doing, even when we do not. If you did not already believe that, I doubt you would have ever picked up this book in the first place. Keep Faith.

"Life is either a daring adventure or nothing."

Hellen Keller

Part 2: The Healing Journey

Section 1
Welcome to Angelscape

Activities Introduction

Section 1 activities are the most widely used in the entire book because they serve as the transition areas into and out of *Angelscape*. The Lotus Pool is used to cleanse and purify the system and to offer a progressive relaxation technique to lull the Journeyer into a meditative state of consciousness. This shift in consciousness provides optimal work receptivity. The TLC Bath (aka: Tender Loving Care) is used as a standard exit and conclusion to every activity. The purpose of it is to return the Journeyer to a normal waking state feeling refreshed and peaceful. It also supports graceful integration of healing shifts, the soothing of distress, and enhanced integrity of the system during rapid changes.

Normally, the Lotus Pool is visited first and then the Journeyer is escorted to whatever *Angelscape* environment is used for the next work activity. That work activity would be completed and then the Journeyer would finish up for the day with the TLC Bath. The first time this activity is done, however, you will just go in, do the activity in the Lotus Pool, and then go straight to the TLC Bath. When you just visit the Lotus Pool and TLC Bath without additional activities, it is called the *Double Dip*. The Double Dip is an excellent meditation strategy that can be plucked from the larger context of the *Angelscape* work quite easily. It is my opinion that anyone who attends to regular energetic cleansing and resiliency strengthening can eventually triumph over any personal issues. Our systems, physical and otherwise, seem to be perfectly capable of self-healing when the obstacles to proper functioning are removed. If you do nothing else with the *Angelscape* work, the Double Dip will serve you very well with minimal time or effort.

Section 1 is also important because it introduces working platforms, conceptual tools, basic skills, and the use of helpers, all of which will be used repeatedly throughout the *Angelscape* journey. The main working platform, or activity structure, used in *Angelscape* is the *"Dip, Drink, and Wrap."* The "Dip" is for the use of healing baths, or the imagery of immersion into a liquid-like healing medium. The "Drink" is the use of imagery of drinking a healing medium. The "Wrap" is being cocooned and sealed within the energies of the healing process, as if being wrapped in a blanket or putting on a robe. This particular technique is powerful because all of the actions are easily visualized as part of the basic skills of living. Everyone knows what it feels like to bathe, drink, and wrap up in a blanket. The sensory memory of having done these things before is more than enough to make the experience as real as possible. The more real something feels, the more successful the visualization. If all else fails, the Journeyer can actually bathe, drink, and wrap up as ways to physically act out the meditation.

The conceptual tools used in this section include the bath, the drink, and the wraps, but it also includes the suction hoses used to imagine congestion being removed from your system. In *Angelscape,* when you need a tool, you simply create it and use it. One of the most important basic skills introduced in section one, and used repeatedly throughout the book, is the *tactile energy breathing* technique. This technique requires you to use your imagination to move energy around your body. It is done by imagining that you are breathing a substance into your body, as if you were hollow, and pulling it or pushing it around. This skill is used often in the book. The Journeyer also gets to experience the imagery of spiritual helpers and the loosening of attachment to the laws of physical reality, which do not apply in *Angelscape.*

Direct Route Activity #1
The *Double Dip*, Entrance and Exit Activities to *Angelscape*

Environment Settings: Lotus Pool and TLC Bath

Note: *This is the only Direct Route activity that is actually two distinct parts. The Lotus Pool Water Breath Cleanse is a necessary part of preparing the Journeyer for the current activity of the day. The TLC Dip is a strategy to assist the Journeyer to integrate and bounce back from work with as much ease, comfort, and grace as possible. These strategies should be used as a matter of course, with awareness and intention, as part of responsible practices for all Angelscape visits.*

Complementary Scenic Route Activities
SR 1 A: Heart Breath
SR 1 B: Sky Float

Part 1
Lotus Pool Water Breath Cleanse

Purpose: The Lotus Pool Water Breath Cleanse provides, cleansing, purification, release of misaligned patterns, preparation for *Angelscape* work, and progressive relaxation and induction to a meditative state of consciousness.

Usage Suggestions: This activity is used as the entrance strategy to every *Angelscape* session. While you are actively going through the *Angelscape* program, I recommend that you visit the Lotus Pool before going to sleep at night. If you feel that you are purging congestion from the activities, use the Lotus Pool as often as you need to in order to keep ahead of the out flowing congestion. There is no such thing as being too energetically clean. Use this activity often.

Activity Props: You may enjoy doing this activity in an actual bath, hot tub, or shower. You can use lotus flower essence as a stand in for the Lotus Nectar and utilize any other tools that you like that would support meditation or cleansing. An indoor water fountain or music that sounds like gurgling water would also be nice.

Summary: In this activity, you will imagine yourself slowly wading into the Lotus Pool until you are at the center. You take a sip of the Lotus Nectar Elixir from one of the lotus flowers floating on the surface of the water. The nectar is an energetic elixir that will help to prepare you for your work. Once you are ready, you will imagine "breathing" the warm, effervescent water in through the soles of your feet on the inhale and then out through your feet on the exhale. It will be as if you were a hollow straw sucking water up and down your body. You will imagine bringing the water up your body in stages, breathing several times at each stage for your first visit. You may take more than one breath to fill up an area that is far away from your feet. A drain at the bottom of the Lotus Pool removes all debris that is purged from your body on the exhale. The water will stay clear, as the Lotus Pool is incorruptible, fully self-cleansing, and holy. Once you are able to pull the water all the way up your body to your head, you will blow it out of the top of your head, like a spout.

There are spiritual helpers that show up while you are doing the water cleansing breath. They can be whatever spiritual figures you trust and prefer. They will have tools available to remove larger debris, congestion, stagnant waste, or anything that needs more attention to be removed. The tools they use can go through your body, as if it is not solid. Their job is to make sure that you are cleansed on every level and to support you in the process in any way necessary. They will get into the Lotus Pool with you, but will remain in the background of your experience and focus. They will work independent of your water breathing, but you may ask them for help if you feel you need it. They may get ahead of you, or lag behind you, depending on where they need to work. The belly, heart, head--or any place in the body that has misalignments or pain--may be areas in which the helpers may focus on more intensely than others. Upon exiting the Lotus Pool, the helpers will put a Work Support Wrap upon you, which may look something like a spa robe.

Helpers: There are usually one or two helpers at the Lotus Pool for the water breathing activity.

New Concepts: Suction Hoses, Lotus Nectar Elixir, Work Support Wrap, "Dip, Drink, Wrap", Double Dip.

Intentions Supporting Activity

- Intentions added from anywhere else in the book that are relevant to this work.

- Cleansing, clearing, and purification of the Whole Self.
- Loosening and breaking up of congestion of any kind, such that it can be gracefully removed in appropriate timing for comfort.
- Cleansing of misalignments and distorted patterns of any kind.
- Removal of inappropriate, negative, parasitic, or harmful influence.
- Optimal relaxation, peace, and feelings of well-being.
- Support for optimal state of consciousness to do work.
- Support for sustained optimal working conditions while in *Angelscape.*
- Support for reminders and prompts for Journeyer to cleanse when needed.
- *Suction Hose*: tool used by the helpers at the station, supports the removal of stubborn blockages (known or unknown), congestion, or other energetic debris in the system.
- *Lotus Nectar Elixir*: energy drink tool that supports shifting of state of consciousness to optimal sensitivity and receptivity, as well as initiating any additional preparation.
- *Work Wrap*: tool that supports optimal working conditions, continued enhanced receptivity, enhanced integrity, and sustainable support to Lotus Nectar Elixir.
- *Dip, Drink, Wrap:* process used in the book that provides imagery of a healing bath, healing drink, and a healing wrap used together to create a synergistic holistic experience that is easily visualized due to its similarity to real world activities.
- *Double Dip:* protocol using the Lotus Pool and TLC Bath to cleanse, clear, and then soothe, comfort, and enhance resiliency. It can be used as maintenance self-care and a meditation session by itself without the *Angelscape* backdrop, if desired.
- Listed intentions reaffirmed as a part of the Cooperative Contract already signed over.
- Engagement of this activity, if a Cooperative Contract has not yet been signed, an affirmation of acceptance of these intentions, corrected in perfection, and brought within Divine Will.

Action Statement:
"I request to enter the Lotus Pool, now please."

Step-by-Step Activity Instructions:

1. Stand at the edge of the Lotus Pool and take a deep breath of fresh air. Notice the sights, colors, sounds, fragrances, and physical sensations of the environment. Pull in as many details as you can and allow yourself to fully enter the moment.
2. Step down onto the first wide stone step within the warm, effervescent water and take another deep breath of fresh air. Your feet and legs may feel a gentle tingling and warmth as you pause to savor the sensations of the water.
3. Move deliberately and slowly down the rest of the stone steps. Allow a deeper sensation of peace and relaxation to wash over you with every step you take into the warm water. Dip your head under the water to complete your submersion once you have reached the center of the pool.
4. Select a lotus flower floating nearby you and sip the nectar from it, as if it were a cup. Allow the nectar to move into your system to prepare you for the work. As you sip the nectar, a pair of spiritual helpers approach and step into the Lotus Pool to support you with the work. The helpers pull out several hoses from the side of the pool and begin working on loosening and gently suctioning clotted congestion from your body. You do not have to attend to them. You are asked to concentrate and attend to your water breathing.
5. You are instructed to imagine "breathing" the warm water of the Lotus Pool in through the soles of your feet and up to your knees, as if your body was a hollow straw. As you exhale, breathe and push the water out of your feet and into the drain at the bottom of the pool. Repeat this 3 times. The water by your feet may look dirty for a moment until the drain moves the debris away. The water turns clear again almost immediately.
6. Next, breathe the water up the rest of your legs to your upper thighs. Pull the water up through your legs on the inhale, and push it out of your feet on the exhale. Repeat this 3 times. Your legs feel buoyant and deeply relaxed.

7. Continue breathing the water up from your feet into your abdominal cavity, filling up your gut, your backside, and your reproductive system. Feel the gentle tickle of the warm bubbles within your belly before you push it back out. Repeat this 3 times or more.
8. Now imagine breathing the water all the way up into your chest cavity next. Take a second breath if you need to. Fill up your hands, arms, and shoulders as well. Imagine your body being three-quarters of the way full of warm cleansing water, and then push it back out of your feet. Repeat 3 times or more. Your spiritual helpers will likely help with the suction hoses at the heart area while you are cleansing your chest cavity.
9. Next, breathe the water up into your throat. Clear your throat, imagine shaking up any stagnation there, and push the water back out of your feet. Take a second breath if you need it. Push it back out of your feet. Repeat this 3 times, or more.
10. The last breath will be a little different. Breathe the water all the way up your body, filling your entire head with the cleansing water. Instead of pushing it back out through your feet on the exhale--push it straight out of the top of your head, like a giant spout. Do this at least 3 times. Try to get your spout "spray" as high as you can.
11. Continue water breathing strongly out of the top of your head until your system feels completely clear. Your helpers may join you in a water spout "contest" to encourage you to blow it up and out as strongly as you can.
12. Your helpers escort you out of the Lotus Pool and place a Work Wrap on you. It may look like a robe, tunic, or some kind of loose fitting wrap. You are now ready to proceed with whatever work you are doing next.
13. Double Dip: Your spiritual helpers walk you over a few yards to the TLC Bath. It looks similar to the Lotus Pool, but the water is thick and syrupy and has shimmering pastel rainbow colors.

Continuing Thoughts

Any place you see or experience water in *Angelscape,* there is an opportunity to cleanse, refresh, or shift your energy in some way. The Lotus Pool is dedicated as a cleanse and transition station, but the lake, the ocean, fountain, swimming hole, and so on, are all filled with sacred healing waters. Go with any urges to swim, drink, anoint, splash, or play in the water anywhere in *Angelscape*.

The visualization of water breathing is a powerful way to reduce anxiety and stress. The cleansing water breaths can reduce the cascade of stress related responses in your body. You can start each morning by visualizing the Lotus Pool Water Breath Cleanse while you take your shower and imagine it during the day any time you feel stressed or anxious.

Part 2
TLC Bath

Environment Setting: Next to Lotus Pool

Purpose: The TLC (Tender Loving Care) Bath is the official exit strategy for the end of every visit to *Angelscape* when any work is done. It is designed to soothe the system, alleviate discomfort, and to coat the system in a buffer that provides a cocooning transition period of enhanced protection, care, and strength.

Usage Suggestions: The TLC Bath is the exit strategy to the end of every *Angelscape* visit. You can also use it when you feel exhausted, worn thin, drained, emotionally overwhelmed, or in any instance that you need to self-soothe and nurture yourself. The TLC Bath is a powerful tool to keep you feeling safe and cozy. Use it as often as you need to use it.

Activity Props: You can use all of the same props you may use for the Lotus Pool. You can also use any tools or props that make you feel comforted, nurtured, and safe, such as, flower essences for “rescue”, homeopathic stress or exhaustion relief, and so on. You may want to wrap yourself up in a cozy comforter after the work, as if the Resiliency Comfort Wrap is actually around you, and have a good nap.

Summary: The TLC Bath is very similar to the Lotus Pool activity, except that its goal is not exclusively to cleanse the system, but to provide soothing and comfort to alleviate symptoms of overwhelm or “detox” as you move through the exercises in the book. It should be used when you exit *Angelscape* as a way to transition back to regular consciousness. It can also be used by itself if you feel uncomfortable or need soothing and assistance to integrate healing work.

You enter into the thick liquid, which you can visualize with a warm light syrup consistency, and imagine breathing it up into your body, coating and soothing everything within. You are given the Graceful Integration Elixir, which will be handed to you by one of the spiritual helpers. When you exit the pool, you will be swaddled in a cozy wrap that is like a cocoon of soothing energies that will surround you and allow you to adjust to the healing shifts with grace.

Helpers: You can use the same helpers as in Lotus Pool activity.

New Concepts: Graceful Integration Elixir, Resiliency Comfort Wrap.

Intentions Supporting Activity

- Intentions added from anywhere else in the book that are relevant to this work.
- Protection, buffering, security, and establishment of appropriate energetic boundaries according to the dynamic needs and sensitivities of the system.
- Cleansing and removal of emotional/energetic debris and congestion released from healing activities.
- Halting and reversal of stress cascade, immediate re-stabilization of system.
- Soothing and TLC for Whole Self, especially emotional body, such that the impact of the work is gracefully accepted and as easy to integrate as possible.
- Soothing of hot spots, pain, or discomfort of any kind, physical or energetic.
- Perfected adjustment with enhanced resiliency, strength, coherence, and integrity, as needed.
- Support to release distorted patterns and to integrate Sacred Self patterns with grace and ease.
- Buffered sensitivities, such that the sensation of being exposed or vulnerable to harsh external environments, or stressors, while in the healing process is alleviated.
- Support for Journeyer to feel loved, supported, and fully cared for during and after the activities in this book.
- Support for the Journeyer to feel competent to handle sensations or symptoms of overwhelm or healing crisis.

- Support for the Journeyer to be prompted to utilize this activity in advance of feeling any discomfort or system stress.
- Support for the Journeyer to remember to use this activity once the sensation of discomfort or system stress is experienced.
- *Graceful Integration Elixir*: energy drink tool that supports gentle integration of healing shifts, such that they are phased in and fully anchored in a comfortable and sustainable way.
- *Resiliency Comfort Wrap*: tool that supports sustained system integrity and strengthening, as well as soothing, comfort, gentle purging of released congestion, and graceful integration of healing shifts.
- Listed intentions reaffirmed as a part of the Cooperative Contract already signed over.
- Engagement of this activity, if a Cooperative Contract has not yet been signed, an affirmation of acceptance of these intentions, corrected in perfection, and brought within Divine Will.

Action Statement:
"I request to enter the TLC Bath, now please."

Step-by-Step Activity Instructions:

1. Your spiritual helpers assist you to enter into the TLC Bath. The fluid is thick and syrupy like a warm and comforting honey or silky lotion. It may be a pastel rainbow of colors, or may change colors to various pastel shades. Walk down the steps of the TLC Bath and sit down. Move your body around to release any stiffness or rigidness.
2. You are instructed to imagine breathing this sweet thick liquid into your body, as with the cleansing water breath at the Lotus Pool. Imagine the liquid thickly coating every part of you, but especially all around your heart and any other areas that seem raw or vulnerable.
3. An attendant approaches the TLC Bath with a kind smile and a cup of Graceful Integration Elixir. Imagine sipping down this elixir, feeling the fluid bring clarity and enhanced sense of stabilization and wellbeing to your system.

4. When you are finished soaking in the TLC bath and have finished your Graceful Integration Elixir, you may exit the bath. Your attendant swaddles you in the Resiliency Comfort Wrap. It is a pastel rainbow colored wrap, securing your whole system in a buffering cocoon of tender loving care.
5. When you are finished, you may leave *Angelscape* or go on to the Scenic Route activities. Do not drive, operate heavy machinery, or do any activities that are dangerous, or that require you to be fully attentive, until you feel fully shifted back to a normal waking state. Take some time to journal or take notes before your memory of the experience fades.

Continuing Thoughts

The Double Dip protocol can be used as often as you wish. The Lotus Pool cleanses and purifies, and the TLC Bath comforts and soothes. Healing can sometimes be viewed as removing congestion from within the system and then bringing stabilization so that progress is made to higher levels of functioning. The Double Dip has all the elements to allow you to remove congestion and bring comfort and stabilization to your system. If you are not ready to engage the *Angelscape* journey, you can easily integrate the Double Dip into your routine instead. It is a powerful, easy to visualize, meditation session that will leave you feeling refreshed and peaceful. It also teaches simple basic skills that can be used without a meditation session; you can use the tactile energy breathing technique without a scenic set up.

Gorgeous lotus flower that you can imagine floating on top of clear effervescent water.

Photograph 119639
by morguefile.com
user: pjhudson

Scenic Route #1 A
Cleansing Heart Breath

Environment Setting: Lotus Pool, TLC Bath

Purpose: The purpose of the Cleansing Heart Breath activity is to provide another protocol for emotional congestion relief, stress relief, and localized tension and pain relief, which can be utilized in or out of the *Angelscape* environment. This breath can be utilized in any of the healing bath environments in *Angelscape.*

Usage Suggestions: This activity targets the cleansing or soothing tactile energy breath to the heart, or other specified area of the body. You can use it as an additional technique any time you visit any of the healing baths in *Angelscape*, or use it directly without visualizing as a way to manage stress. Use it as you feel prompted.

Activity Props: You can do this activity in a bathtub or other type of water. You may use a safe warming cream (gentle muscle rub or vapor rub cream) on your heart area to support the sensation of localized warmth, which is an important element to relieving stress concentrated at the heart area.

Summary: The Heart Breath is a modification on the Water Breath Cleanse activity. The Water Breath Cleanse moves the water like a pillar through your body, but the Heart Breath moves the water directly into the heart area and focuses on filling up only that region of the body. The inhale and exhale pulls the water in and pushes the water out from the heart center of the body, removing emotional congestion and stress that often concentrates in this area.

The Heart Breath as used in the TLC Bath brings specialized comfort and care directly to the emotional body. Since some of the work in *Angelscape* deals with purging old pain, the emotional body can sometimes feel stressed. Use the Heart Breath in both the Lotus Pool and the TLC Bath to experience the range of assistance possible. The Heart Breath can be modified to any part of the body that is experiencing trauma or distress.

Helpers: You may use the same helpers as Lotus Pool activity.

New Concepts: None

Intentions Supporting Activity

- Intentions added from anywhere else in the book that are relevant to this work.
- Support for the loosening and removal of emotional congestion.
- Support for stress-reduction and deep relaxation.
- Release from localized tension or pain.
- Cleansing of specific energy centers, or areas of body, as needed.
- Support to move healing energies where needed in body.
- Support for proactive and positive self soothing and coping skills.
- Support to utilize the tactile energy breathing technique in practical ways for self soothing.
- Support for the Journeyer to seek professional care if personal needs require it.
- Listed intentions reaffirmed as a part of the Cooperative Contract already signed over.
- Engagement of this activity, if a Cooperative Contract has not yet been signed, an affirmation of acceptance of these intentions, corrected in perfection, and brought within Divine Will.

Action Statement:

"I request to initiate the Heart Cleansing Breath, now please."

Step-by-Step Activity Instructions:

1. Your helpers escort you into the Lotus Pool or TLC Bath, as you select. They have all necessary tools available if they are needed. Otherwise, they will stand out of your way and remain in the background.
2. You are instructed to imagine breathing the warm fluid of the bath directly into your heart and chest cavity. Pull the fluid in on the inhale and push it back out on the exhale. Feel the fluid filling up the entire chest cavity, releasing tension, stress, and congestion.
3. You are asked if there are any other areas in your body that feel tense or tender. If so, you may do the direct water breath into those areas, just like you completed for the Heart

Breath. When you have used the Heart Breath in all the areas you wish to work upon, your helpers will swaddle you in the Resiliency Comfort Wrap.

4. When you are finished, you may leave *Angelscape*, or go on to the next Scenic Route activity. Do not drive, operate heavy machinery, or do any activities that are dangerous, or that require you to be fully attentive, until you feel fully shifted back to a normal waking state. Take some time to journal or take notes before your memory of the experience fades.

Continuing Thoughts

The cleansing breath work is a powerful tool to release tension and congestion anywhere in the body. It is also a powerful way to imagine the movement of healing and helpful energies in the body. The heart center of the body is where most of us tend to hold our emotional, and often physical, tension. Other parts of your body may hold tension or pain, or feel otherwise heavy and in need of cleansing and revitalization. Practice using the cleansing water breath on any area of the body or any other energy center. This technique is the most easily adapted to non-meditative stress relief while you are on the go during the regular workday. You do not have to imagine the Lotus Pool to imagine breathing into your heart area if you do not have the privacy to do so. You can simply breathe.

The water in both baths should have an energetic quality. This photo can help you imagine the water being bubbly.

Photograph 197912 by morguefile.com user: cooee

Scenic Route #1 B
Sky Float

Environment Setting: Lotus Pool or TLC Bath

Purpose: The Sky Float activity promotes awareness expansion and consciousness fluidity, rapport building with helpers, embryonic nurturing, relaxation, body/mind fluidity, and awareness toggling skills building.

Usage Suggestions: This activity is helpful to develop a sense of expanded awareness. If you like doing the activity, you can integrate it into your meditations. If you do not like it, you do not have to do it again. Use it as you feel prompted.

Activity Props: You can set up this activity in a physical way by asking a trusted friend to support you while you float in a pool looking at the sky. You can use some of the same props used in the other section activities to support your visualization skills as desired. I recommend taping this activity ahead of time because you should allow yourself to be "right out of it". It will be easier to listen to the instructions than to read them.

Summary: The Sky Float is an awareness shifting activity that you can do as part of your transition into *Angelscape*. Once you have walked into the Lotus Pool and the helpers have joined you, simply float in the water on your back looking at the sky. You breathe in the essence of the sunlit sky and then toggle your conscious awareness from your body to the sky. You fill the sky with your awareness, if you can, to give you a sense of having no physical boundary. You fill up a cloud in the sky with your awareness if you need some boundaries, and then slowly build up your ability to fill up the sky.

The instructions are written as if you are looking at a sunlit sky during the day, but if you prefer, you can star hop into a night sky if that feels more natural to you. The idea is to loosen the concept of your consciousness as being bound to your physical body, such that you can learn to appreciate yourself in a more spiritual and fluid form. You may use either the Lotus Pool or the TLC Bath for this activity; select whichever is most comfortable for you. Initiate it after you have soaked and completed the water breathing work. This activity is best done when you are relaxed and loose.

Helpers: Use the same helpers as the Lotus Pool activity. You will imagine them gently supporting your back so that you can go completely limp, trusting that you will be supported to remain above the water.

New Concepts: None

Intentions Supporting Activity

- Intentions added from anywhere else in the book that are relevant to this work.
- Support for an expanding sense of awareness.
- Soothing deep relaxation.
- Release from mundane concerns, *"getting out of ones own skin"*.
- Support for the building of rapport and trust with spiritual helpers.
- Pre-birth embryonic re-nurturing and re-patterning, if needed.
- Support to easily toggle between different states of consciousness.
- Support to experience the self as pure consciousness without boundaries.
- Support to experience the self as being a part of All Creation.
- Support to access deeper parts of the self, as needed.
- Listed intentions reaffirmed as a part of the Cooperative Contract already signed over.
- Engagement of this activity, if a Cooperative Contract has not yet been signed, an affirmation of acceptance of these intentions, corrected in perfection, and brought within Divine Will.

Action Statement:
"I request to initiate the Sky Float, now please."

Step-by-Step Activity Instructions:

1. After you have completed your breathing work in either the Lotus Pool or the TLC Bath, allow yourself to float backwards upon your back. Your helpers will stand next to you on each side to keep you perfectly supported and safe.
2. You are instructed to take a deep breath and go as buoyantly limp in the warm water as you can. You notice that the

helpers keep your body at a perfect level in the water so that your face remains above the water line.

3. Gaze at the bright and beautiful sky above you. The sun is shining in the company of fluffy white clouds. Imagine breathing in the essence of the sky into every part of your floating body. Imagine the sky itself is filling you up until your body is the same color as the sky.
4. Allow your awareness to move up into the sky and into one of the fluffy white clouds far above you. Imagine that you are floating perfectly supported in the sky. Fill up the whole cloud with your awareness. Become the cloud.
5. Now allow yourself to look down at your floating body in the Lotus Pool. You look so small, just a fuzzy dot surrounded by a quilt work of countryside.
6. Slowly lower your awareness down through the sky, moving closer to your floating body, like an elevator moving from the penthouse to the ground floor. Your body gets larger and larger in your perspective as you move closer to it.
7. Now, move your awareness back into your floating body until you inhabit it completely. Wiggle your toes in the water and take a deep breath.
8. Place your awareness on your left big toe wiggling in the water. Imagine moving the seat of your consciousness into your big toe, as if your big toe was the container for your mind.
9. Imagine wiggling your body gently in the water, as if you are making the command to move your body from within your big toe.
10. Move the seat of your awareness back to your head and focus your attention on the sky again. Watch the clouds get fainter until they finally disappear and all that you can see is deep blue sky.
11. Move your awareness into the blue of the sky and fill it up with as much of your awareness as you can. Disburse yourself into the blue sky and become the sky.
12. When you are ready, move your awareness back to your floating body. Your helpers will gently lower your feet and legs into the pool so that you are standing again. Gently move your body until your awareness is anchored fully

within it. Your helpers assist you out of the TLC Bath and swaddle you with the Resiliency Comfort Wrap.

13. When you are finished, you may leave *Angelscape*. Do not drive, operate heavy machinery, or do any activities that are dangerous, or that require you to be fully attentive, until you feel fully shifted back to a normal waking state. Take some time to journal or take notes before your memory of the experience fades.

Continuing Thoughts

This activity is designed to help you toggle your awareness and consciousness from small to large to small, from within to without to within, from contained to uncontained to contained again. This ability to move your awareness assists you to access deeper aspects of your own consciousness from an awake and aware position. The ability to be aware of many levels of being will help you to gain mastery over parts of yourself that currently function outside of your awareness and which may limit or act in opposition to your well-being, such as, unconscious perceptual distortions, negative or limiting scripts or mind talk, and so on.

You may switch up where you place your awareness and play with those concepts in whatever way you wish. You may move your awareness into and out of anything in *Angelscape*. For example, you could go from cloud to body, body to lotus flower, flower to leaf, leaf to tree, tree to bird, bird to another tree, another leaf, to a ladybug, back to the leaf, into the tree, into the roots, and into the ground, becoming the countryside. You can also practice moving the seat of your consciousness from your head to other parts of your body, such as your heart, your fingers, organs, and so on.

Summary and Wrap Up

Complementary Activities

- Take a sea salt bath or an herbal cleansing bath.
- Burn ceremonial incense or cleansing herbs, such as, frankincense, white sage, sweet grass.
- Research physical body detoxification techniques.
- Research or make an appointment for a colonic (deep bowel cleansing).
- Clean your house, attic, closets, pantry, or refrigerator.

- Throw away items you no longer need.
- Find music that you like for the Lotus Pool and TLC Bath activities.

Project Ideas

You can make your own special wraps to correspond with the wraps you use in *Angelscape*. Even if you are not a tailor, you can still buy a yard or two of your favorite fabric and use fabric paints or simple stitches to add stone beads, decorations, or meaningful items to create your special "wrap".

Reflection Questions

1. Describe how you were feeling before and after the activities.
2. What were the most vivid details of your imagery during the activities?
3. Describe your helpers, the tools, and their assistance.
4. What surprised you the most about your experiences?
5. What was your favorite activity in Section 1?
6. What was your least favorite activity in Section 1?
7. Can you integrate your new skills into your more familiar practices?
8. Were there any details that seemed highlighted to you that you might want to think about?
9. Do you feel inspired to do any research in any other related area? If so, what is it?
10. What ways have you used to cleanse yourself emotionally, spiritually, or mentally?
11. What areas of your body seemed to have the most congestion? Do you know why?

Focus Group Feedback

Sharon

Water Breath Cleanse

The lotus pool is one of my favorite places. I love the peace, serenity and joyful energy that surround it. I had three helpers, two women who supported my arms on both sides, and a very large man in the front who did all the vacuuming. At the bottom of the pool, in a circle surrounding my feet, were pink quartz crystals about the size of grapefruits. Throughout the water breathing, the man vacuumed my whole body and energy centers, but he especially concentrated on my head and neck areas, like my ears, eyes, and throat.

Before doing the water breathing, I was very tired, heavy and foggy. After the session, although I still felt tired, I felt much lighter and clearer. The best part of the activity was the peace and solitude, the lifting of the "burden" so to speak, and coming away feeling lighter and "cleaner". It was very nice and refreshing.

Laura

Water Breath Cleanse

It was a balmy night setting as I walked into the Lotus Pool. The water had an iridescent green glow to it, like a swimming pool at night with a green light on below the surface. The water itself was *thickish*--like it had a dense quality to it, but at the same time *not*. It was both light, like good bath oil, and soft, with a silky texture. "Pure" comes to mind--extremely "pure". I wanted to drink it as I walked in, and did--it was sweet and refreshing. As I went in, my body became somewhat translucent, because I felt as if the water didn't come exclusively up through my feet, but flowed through my body at all levels simultaneously.

There were two angelic presences with me who began to help with the clearing and cleansing process. Their work seemed focused on the lower half of my body, the first two energy centers. It was quite a process to clear and balance them. I did not get the "water spout" element, because I felt like I was a *part* of the water in some way. It flowed through my form just washing around and through every molecule. Before I began, I felt tired from the day--afterwards I felt squeaky clean and extremely relaxed with not a care in the world. I did feel like I needed to go directly to bed and get some sleep though. It was such a relaxing and comforting experience. I think so many people will love it. I knew I was in sacred space.

TLC Bath

I knew without a doubt I needed this! It felt warm and safe. I felt "softened around the edges". It was as if I could be "softer" about some of the things that I've had to be more rigid about in life without losing the core values I felt were important.

I seemed to be in almond oil--I felt and smelled it clearly. The towel I wrapped up in was sitting on a stool waiting for me to get out. I was in quiet solitude, no helpers around, but it seemed to be what I needed the most. Quiet time is very healing to me. I had the sense that if I stayed in the oil much longer, I'd have an out-of-body experience and be gone for a while. It didn't seem a good time for that, so I made a conscious decision to get out, stay present, and literally fell asleep shortly after finishing the exercise.

Lourdes

Nectar Sip

I had an angel greet me and another one walk me down the steps of the Lotus Pool. There were lotus flowers in the pool and they floated over to me. I was instructed to sit in the water and drink the nectar. The nectar was light, but warmed my body like a sip of brandy. As I drank it, a green light began to glow within my forehead. As it flowed through my body, the light started becoming golden. I started crying and releasing some emotions that felt as if they came out of nowhere. As my tears flowed, an angel put his hand on my back behind my heart center. As the release continued, I was given an amber/golden citrine colored pendant to wear over my heart center. It infused my body with a golden ray, which brought about a sense of tranquility. I got up and was given a white fuzzy robe, and was directed to sit down on a chaise lounge chair to relax.

Water Breath Cleanse

Before starting this exercise, I was cold. The angel helpers led me to the center of the pool. At the center, the angels got ready to suction off the unwanted energy. As I started doing the exercise, I started feeling a warmth in my feet. This is unusual, because my feet are usually cold. As the warm water rose up my body, I felt lighter and started seeing the colors of indigo and purple. When the water made its way up to my abdominal cavity, I felt myself starting to cough and my stomach started rumbling (even though I had eaten a half an hour before the exercise). Pushing the water up to my head, the color changed to red. By the time I was spouting it out, there were water angels suctioning off my heart and throat chakras along with hoses on my back where my lungs are.

Heart Breath Cleanse

I entered *Angelscape* and as soon as I got there, I was filled with lightness and joy. I skipped and twirled all the way to the Lotus Pool. I was delighted to go to the pool. As I went into the pool, my angel attendants appeared and said they would be at my side if needed. As soon as I started breathing into my heart chakra, I saw the color green. It was warm and comforting. As this cleansing continued, I found my breaths getting longer and I was feeling warmer. The water made its way into my stomach area and it felt as if a warm balm was being placed on this energy center. After a while, I felt well enough to get up out of the pool. I was wrapped up in a soft comfortable white robe and sat down in my favorite chair. I drank another herbal concoction in total peace.

Sky Float

This was the hardest activity for me. I couldn't relax enough. I didn't like the idea of floating, and becoming "one" with the clouds and sky was difficult for me. For some reason, I didn't feel secure on my back and felt lost when I tried becoming one with the cloud. To help me, I gave up on the float and did a water cleansing breath, which helped me a great deal.

Lori

Water Breath Cleanse

When I got into the Lotus Pool, I heard babbling water and I felt the fizzies. I had actual rose fizzy bath bombs in the bathtub with me. My angels and guides were sitting along side with their feet dangling in the pool. I didn't actually see them, I just knew they were "there". There were two helpers at the Lotus Pool with the whitest skin and large blue eyes. One of my totems was there as well, a hawk with a watchful eye, which I could see and hear it as it circled. There were also lots of butterflies, and I could hear beautiful birds. I even saw a tiny frog and he also had blue eyes.

It was super peaceful, but I also somewhat dreaded what was going to happen. I don't know any other way to explain it; dread might be a bit too strong. I felt my angels give me the message, "It's ok. It's ok." When I got into the water, the two helpers came and started to massage the center of my back and chest. I started feeling heat and could finally relax. The pool was a deep blue color; I loved the color, so surreal and outstanding! I then started the breathing work. When I started breathing the water, it was coming up as bright white with a blue tinge to it. I was okay until I got to my chest. I realized that my arms were crossed over my chest in both the meditation and in my actual physical position.

The helpers were immediately by my side and I could see my guides and angels sitting in front of me, emitting a soft green light. When I tried to get the water to my heart, I immediately saw a huge black spot. The water was actually going *around* it. I realized this is what they had been massaging to try to break it up. As the water went around the black spot, I could feel it loosen, and then they sucked some of it up. It was so compact, however, and I didn't really want to let go of it. The helpers gave gentle reassurances that it was *okay* and that we would take our time to "dissolve" it. I kept thinking, "but it's there to protect me". They told me gently, *no*, and that they would slowly remove it because it was no longer serving me and was preventing me from moving forward. Glowing water kept going around it with each breath to dissolve it a little more, but it was really solid. I believed this black spot was a self-protective barrier that I had put up and I was a little scared to release it. I thought I would be vulnerable if it was removed. But again, I got reassurance that we would move slowly and it was time for me to release it.

It got a little uncomfortable, all the pressure I felt there, and I had to end the session. I kept the water pushing around it until it spilled out the top of my head, but the black spot was still not removed. That is why I stopped. I was crying and scared, like I was letting go of something really, *really* old. Rationally, I knew it was time to let it go, and that the spot was not good for me, but I still felt really confused--supported, but scared too. I was *very, very* emotional.

Author's Note: *About two months passed and I contacted Lori to see how she was doing. I updated the Cooperative Contract to include support and assistance through avoidance and internal interference. Once Lori signed her Cooperative Contract, she immediately rejoined the group and actively began working again.*

Lori's Water Breath Cleanse Continued…

The second time around my helpers and I started again. I felt like I was ready to let it all go, and to start the activity fresh. I consciously was ready to release the pressure that I had come to like and live with, even though I guess it was not good for me. I felt protected by the black spot, as if nothing could hurt me, even though that was not the truth. I understand that now. It also blocked the good energy, the healing energy I needed. That's what my helpers made me understand. The water tingled as it went up to my black spot this time. The helpers sucked up the majority of it, they kind of "cut it up" before it was sucked up, but nothing hurt. I felt the pressure release very slowly and I finally began to feel clean once I could get a good amount of water up into my throat. Then the coolest thing happened! I felt a *pop* when I got to my forehead! I actually *heard* it too. I'm not sure what that was, but it was neat. I found I could even get a bit of water to come off my head like a spout, not really high, just a little spray, but my guides were clapping! I felt so clean and the pool was bubbling. During all this, I looked down into the water a few times and saw black draining from my feet, but it kind of just faded away in the water. The water was cloudy for a second or two and then returned to the deep sparkling blue.

Heart Breath

Wow, I found this extremely powerful. It helped me to clear up and come to an understanding about so many emotions. I felt a tingling sensation and the most wonderful feeling of warmth. The Lotus Pool Water Breath activity was challenging to me, but this was not. I believe that I needed to do the hard work in the first water breathing activity in order for this one to be a good experience. This almost felt like a soothing bandage--hard to describe, but very calming. I also used this at work today and it helped once again clear things. I never really realized how much it helps to take *deep* breaths during stressful times at work. I intentionally did it today at work when I felt overwhelmed by deadlines. It made me feel less negative and less aggressive.

Cee

Water Breath Cleanse

I enjoyed inhaling the fizzy warm water of the Lotus pool through my feet and up my legs. It was invigorating and energizing. As I was using the breathing technique up to my abdominal cavity, it seemed to take much longer to energize. By the time I got to the chest/heart cavity, I needed my helper to use suction to clear some pretty nasty gunk out. That took a while and sounded like a vacuum that was trying to suck up chunks of stuff. It went more smoothly after the helpers suctioned my chest area of the chunky stuff. Breathing the water out of the top of my head felt great, especially as I got better at it. My helper was laughing his head off when the water blew past the top of a tree as I exhaled. Very enjoyable from the start, but it took some practice.

Section 2
Meet Angelscape Helpers

Activities Introduction

The bulk of the work done in *Angelscape* is done with helpers of various kinds. These helpers are symbolic of the active and interactive assistance available through faith in God and a spiritual reality. Their purpose is to act as the "humanized" conceptual tool of divine intervention because trying to imagine God is just too big and abstract. They are used in the guided imagery to set up a tangible scene that we can wrap our heads around and work with in ways that are familiar to us. They also provide the bridge between the *Angelscape* activities and your own unique perspective.

The spiritual helpers, or Divine Advocates, that are assigned in this activity will depend upon your own religious and spiritual beliefs. You will experience what is in alignment with those beliefs. If your personal beliefs prevent you from using Divine Advocates of any "personality", you may elect to use beings of pure light instead. If you do not have a preference, the four main archangels of Michael, Gabriel, Raphael, and Uriel seem to work well for people. There may be many nameless helpers doing various tasks, depending on how you want to imagine the structure of your environment. I use the term Divine Advocate when describing one of your main helpers. I use the general term "helper" for the less defined general workers that are found throughout *Angelscape.*

Most of us have the strong desire to be safe and to have our very own "Guardian Angel". *Angelscape* addresses this by providing the Journeyer, not just one Guardian Angel, but teams of them. There are three main teams of Divine Advocates that have specialized duties: the Guardian Team, the Healing Team, and the Guide Team. The Direct Route activity places a system of spiritual and energetic protection around you, all of your important environments, and networks of connection (family, and so on). Maintaining healthy boundaries between yourself and "what's out there" is important, regardless of what level of reality you are addressing. The Guardian Angel Shield provides a conceptual and spiritual tool that gives support for the energetic and spiritual boundaries that you need for your wellbeing and system integrity.

The Scenic Route activities assign your Divine Advocates as well as bringing you into an alignment with all the assistance you require through God as a centering focal point. You will stand along with your most beloved spiritual figures to understand that you are not alone in your journey, and that perhaps you never were. You are brought through several bonding experiences with your Divine Advocates so that you can feel them as strongly as possible through your imagination. Your faith in their ability to be of service to you through God and to help nurture and care for you is one of the main ingredients in the success of your journey. Some people find this section to be very touching and deeply emotional. Remember that it is okay to use your imagination, because that is what this book is about. But your imagination is the key and tool to a deeper connection with your spiritual reality. Be like a little child and allow your imagination and sense of wonder guide your way. We do not have to know it all. We just have to show up and let things unfold without getting in our own way.

The Chamber of Light has a domed ceiling that lets in sunlight. Imagine the hole larger, open, with streaming sunlight surrounding an Eternal Flame.

Photograph 204267
by morguefile.com
user: Alvimann

Direct Route Activity #2
Anchoring the Guardian Angel Shield

Environment Setting: Chamber of Light

Complementary Scenic Route Activities
SR 2 A: Divine Advocate Guide Assignments
SR 2 B: Intuition Support and Gifting

Purpose: The Guardian Angel Shield is anchored as a permanent energy construct of protection, shielding, and buffering from anything not in alignment with Divine Will, or that which is overwhelming to the system.

Usage Suggestions: Anchoring the Guardian Angel Shield is something you only have to do once, but if you want to reaffirm the work through the guided imagery as a way to feel reconnected, you may do that. You can reaffirm the presence of your Guardian Angel Shield daily, or when entering situations that call for it, by saying, *"I reaffirm the presence of my Guardian Angel Shield."*

Activity Props: You can use pictures of your favorite religious/spiritual figures, candles, a fireplace to imagine the Eternal Flame, or you can do your meditation in an actual church or temple setting.

Summary: You will enter into the Chamber of Light and approach the Eternal Flame of God's Grace and Love. A Divine Advocate walks through the Eternal Flame to stand near you. Walking through the Eternal Flame of God's Grace and Love to approach you symbolizes that your advocates only connect to you through, and under the authority of, God. The Divine Advocate takes fire from the Eternal Flame with his/her Sword of Light and blows it into a large sphere that is anchored around you for protection. The Guardian Angel Shield is also provided around relevant environments and personal connections.

Helpers: Archangel Michael, or whichever Divine Advocate you select for the duty of anchoring the Guardian Angel Shield.

New Concepts: Candles, Divine Advocate's Sword of Light, Guardian Angel Shield, "All Assistance", "Highest Outcome".

Intentions Supporting Activity

- Intentions added from anywhere else in the book that are relevant to this work.
- Anchoring of Guardian Angel Shield permanently to Whole Self and systems of self.
- Protection from harm, interference, nuisance, or anything functioning outside of Divine Will of any kind or from any level or direction.
- Protection and shielding from the impact of chaos, distress, or any situation that destabilizes functional competency, well being, or safety.
- Buffering and shielding of Whole Self to augment comfort and mitigate overwhelm.
- All Assistance, influence, and interconnections of any kind filtered through God and brought within Divine Will.
- Support for the Journeyer to feel safe, comforted, nurtured, and beloved.
- Enhanced strength and resiliency to all systems, such that vulnerabilities are fully sealed under all appropriate protections with perfected integrity.
- Support for Journeyer to call for the Guardian Angel Shield to be provided to other environments, situations, or people, as appropriate within Divine Will.
- Placement of the Guardian Angel Shield to be understood as part of any prayerful request through the platform of lighting candles in the Chamber of Light.
- *Candles*: used as symbolic prayer requests for the Highest Outcome, support, blessing, and assistance to flow to the intended subject through an outpouring of God's Grace and Love within Divine Will.
- *Divine Advocate's Sword of Light*: used by the Divine Advocate(s), the Sword of Light symbolizes a tool of action of God's Divine Will and authority.
- *Guardian Angel Shield*: spiritual and energetic security placed around people, places, or things to provide active divine protection, buffering, and shielding within Divine Will. It also is used as a structure of care, support, nurturing, delivery of appropriate spiritual resources, and strengthening.

- *All Assistance:* term describing all possible assistance provided from spiritual resources that are within free will and Divine Will limitations to support the Highest Outcome.
- *Highest Outcome:* term describing the best, highest, and most beneficial unfolding potential possible within Divine Will, given the situation, free will choices, and circumstances (aka: Highest Possible Outcome, or best possible conclusion).
- Listed intentions reaffirmed as part of the Cooperative Contract already signed over.
- Engagement of this activity, if a Cooperative Contract has not yet been signed, an affirmation of acceptance of these intentions, corrected in perfection, and brought within Divine Will.

Action Statement:
"I request to anchor the Guardian Angel Shield, now please."

Step-by-Step Activity Instructions:

1. Enter *Angelscape* at the Lotus Pool. Complete the spouting Water Breath Cleanse, sip your Lotus Nectar Elixir, and put on your Work Wrap to prepare for your journey. When you feel ready, you may continue.
2. A helper escorts you to the Chamber of Light. As you enter the building, you notice the candles and the smell of flowers. You approach the Eternal Flame of God's Grace and Love, which is burning brightly under the streaming sunlight from above. Light a candle on behalf of your care and protection. Offer up your favorite prayer if you would like.
3. When you are ready, imagine a figure standing on the opposite side of the Eternal Flame. This figure walks into the Eternal Flames of God's Grace and Love and emerges through it to greet you. You may request a specific Divine Advocate, or allow your advocate to approach you as the Archangel Michael.
4. The advocate that has emerged is holding a flaming Sword of Light. The Divine Advocate reaches back into the Eternal Flame with the Sword of Light and spins it, as if part of the Eternal Flame was molten glass being formed into a vessel. This vessel is made larger and larger until it is round and able to fully enclose you within it. This vessel is the

Guardian Angel Shield, forged from the Eternal Flame of God's Grace and Love.

5. Imagine this large bubble of light being slipped over and around your Whole Self. Your advocate seals the vessel around you and taps it three times with the tip of his/her Sword of Light. The bubble vibrates, hums, and then slowly fades from your immediate sight. It has become a part of your spiritual energy field and will remain there as permanent protection.
6. The Divine Advocate then forms several other Guardian Angel Shields from the Eternal Flames. You are asked to imagine your home, your workspace, your car, and any other environments that you feel you would like more divine protection or buffering. Imagine the Guardian Angel Shields being placed and activated around the environments you have selected.
7. When you are finished, you may continue with the Scenic Route activities, or your main Divine Advocate escorts you to the TLC Bath. Once at the TLC Bath, you will coat yourself in the soothing energies, sip your Graceful Integration Elixir, and then wrap yourself in the Resiliency Comfort Wrap. Do not drive, operate heavy machinery, or do any activities that are dangerous, or that require you to be fully attentive, until you feel fully shifted back to a normal waking state. Take some time to journal or take notes before your memory of the experience fades.

Continuing Thoughts

Reaffirm the Guardian Angel Shield, using the Action Statement below, any time you feel like there is increased danger or risk, such as when you get into a car, go into public, or enter into an actual dangerous situation or environment. You may also wish to reaffirm the Guardian Angel Shield before bedtime, or any time you feel "creeped out" or agitated for any reason. Distribution of the Guardian Angel Shield is automatically requested for the subject of any candle lighting session or activity because it falls within the category of "All Assistance".

Action Statement:

"I reaffirm the Guardian Angel Shield, now please."

Lighting Candles

The candles that you light in the Chamber of Light, or that you intend to be lit through visualization or direct request, represent a request for all assistance and care possible for the intended subject or issue within Divine Will. This means that you have prearranged for the candle to represent an entire set of intentions that might apply to any given situation, but that you are allowing God to perfect that prayer in the most appropriate way. You can go into the Chamber of Light as a meditative session and light as many candles as you wish.

You may also intend for a candle to be lit in the Chamber of Light by requesting it directly, such as when you are on the go and cannot take the time to imagine the Chamber of Light. I often visually imagine a candle superimposed upon people that I wish to pray for and have used that as my "short hand" version of going into the Chamber of Light to make a formalized request. Using this method, I can quickly and easily light a candle for someone using my imagination.

Prayers as Cooperative Contracts

It is my opinion that the *Angelscape* work is potent because of the clear synergy between Divine Will and free will. The Cooperative Contract concept lists out our clear goals and intentions, but it also allows for God to correct and perfect them--and then gives our voluntary free will permission to receive whatever spiritual help we need to reach our goals. Many well-known and beloved prayers may make excellent types of cooperative contracts. You may sign over your favorite prayer(s), just like a cooperative contract, as a way to show your alignment with the intentions of the prayer and to be clear that you grant permission to receive the assistance provided through the prayer. For example, the "Lord's Prayer" is extremely well adapted to being used like a cooperative contract, as is the Jewish "Shema" and many others. If you would like to try this method of prayer empowerment, just imagine signing the prayer like a contract and then tossing it into the Eternal Flame of God's Grace and Love to place it into God's Hands.

Scenic Route #2 A
Divine Advocate Guide Assignments

Environment Setting: Chamber of Light

Purpose: Divine Advocates and specialized teams are officially assigned and synchronized with you through God.

Usage Suggestions: This is a ceremonial process by which you officially receive and acknowledge your Divine Advocates and the close working teams that will follow you throughout life. You do not have to do this activity again, but if you feel prompted to work with new or additional Divine Advocates in the future, you should request for them to be placed in *Synchronization* with you *through* God. This process requests that those you select for your spiritual advocacy are, in fact, under the authority and oversight of God/Divine Will, and not acting independent of it, or against it.

Activity Props: You can use the same props here as described in the Direct Route activity; pictures of your favorite religious/spiritual figures, candles, a fireplace to imagine the Eternal Flame, or you can do your meditation in an actual church or temple setting.

Summary: In this activity, you will receive three main teams of advocates: a Guardian Team, Healing Team, and a Guide Team. Once your advocates and teams are assigned, you are brought through *All Assistance Synchronization*, which empowers your advocates and teams to use all possible resources of assistance available within creation to assist you as needed. Synchronization is the process of taking many parts and placing all parts into a system of wholeness through God as the centering and balancing foundation. Some people call this atonement (being "at one"), or being in *Divine Alignment.*

You can imagine this synchronization process to look like a flower with many petals. The petals are the many individual parts and the center of the flower, indeed, the entire flower, is God. All petals relate to each other through the center as the unifying foundation. In this respect, All Assistance Synchronization places the Journeyer in proper alignment and connection to any source of assistance, healing, and support from any layer, level, or aspect of creation (natural or spiritual), so long as it is *through God* as the centering foundation, within Divine Will, and in alignment with the Journeyer's highest good and free will acceptance. Your Divine Advocates will generally walk to you through the Eternal Flame of God's Grace and Love to symbolize that they work *through* God and not separate from Him.

Helpers: The helpers are assigned here. Select your most beloved spiritual figure to be your main Divine Advocate as they will be the "director" for the rest of your journey.

New Concepts: Guardian Team, Healing Team, Guide Team, Synchronization/Divine Alignment, All Assistance Synchronization.

Intentions Supporting Activity

- Intentions added from anywhere else in the book that are relevant to this work.
- All Assistance, as appropriate, for any matter that needs attention.
- All Divine Advocates under full authority and oversight of God/Divine Will.
- Divine Advocates, and specialized teams selected, assigned, and activated for duty.
- All Assistance Synchronization between Whole Self and All Assistance available through the agency of God's Grace and Love.
- All Assistance empowered with the Presence of God, intelligent and self-regulating.
- Divine Advocates and teams moderated, updated, and adjusted to meet emerging needs.
- Divine Advocates and teams to provide All Assistance to the Journeyer, and relevant networks of connection, in any way possible within Divine Will.
- Protection and care provided to environments and networks of relationships when possible under Divine Will.
- Adjustment of events, circumstances, and points of convergence with other influences to advocate for Journeyer's highest and best good, when necessary.
- Support for appropriate communications, warnings, guidance, or prompts from Divine Advocates, when needed.

- Support for the cultivation of skills and opening of sensitivities required for basic communication and clarity with Divine Advocates.
- Divine Advocates to be in alignment with Journeyer's personal beliefs, such that maximum comfort and spiritual alignment is achieved.
- *Guardian Team*: divinely aligned spiritual helpers who specialize in keeping you and yours safe from all harm or anything not present within Divine Will.
- *Healing Team*: divinely aligned spiritual helpers who specialize in the rectification of damage or distortion of any kind from your Sacred Self Template, including physical, mental, emotional, or spiritual healing.
- *Guide Team*: divinely aligned spiritual helpers who specialize in providing you with actionable guidance for healing, reflection, choices, decisions, and events of consequence, such that you may choose the Highest Outcome possible within Divine Will.
- *Synchronization/Divine Alignment*: Synchronization is the process of taking many parts and placing all parts into a system of wholeness through God as the centering and balancing foundation. Some people call this atonement (being "at one"), or being in *Divine Alignment.*
- *All Assistance Synchronization* protocol: places the Journeyer in proper alignment and connection to any source of assistance, healing, and support from any layer, level, or aspect of creation (natural or spiritual). It places God as the centering foundation of all assistance by aligning all sources of guidance or assistance under Divine Will and in compliance with the Journeyer's highest good and free will acceptance.
- Listed intentions reaffirmed as part of the Cooperative Contract already signed over.
- Engagement of this activity, if a Cooperative Contract has not yet been signed, an affirmation of acceptance of these intentions, corrected in perfection, and brought within Divine Will.

Action Statement:
"I request to initiate the Divine Advocate Guide Assignments, now please."

Note: *Skip to step 3 if you are coming immediately from the previous activity.*

Step-by-Step Activity Instructions:

1. Enter *Angelscape* at the Lotus Pool. Complete the spouting Water Breath Cleanse, sip your Lotus Nectar Elixir, and put on your Work Wrap to prepare for your journey. When you feel ready, you may continue.
2. A helper escorts you to the Chamber of Light to stand in front of the Eternal Flames of God's Grace and Love.
3. Imagine your most beloved spiritual figure emerging from within the Eternal Flame of God's Grace and Love. This spiritual figure will stand in as your main Divine Advocate and main "touch point" for your interactions in *Angelscape.* You may greet him/her in whatever way seems appropriate. When you have finished greeting your main Divine Advocate, you may continue.
4. Imagine a small group of advocates forming on the opposite side of the Eternal Flame. They are your assigned Guardian Team. Watch them walk through the Eternal Flame, nod to you, and take their place around you.
5. The next group of advocates, your Healing Team, assembles on the opposite side of the Eternal Flame before walking through it. They also nod to you, and take their place around you.
6. The next group of advocates, your Guide Team, assembles on the opposite side of the Eternal Flame. Like the others, they walk through it, nod, and then stand near you.
7. Your Divine Advocates smile at you as they hold hands and form a large circle around the Eternal Flame of God's Grace and Love. You are a part of the circle, holding the hands of your closest Divine Advocates on either side.
8. Your closest Divine Advocate requests to initiate the "*All Assistance Synchronization*". You can feel a movement of energy swirling around the group, bringing your energies and

those of your Divine Advocates and All Assistance into Divine Alignment and balance through God.

9. When the energies of the synchronization subside, you may go on to the next Scenic Route activity, the Intuition Support and Gifting, or end your session for the day. If you wish to go on to the next activity, do so now. If not, your Guardian Team will surround you, and like the Guardian Angel Shield, may slowly fade from your immediate view. The other teams may file back through the flames, or fade from your view, depending on their purpose and work. You will see them again as your helpers in the appropriate activities.
10. If you are done for the day, your Divine Advocate escorts you to the TLC Bath where you will coat yourself in the soothing energies, sip your Graceful Integration Elixir, and then wrap yourself in the Resiliency Comfort Wrap. Do not drive, operate heavy machinery, or do any activities that are dangerous, or that require you to be fully attentive, until you feel fully shifted back to a normal waking state. Take some time to journal or take notes before your memory of the experience fades.

Continuing Thoughts

The teams of helpers are used for various purposes. The Guardian Team is less interactive with you, besides warning you when you need to be careful. You can establish a "warning code" with your Guardian Team that they may use to let you know when you should be extra careful. This can be a color, shape, sound, or a buzz sensation somewhere easily felt in your body. Otherwise, the Guardian Team stays out of view as mostly background workers. The Healing and Guide Teams are far more interactive because you work with them in *Angelscape* to get your work activities completed. You will likely establish strong rapport with these Divine Advocates through the highly interactive nature of their purpose.

Scenic Route #2 B
Intuition Support and Gifting

Environment Setting: Chamber of Light

Purpose: The Intuition Support and Gifting activity provides a platform to boost your intuition, establish rapport and communication with your Divine Advocates, and to provide whatever gifts would be helpful to you as conceptual tools to enhance work receptivity or clarity.

Usage Suggestions: This activity is a gifting ceremony in which you receive conceptual tools to help you be more receptive and open to divine guidance and assistance. You do not have to do this ceremony again, but you will want to integrate the use of your gifted tools into whatever routine you use to prepare for spiritual work sessions. You can always ask for updates to gifts at anytime, without an official ceremony.

Activity Props: You can use flower essences, essential oil, or holy water for anointing your forehead, or you can wear a special hat, scarf, or head gear that reminds you of given gifts.

Summary: This activity is facilitated by your assigned Divine Advocates in order for you to be able to boost and enhance your spiritual sensitivities for work or communication related tasks. One or more of your Divine Advocates will approach you from the Eternal Flame and kiss your forehead, eyes, and ears. They may perform other sensitivity opening activities, depending upon your individual needs. You will be given one or many tools to help boost and enhance your intuitive receptivity. These tools may take the form of gifts, such as, jewelry, a hat, head wraps, headphones, glasses, or any other object that you would symbolically link with heightened and increased ability to sense your spiritual guidance or communication (seeing, hearing, speaking, and envisioning).

Helpers: Your assigned Divine Advocates are present for this activity. Some may stay in the background. You may be approached by just one Divine Advocate for the work and gifting (typically the Divine Advocate that you consider your main advocate) or you may be approached by leaders of each of the main three teams.

New Concepts: Gifts

Intentions Supporting Activity

- Intentions added from anywhere else in the book that are relevant to this work.
- All Assistance, as appropriate, for any matter that needs attention.
- Enhanced resonance and protected interaction with Divine Advocates.
- Short-term boost in intuitive receptivity for work and communication with Divine Advocates.
- Imagery and sensation enhancement for work within *Angelscape*.
- Long-term intuition and sensitivity expansion, appropriately paced.
- Cleansing or operational augmentation of intuitive energy centers.
- Removal of static, interference, or inappropriate contact of any kind.
- Mitigation, decrease, or removal of perceptual bias, miscommunication, or misunderstanding.
- Support for communication and intuition to be seen on a broad scope, such as repetitive messages, or events that seem to be "trying to tell you something".
- Support to embrace intuitive capabilities for what they are and to cultivate natural skills.
- Support for Journeyer not to place comparison between personal abilities and those of others, or to be inappropriately subordinated by anyone with seeming more expansive capabilities.
- Support to work with others to enhance intuitive entrainment, layered meaning, cooperative intuitive teamwork, exploration, and investigation.
- Tools gifted to provide individualized assistance to enhance intuitive receptivity and other stated intentions.
- *Gifts*: gifts and other symbolic or practical tools are often given to the Journeyer by his/her Divine Advocates. Gifts assist the Journeyer to acquire a new skill, new technique, or to enhance functioning in some way.
- Listed intentions reaffirmed as part of the Cooperative Contract already signed over.

- Engagement of this activity, if a Cooperative Contract has not yet been signed, an affirmation of acceptance of these intentions, corrected in perfection, and brought within Divine Will.

Action Statement:
"I request to initiate the Intuition Support and Gifting, now please."

Note: *Skip to step 4 if you are coming immediately from the previous activity.*

Step-by-Step Activity Instructions:

1. Enter *Angelscape* at the Lotus Pool. Complete the spouting Water Breath Cleanse, sip your Lotus Nectar Elixir, and put on your Work Wrap to prepare for your journey. When you feel ready, you may continue.
2. A helper escorts you to the Chamber of Light to stand in front of the Eternal Flame of God's Grace and Love. You may light a candle for the support of your intuition or offer up your favorite prayer, as you see fit.
3. When you are ready, you see your Divine Advocates assemble on the opposite side of the Eternal Flame. As always, they walk through the Eternal Flame to greet you, symbolizing their connection to you through God.
4. A Divine Advocate approaches you and places a kiss upon your forehead, on both ears, and on both eyes. You may feel a tingle of energy move through those areas or through your body. Your Divine Advocate may perform other activities, according to your needs, or s/he may be finished with this part of the work.
5. The Divine Advocate will place upon you, or give to you, some kind of gift or tools that will assist you with intuition support and enhancement from now on. Accept the blessing with thanks and gratitude. You may light a candle for thanks and gratitude if you would like.
6. Other Divine Advocates may approach you to repeat the kiss of enhanced intuition and/or gifting activities, as appropriate.
7. When you are finished, your main Divine Advocate escorts you to the TLC Bath where you will coat yourself in the soothing energies, sip your Graceful Integration Elixir, and

then wrap yourself in the Resiliency Comfort Wrap. Do not drive, operate heavy machinery, or do any activities that are dangerous, or that require you to be fully attentive, until you feel fully shifted back to a normal waking state. Take some time to journal or take notes before your memory of the experience fades.

Continuing Thoughts

Discernment: Discernment is the ability to tell what is authentic and usable from what is false or not usable. Often part of our intuition enhancement process covers “discernment training”. It is possible that you will be given completely absurd information that is neither relevant or useful, or obviously wrong. It is to help you develop the ability to discern what is authentic from what is absurd and distorted. It is your responsibility to reject, refuse, and dismiss absurdity. There is a famous saying from Voltaire that says, “If one can make you believe in absurdities, they can make you commit atrocities.”

Be willing to say, “I refuse that,” *even to your Divine Advocates*, if the information feels wrong to you. You are ultimately responsible for conclusions you make and the directions you take, regardless of the spiritual guidance you believe you are getting. A quick rule of thumb is that authentic information increases love, peace, faith, direction, capacity, and well-being and absurd or distorted information increases fear, suspicion, despondency, feelings of abandonment, helplessness, and so on. Expect to be tested so that you learn to develop those necessary and critical skills more fully. Be mindful that even those with usually good discernment skills can have challenges when confronted with things that rub against their own issues.

“Coming together is a beginning; keeping together is progress; working together is success.”

Henry Ford

Summary and Wrap Up

Complementary Activities

- Add favorite spiritual prayers or practices for protection into your *Angelscape* routine.
- Research topics on psychic and spiritual protection.
- Research your Divine Advocates qualities and work focus.
- Research topics on enhancing clairvoyance, intuition, and receptivity.
- Find friends/buddies for team intuition supported work sessions.

Project Ideas

You can create an intuition support garment--such as the Work Wrap imagined upon getting out of the Lotus Pool--that you can wear before you do your sessions in order to help you to maintain your “role” as Journeyer. You may have already designated an actual robe or wrap for this purpose. If so, you might consider sewing beads, buttons, or other objects that remind you of gifts given to you in the Intuition Support and Gifting activity. You can also create a special hat for yourself that you can sew stone beads, buttons, or other supportive pieces to imagine putting on your “intuition cap” before working.

If you do not like commercially created guidance cards, which may not be in full alignment with your religious or spiritual beliefs, you can create your own using pre-perforated blank business cards. You can use words, phrases, prayers, mantras, symbols, pictures, and so on. Select what is meaningful to you. Put the message on just one side and make the top side the same on all cards so you do not know which one is which. Pull one card or many, or shuffle them until one naturally falls from the stack to receive what information you can.

Reflection Questions

1. Describe how you were feeling before and after the activities.
2. What were the most vivid details of your imagery during the activities?
3. Describe your helpers, the tools, and their assistance.
4. What surprised you the most about your experiences?
5. What was your favorite activity in Section 2?

6. What was your least favorite activity in Section 2?
7. Can you integrate your new skills into your more familiar practices?
8. Were there any details that seemed highlighted to you that you might want to think about?
9. Do you feel inspired to do any research in any other related area? If so, what is it?
10. What was your experience with distributing the Guardian Angel Shield protection to other environments?
11. What ways have you used to protect yourself emotionally, spiritually, or mentally?
12. What tools or gifts did you receive to help enhance your intuitive receptivity?
13. What methods do you usually use to interact with your spiritual guidance?
14. What other procedure(s), if any, did your Divine Advocate facilitate to help open your intuitive sensitivities?
15. Who were your Divine Advocates? Any surprises? What area of expertise do these Divine Advocates usually address?
16. What do you think their divine characteristics have to do with their selection as your helpers?

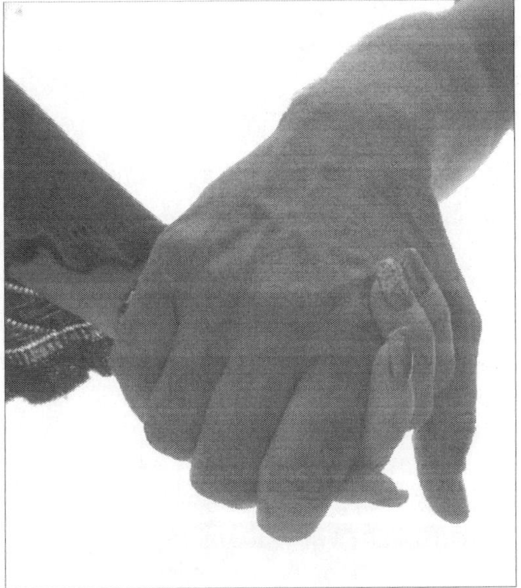

Have faith that you are not alone, even if you cannot always see your company.

Photograph 115356
by morguefile.com
user: taliesin

Focus Group Feedback

Sharon

Guide Assignment

Walking into the Chamber of Light is always a calm, peaceful and centering experience. No matter what kind of day you are having, once you enter into the chamber, things seem to come into perspective and settle down. It is like stepping out of a rainstorm and feeling relieved you are home. The advocate that stepped out of the flame holding the Sword of Light was Jesus. Jesus and Archangel Michael were members of each of my three main teams.

When the team encircled me and started the synchronization process, a strong wind came down and encircled us, like a tornado sweeping around the group. The wind actually "blew" through each person, and when it did, that person's energy or essence merged with the person next to him, and so on around the circle, until the whole circle was connected in one unified energy field.

When that was complete, the "tornado" rose spinning, swirling up through the sky dome and then out. My Guardian Team encircled me closely, like a big hug, and then faded away. The most vivid detail of my imagery was the realization of the amount of "help" and support that is available to you just for the asking. The unconditional love coming from the whole team felt like they were saying, "We are here for you and we've got your back. Have no worries." I like that. The warning code that my Guardian Team will use to flash me is a red star.

Laura

Guardian Angel Shield, Synchronization, Gifting

I took a break for a moment and then returned to the chamber for the Guardian Angel Shield activity. I sat and began deep breathing. I felt the need to physically ground myself before continuing. As the Guardian Angel Shield was positioned around me, there was a feeling of total peace and safety. I felt a strong connection through the top of my head and out the dome of the building, as though it was more of a column than a bubble. The synchronization process brought a cycling of energy in a clockwise direction. This really affected my spiritual and intuitive energy centers. My "warning code" is a verbal one, which comes as a spoken word in my mind, as well as a physical sensation in my solar plexus.

I moved right into the gifting of tools. The "kiss", in my case, was an anointing with jasmine oil. I received a box of crystals--no surprise there- -

some in the form of pendants to be worn in different situations, some loose, and some larger for strategic placement--either in my home, vehicle, or anywhere I wish to anchor that specific energy.

Lourdes

Guardian Angel Shield and All Assistance Synchronization

The Guardian Angel Shield exercise felt very comfortable and right for me. Before starting this exercise, I had a headache and just didn't feel right. I went into *Angelscape* and into the Chamber of Light. While there, Archangel Michael came and fashioned a sphere for me. I did feel a buzz as the sphere encapsulated me. Loved it. When everyone had come out of the flame, we held hands around it and felt the energy connect through each of us. What a wonderful feeling. After this was done, and my thanks had been said, they all walked back through the flame. I came home with a lightened headache and a more tranquil piece of mind.

Intuitive Gifting

For the Intuitive Gifts, I went to *Angelscape* and met up with Archangel Michael and he walked beside me to the Chamber of Light. While contemplating the flame, the archangels came to bless my senses and give me gifts. All of the gifts were psychic in nature and were to help me communicate through my senses better. After the archangels came, the female Divine Advocates arrived and also blessed me. After receiving my gifts, and saying thank you, we all joined hands around the fire and shared in its energy. What I felt during this exercise was a warmth in my ears. I was cold before starting the exercise and then got really warm during it. In fact, I was feeling an energetic buzz during the whole exercise. I did not want to end this exercise at all!

Section 3
The Little Ones

Activities Introduction

The focus in Section 3 will be on healing and correcting distorted views and perceptions about the self. It will also work to reconnect us with our innocence and playfulness that tends to be lost as we get older. Most of our limiting inner scripts, or perceptual distortions are created in childhood. Children are, by developmental nature, egocentric, meaning, they believe *everything* is about them in some way. They do not have the capacity to separate themselves from things happening to or around them, and so they "internalize" things (see themselves as the problem) that are not authentically theirs. Unconscious beliefs from this process are forged in the system and become the "issues" we carry on into adulthood. Many of these issues are false, limiting, negative, self-destructive, or erode our faith in our own goodness and intrinsic value.

The process of healing involves assembling and addressing our inner children, what I call the "*Little Ones*", and identifying the distorted beliefs and perceptions that they have held. Many of these parts are full of intense emotion, which needs to be cleansed and released. We are *not* going into this activity to wallow in events of the past, but to gracefully-- and without further pain--address the distortions, release the held pain and suffering, and re-nurture the essence of our own innocence until it is prepared to be whole again. Some of this work will be done with conscious action on our part, but much of it will be done behind the scenes and outside of our awareness by our Divine Advocates. That is the beauty of working with a cooperative spiritual reality; we can do this in a way that is comfortable and supported.

You may use the Baby Double Dip as a way to be more proactive with the cleansing of held pain and care of your Little One(s). Some Little Ones may need to talk to you and reconnect with you more intimately than the amphitheater setting allows in the Direct Route activity. However, this more intimate interaction with Little Ones is designed for people who have *mild to moderate* issues to release. If you find that engaging your Little One(s) is too overwhelming, please go to a qualified therapist to walk you through it. You deserve proper and competent support to move through severe emotional congestion. If you try it and it seems fine, that is okay too. You may have already cleared significant layers of congestion through the Lotus Pool Water Breath Cleanse to be able to do the work with the Little Ones. It is obviously *good* to get stagnant emotional gunk out of your system, but be kind to yourself and treat yourself with respect and compassion. Go as slowly as needed. Listen to your inner prompts to move forward, or to rest and allow yourself to rebalance.

The TLC Bath exit protocol is particularly important to utilize during this section of the work because it is designed to soothe a beleaguered system and help the healing shifts be graceful and kind. Do not forget to use it any time you need to use it, even if you have not gone on a full *Angelscape* visit. Since the Baby Double Dip is essentially the same, but child appropriate, you can imagine using either area for this work. If your Little Ones are being shown to you as needing a lot of washing and TLC, please be sure to include them in an enthusiastic schedule of Double Dipping while you are going through this particular section.

The ultimate goal of this work is to re-establish a sense of authentic self-worth, competency, resiliency, and a positive self-image by releasing distorted perceptions and scripts, unexpressed pain, and re-embracing the innocence and joy that were compromised by events that may have been too big for a child to process. In short, we are "dropping the kids off for healing" and then moving along while they are being cared for on a spiritual level. We will reunite with them later, when they have completed the healing work necessary before being brought back into our active systems.

The Garden is visualized with plenty of butterflies, symbolizing transformation.

Photograph 197942 by morguefile.com user: lightfoot

Direct Route Activity #3
Little One Healing and Restoration

Environment Setting: Garden of the Little Ones

Complementary Scenic Route Activities
SR 3 A: Baby Pool Double Dip
SR 3 B: The Wishing Well

Purpose: The goal of this activity is to provide a path of healing for hidden parts of ourselves that function mainly outside of our awareness and manifest through unconscious influence.

Usage Suggestions: This activity is meant to be a full sweeping experience, such that *all* inner children are called forth and brought into a healing process. However, if you feel strongly prompted to do this activity again to follow up and make sure it is done fully and completely, you may do this again, or as often as you feel the need.

Activity Props: You can use pictures of yourself as a child, or pictures of other children that remind you of an emotion. Have scraps of paper handy to write down distortions that you acknowledge so you can have the satisfaction of actually ripping them up. You may want to have other art supplies for this activity, such as crayons, construction paper, markers, and so on. I also highly recommend the "rescue" type flower essence, the five-flower blend, or any other blends especially designed to help distressed children.

Summary: You will enter into the Garden of the Little Ones and sit down in the amphitheater by yourself. One of your Divine Advocates steps onto the stage of the outdoor theater and bangs on a *gong* that is a prop on the stage. In response to the resounding gong, your inner children begin filling the amphitheater. Once the amphitheater is full of your inner children from every developmental stage in your life (some may be adults), the Divine Advocate addresses the audience of children. The children are told by your Divine Advocate that no matter what has happened, what they have done, or what was done to them, that they are beautiful, valued, and beloved children of God. They are told that anything within them or from outside of them that says anything different about their natures is *lying* to them--and that it is time to throw away those lies.

The children are instructed to pull out the pieces of tattered paper, which are the inner scripts and distorted perceptions that they have held, and to pass them up to the stage. The children pull out scripts of paper that say things that are not true, that they falsely believed, and which still influence unconscious functioning into the current day. The ugly and tattered scripts of paper are all passed up to the front where they are collected. The Divine Advocate pulls out five of the most common distortions about the self and the entire audience gets to yell out that the distortion is false and to replace it with what is true. The tattered and ugly papers are ripped up, thrown into the air, and become butterflies. The beautiful butterflies fly through the audience of children and turn into glowing clouds of sparkles that fall over the children like fairy dust. The children smile and begin to yawn. The adult attendants come around, wrap the children up in their own cocoon like swaddling blanket, and carry them off to complete the healing work in a "butterfly sleep".

Helpers: If you have no preference, the Archangels' Gabriel and Raphael may be part of helpers that show up here. It is also possible that trusted and beloved adult figures from your past act with the healing team in this activity (grandparents, and so on). Many times the figures are seen as female, but it depends on your personal needs and wishes.

New Concepts: Gong, Scripts (of paper), Butterfly Dust, Swaddling Cocoon Wraps, Little Ones, "Tag, Refuse, Rescript", Butterfly Sleep.

Intentions Supporting Activity

- Intentions added from anywhere else in the book that are relevant to this work.
- All Assistance, as appropriate, for any matter that needs attention.
- Gathering of all dissociated parts of self, inner children, and parts of self holding distorted scripts which negatively impact current functioning.
- Release, refusal, and relinquishing of negative and distorted scripts about the self.
- Rescripting and replacement of distortions with authentic truth about the self.
- Rectification of accumulation and cascading distortions and damage from point of origin.

- Healing, comfort, care, nurturing, and rectification of damage upon inner children.
- Graceful release of pain without the need to remember or re-experience traumatic events.
- Cocooning of inner children for complete healing, respite, and preparation for re-integration.
- Little Ones that remain to interact during Scenic Route activities, also are provided all care and placed into all healing protocols, regardless of showing up for other work.
- Reclaiming and restoration of the Sacred Child within and the restoration of innocence.
- Support for reflection, identification, and continued follow up and healing of childhood issues and distorted scripts as they emerge.
- Support for easy tagging and flushing of distortions in waking state.
- Nurturing and unconditional love to fill the Whole Self from spiritual sources (God) if earthly sources (parents) are/were insufficient.
- Support to release what no longer serves the self so that an authentic relationship with the present and future is encouraged and highlighted.
- Support to heal and rectify distorted perceptions associated with subjects, beliefs, and conclusions related to the matters other than the self.
- *Gong*: a tool used in *Angelscape* by the Divine Advocates as a way to summon and call all relevant aspects, players, or necessary participants to activities that require the Journeyer to imagine and work with more than his/her immediate self.
- *Scripts*: symbolized by pieces of paper, or scripts like in a theater, to communicate and reveal perceptual distortions held in the system. It also is used to provide a tangible conceptual process to "Tag, Refuse, Rescript" the distortions, and to usher in the healing and transformation of dysfunction. The "Re-script" can also be symbolized by something written on paper, but is viewed as the corrected and perfected message, vision, or potential outcome that replaces the distorted one.

- *Butterfly Dust*: a tool used to symbolize the beginning of the transformational healing sleep provided to the Little Ones in order to restore them back into the system.
- *Swaddling Cocoon Wrap*: a specialized care wrap, designed for the Little Ones to be perfectly buffered and comfortable, while in the healing sleep. It is like the cocoon of a butterfly that provides the necessary sacred space for complete transformation. They will emerge as happy children, completely prepared to re-integrate with the Whole/Sacred Self when it is time.
- *Little Ones:* term used to describe Journeyer's "inner children" or aspects of the self that are child-like, or that symbolize the Journeyer at a critical events or point of consequence. The Little Ones are seen as being parts of the self that function in an unconscious way. They may hold limiting, distorted, or dysfunctional perceptions about the self or the larger world. They also retain the innocence, inner joy, and wonder that is often lost as we grow older.
- *"Tag, Refuse, Rescript"*: protocol to initiate identification, cleansing, and positive script replacement of perceptual distortions. It supports the Journeyer to be mindful of inner distortions and provides a plan of action to combat distortions as they are "tagged". The energetic support can be called for in full by any of the individual command words, if used with that intention.
- *Butterfly Sleep*: the healing sleep that the Little Ones take after releasing distortion that they have held within unseen parts of the self. This is a comfortable and graceful process whereby the inner children do not experience any additional distress or pain.
- Listed intentions reaffirmed as part of the Cooperative Contract already signed over.
- Engagement of this activity, if a Cooperative Contract has not yet been signed, an affirmation of acceptance of these intentions, corrected in perfection, and brought within Divine Will.

Action Statement:
"I request to initiate Little One Healing and Restoration, now please."

Step-by-Step Activity Instructions:

1. Enter *Angelscape* at the Lotus Pool. Complete the spouting Water Breath Cleanse, sip your Lotus Nectar Elixir, and put on your Work Wrap to prepare for your journey. When you feel ready, you may continue.
2. A helper escorts you to the Garden of the Little Ones. Once there, you are brought to an outdoor amphitheater to take a seat. Your Divine Advocate steps onto the stage, bangs a large gong three times, and calls for all of the Little Ones to gather into the amphitheater. The children arrive, sit down, and wait for the Divine Advocate to speak.
3. Imagine the Divine Advocate telling the audience of children that they are beautiful, valued, and beloved children of God--regardless of what has ever happened in their lives. They are told that anything that says anything different is lying to them and that they are to pass those lies up to the stage. The children pull out ugly scripts of paper and pass them to the stage.
4. The Divine Advocate collects all of the tattered scripts of paper and puts them into a bag. S/he pulls out the top five distortions, most of which form the structure of all the rest that are in the bag. The five main distortions are, "I am.... 1) ugly 2) stupid 3) evil 4) worthless 5) powerless." Some of the children weep and bury their faces in their hands when these distortions are read aloud. Sweet grandmotherly figures may move into the crowd to comfort and bring a sense of safety to any of the Little Ones who require it.
5. The Divine Advocate instructs the children to stamp their feet and yell, "*False!*" to each one of the distortions and then to yell out and embrace the replacement that s/he gives them.

DISTORTION		**REPLACEMENT**
Ugly	FALSE!	**I am beautiful!**
Stupid	FALSE!	**I am smart!**
Evil	FALSE!	**I am innocent!**
Worthless	FALSE!	**I am precious!**
Powerless	FALSE!	**I am strong!**

6. The Divine Advocate invites some of the older children onto the stage to pull out more distortions to refuse and rescript

for everyone in the audience until they feel they have covered all of the main ones. Imagine the children then ripping up all of the distorted scripts, including the ones in the bag that were not read. Some of the children seem to take great relief in this action and make confetti out of the ugly pieces of paper. The confetti is gathered up and placed back into the bag and the volunteers sit back down.

7. The Divine Advocate smiles at the children and says, *"We ask God to transform these lies into what is good and true, and for the children to be healed with Grace of their suffering and pain, now please."* The children nod and say, *"Yes, please."*
8. Imagine that the bag holding the confetti begins to glow with a golden light, emitting a high pitch, humming sound. It bursts open in a dazzling flash of bright light. As the sparkles clear, the children are delighted to witness that small armies of beautiful little butterflies have been created from the bag of confetti. The butterflies spread out over the audience of children and gently pop into small clouds of sparkly golden dust that settles over the children. The children giggle and cheer as if it is thc bcst magic show they have ever seen.
9. The golden butterfly dust begins to sink into the audience of children. They begin to stretch and yawn. The healing dust makes them drowsy and peaceful. Adult attendants come around with blankets and wrap each of the children up in a cocoon like swaddling. They are gently carried off to a special healing area. The children will sleep through the rest of the healing process, which will purge them of their emotional pain and any lingering damage. They will emerge as happy children, completely prepared to re-integrate with the Whole/Sacred Self when it is time.
10. When you are finished, you may continue with the Scenic Route activities, or your main Divine Advocate escorts you to the TLC Bath where you will coat yourself in the soothing energies, sip your Graceful Integration Elixir, and then wrap yourself in the Resiliency Comfort Wrap. Do not drive, operate heavy machinery, or do any activities that are dangerous, or that require you to be fully attentive, until you feel fully shifted back to a normal waking state. Take some

time to journal or take notes before your memory of the experience fades.

Continuing Thoughts

Perceptions are not just about how we view ourselves, but how we view others, our world, and life. Perceptions are the filters through which we assess, categorize, and process everything that goes on around us. News is just news--whether it is good news or bad news often depends on our perception and assessment of it. As you rectify and heal distorted perceptions about yourself, you may find that you begin to identify distorted perceptions about the larger systems within which you function. You rectify those distortions in the same way as you rectify the ones functioning internally. You first must identify them, then refuse them, then replace them with something positive and authentic. It essentially comes down to this; if you want to change your world, first you need to change your perception of it.

The Garden has an outdoor amphitheater, which is used when addressing the children or when playing out a challenge.

Photograph 69496
by morguefile.com
user: xandert

Scenic Route #3 A
Baby Pool Double Dip

Environment Setting: Garden of the Little Ones

Purpose: This activity provides all of the cleansing and soothing support provided by the Lotus Pool and TLC Bath in an age appropriate setting for the Little Ones. It provides an opportunity for the release of childhood pain and suffering and allows the adult self to connect with and create a nurturing relationship with his/her own inner children.

Usage Suggestions: The baby pools are child appropriate versions of the Lotus Pool and TLC Baths. When you first encounter your Little Ones, you may wish to engage this activity until no more Little Ones show up, or to use it as a fun activity you can do with your Little Ones at any time to play, splash, and enjoy one another's company.

Activity Props: You can use any of the props already described in the Lotus Pool/TLC Bath activities, such as, actual bath, hot tub, or shower, and so on. You can also use the props described in the Direct Route activity #3, such as, childhood pictures, art supplies, and flower essences for distressed children. Other good ideas include a bottle of bubbles, bath toys, fun bath extras (bath fizzes, scented bath salt, dried flowers, or other pamper yourself items), and a soft cozy towel to dry off. If you made yourself an actual TLC wrap, you can use it after you are finished.

Summary: This activity is provided as a way for you to consciously participate in the purging of held pain and grief within the system, as symbolized by the Little One that holds it. It is almost identical to the Double Dip protocol as facilitated in Section #1, except that you are joining your inner child(ren) in a child-sized version of it. You will be helping your Little Ones to cleanse and purge their pain before sending them for more intensive healing with the Divine Advocates through the Butterfly Sleep. Only the inner children who are ready and eager to cleanse will be selected for conscious interactive cleansing by the Journeyer. All others will go through a perfected cleansing and healing process through the agency of the Divine Advocates under the Grace of God, and outside of conscious awareness.

This activity is child friendly and meant to put your Little Ones at ease so that they can do the cleansing and soothing along with you. You will be functioning as the caring adult in this situation, although there may be other helpers around. You will do the water breath cleansing in the baby pool and show the child(ren) how to use the water to cleanse themselves until you are all spouting the water joyfully into the air. Special scrubbing bubbles are placed in the pool and given as an elixir energy drink for the children to better imagine cleaning up on the inside. It is important for you to keep a light and playful attitude. If you need to talk to the Little Ones, keep your explanations simple, as if talking to real children. Reassure them, help them to understand that whatever happened was not their fault, and that it is time to release feeling bad so that they can play and have fun again. Most of all, reassure them that they are deeply loved and wanted. They carry pieces of your authentic Sacred Self that are valuable and important to you.

If, for any reason, you feel that you need to stop the session early due to overwhelm, or if you run out of time, be sure to communicate to your Little One that it is time for them to go back to their Butterfly Sleep and that you love them and will see them again soon. It is normal for this activity to be emotionally evocative. If you need a good cry, have a good cry. Do not hold it in. Purging requires tissues. There is no way to get around it, except to go through it.

Helpers: The same helpers as the Direct Route activity, or any others you prefer. *You* are the main dedicated helper in this activity.

New Concepts: Angelic Scrubbing Bubbles Elixir, Twirly Straw Suction Hose, and the All Better Elixir

Intentions Supporting Activity

- Intentions added from anywhere else in the book that are relevant to this work.
- All Assistance, as appropriate, for any matter that needs attention.
- Cleansing of pain and suffering held within the system of self, or within inner child(ren), without the need to re-experience or remember originating trauma.
- Appropriate selection of inner children, such that only those who are ready to cleanse gracefully are brought for interactive cleansing with Journeyer.

- Inner child(ren) who are too traumatized for conscious interactive cleansing, to be healed and cleansed in perfection by Divine Advocates through God, outside of awareness.
- Perfected nurturing, comfort, and care provided to all parts of self.
- Reconnection to lost innocence, or lost parts of self.
- Releasing of shame, guilt, or sense of being corrupted or dirty.
- Release of patterns of victimization, helplessness, and predation.
- Enhanced resiliency, emotional integrity, and strength.
- Preparation for reintegration of lost, suppressed, or disassociated parts of self.
- Release from distorted perceptions, conclusions about life, or conclusions about the nature of reality as held in error by inner child(ren).
- Support and permission to be playful, spontaneous, and childlike in ways that nurture and bring joy to living.
- Rectification of distorted attitudes, behaviors, and perceptions about sexuality, intimacy, or relationships as held in error by inner child(ren).
- Healing with Grace, Ease, Mercy, Compassion, and Love, such that all inner children feel safe, acknowledged, perfectly nurtured, and able to express themselves without fear.
- *Angelic Scrubbing Bubbles*: used as an internal scrubbing medium, to remove congestion of any kind, stagnated emotional waste, and unshed tears.
- *Twirly Suction Hose*: identical in function to the adult version found in the Lotus Pool, except in a fun, child friendly appearance.
- *All Better Elixir*: identical to the Graceful Integration Elixir, but specialized to Little One soothing, comfort, and integration needs.
- Listed intentions reaffirmed as part of the Cooperative Contract already signed over.
- Engagement of this activity, if a Cooperative Contract has not yet been signed, an affirmation of acceptance of these intentions, corrected in perfection, and brought within Divine Will.

Action Statement:
"I request to initiate the Baby Pool Double Dip, now please."

Note: *Skip to step 2 if you are coming immediately from the previous activity.*

Step-by-Step Activity Instructions:

1. Enter *Angelscape* at the Lotus Pool. Complete the spouting Water Breath Cleanse, sip your Lotus Nectar Elixir, and put on your Work Wrap to prepare for your journey. When you feel ready, you may continue.
2. A helper escorts you to the Garden of the Little Ones. Once there, you are brought to the baby pool area. There are two child-sized pools that mimic the Lotus Pool and the TLC Bath areas with which you are familiar, as well as other water play areas, including a little waterfall shower. Imagine that this area is similar to the kiddie section of your local water park, but private and soothing.
3. Get into the Baby Lotus Pool and locate the Twirly Suction Hose and the bottle of Angelic Scrubbing Bubbles. When you are ready, tell your helper to bring in the Little One(s) that are most interested and enthusiastic to play in the cleansing water with you. The Divine Advocate and/or adult helpers stay nearby to assist the work and to provide support.
4. Imagine your appropriate Little Ones being brought to the pool areas. Greet your Little Ones and allow them to get used to the water and to find toys that they like. Let them pour the Angelic Scrubbing Bubbles into the pool and then let them drink some of it. Imagine that the bubbles begin to froth and grow as the children reluctantly smile and get more interested in the pool. Let the children play with the Twirly Suction Hose in the pool so that they get used to the sounds.
5. When the children seem comfortable, begin to do the Water Breath Cleanse that you learned in the big Lotus Pool. Imagine the children watching you, finding it interesting how the water comes out foggy, but then immediately clears. Continue with the progressive cleansing with a smile on your face. Imagine that one of the helpers that the children know already joins you in the baby pool and uses the Twirly Suction Hose to gently suction out congested debris from

your body. You giggle to show that it tickles a little bit. Make it look like fun.

6. Once you are fully cleansed, do several dramatic and fun "water spouts" out of the top of your head. Imagine the children giggling with delight at the spray of water as they ask you to show them how to do it. Talk them through the water breath cleansing activity while the helpers playfully suction out the congestion. Keep the mood upbeat and soothing. Watch as the children feel progressively lighter, more joyful, and more playful.
7. Finish off your water breathing cleanses by having everyone spout the water cheerfully and exuberantly out of the tops of your heads. Imagine the mist from the spray of the spouts throwing rainbows all over the garden. When it feels time to move along, announce to your Little Ones that it is time to get into the other baby pool, the Baby TLC Bath. Take their hands and go into the thick and gooey bath.
8. Imagine showing your Little Ones how to breathe in the thick, gooey liquid. Let them know that it coats them in feel-good comfort and makes everything All Better. Your helpers approach the pool with All Better Elixir drinks with twirly straws. The children drink them up, have some cookies, and then begin to yawn and stretch.
9. The helpers come with the Swaddling Cocoon Wraps and gently cuddle the children in their sweet little cocoons to prepare for their healing sleep. Kiss them good-bye and let them know that you will see them again soon. You may give them a token gift, such as a stuffed animal or baby blanket that they can hold onto until you see them again. Allow them to give you a gift, if they have one for you, which you can hold onto until you see them again.
10. When you are finished, you may continue with the next Scenic Route activity, or your main Divine Advocate escorts you to the TLC Bath where you will coat yourself in the soothing energies, sip your Graceful Integration Elixir, and then wrap yourself in the Resiliency Comfort Wrap. Do not drive, operate heavy machinery, or do any activities that are dangerous, or that require you to be fully attentive, until you feel fully shifted back to a normal waking state. Take some

time to journal or take notes before your memory of the experience fades.

Continuing Thoughts

You can get creative with the process of cleansing the Little Ones. You may bring them to a small waterfall, a swimming hole, the beach, a lake, or whatever watery environment you think the children will respond to in a favorable way. This process of purging pain and energetic/emotional congestion can be used as a continuing tool of releasing anything that no longer serves the self from any part of you from any age. Teenaged selves tend to have a lot of emotional congestion; you can take them to an age appropriate area for their cleansing if you feel the need.

You may go back to this activity several times if you feel prompted to do that. As you release excess pain and congestion in the system, it may allow for other parts of yourself to be ready and eager to do the same thing. You may wish to do several baby pool trips to take care of Little Ones from each developmental stage of childhood. You may want to focus on one child at a time, or feel prompted to work with several that you know have had a burden that they are ready to release.

Parents can use this imagery to help their children to purge excess congestion and to do a full energy cleanse. Allow them to imagine the activity while in a bubble bath. Make it fun and exciting. Teaching them the skills of purging emotional congestion give them greater strategies to cope with pressures, which will assist them not to internalize situations that are outside of their ability to understand. The more capable they are to release negative emotions, the more intact the structure of their system will remain, and the less 'fixing' they will need to do as adults.

Life can get messy.
Cleanse often.

Photograph 46318
by morguefile.com
user: anitapatterson

Scenic Route #3 B
Wishing Well

Environment Setting: Garden of the Little Ones, Sacred Well

Purpose: The Wishing Well activity helps to reconnect you to your dreams, hopes, and visions for the future. You can reconnect with your early passions, interests, talents, and skills that may have been abandoned over the years.

Usage Suggestion: The Wishing Well activity can be used any time you want to empower your dreams or wishes. It can be integrated into manifestation techniques as well as being a place for you to connect to the optimism and hope of a bright future.

Activity Props: You can do this activity at an actual fountain, wishing well, or body of water that it would be okay for you to toss in a coin. You might also like to have art supplies on hand that you can use to draw out some of your dreams and visions.

Summary: You will go to the Garden of the Little Ones, where you are met by a Little One. The child takes your hand and walks you to the back corner of the garden. A large stone wall frames a lion's head spout that empties into a fountain. The Little One talks to you about some of your childhood dreams and wishes that may be relevant to your path in life today. You discuss your current wishes and throw the coin into the fountain to express it. After each coin toss, you sip the clear wishing water, which is a vibrational energy drink.

The Wishing Well is a place for expressing positive visions of the future. It is a place of constructing your desires, your path of service, and your contributions to the world. The Wishing Well is placed in an area designated for children because children know how to dream big and without apology. You are encouraged to dream big and joyfully imagine the highest possible outcome for yourself, your family, and the world at large. The Wishing Well is used as a platform for you to begin articulating your vision of a positive future and to begin the movement of support and energy to its clarification or manifestation within Divine Will.

Helpers: A well-adjusted and happy Little One is a helper to you in this activity. Any of your Divine Advocates, especially from your Guide

Team, may join you to help guide your vision and to provide feedback, if you need it.

New Concepts: Wishing Coin, Wishing Well Elixir.

Intentions Supporting Activity

- Intentions added from anywhere else in the book that are relevant to this work.
- All Assistance, as appropriate, for any matter that needs attention.
- Reconnection to childhood hopes, dreams, and visions for the future.
- Reconnection to untapped talents, skills, and abilities.
- Support to see the future as promising, exciting, hopeful, and positive.
- Guidance and support to clarify highest path in life.
- Support to be grateful for current path in life, life lessons, and challenges overcome.
- Acknowledgement of many blessings and successes.
- Releasing of disappointment for paths not taken, seeing wisdom of the path of your experiences.
- Empowerment to tackle new challenges, projects, or dreams.
- Voluntary alignment of wishes with Divine Will, responsible and mature use of creative powers of manifestation.
- Increasing feelings of empowerment, courage, and strength to accomplish what you feel you are called to accomplish.
- Path support, guidance, clarity, and course correction, as needed or beneficial.
- Roadblocks and obstacles provided to discourage improper paths.
- Serendipity and synchronistic opportunities to encourage movement onto the highest possible path.
- Protection from diversion or sabotage of any kind, from any direction.
- *Wishing Coin*: used to symbolize a particular wish or hope that you would like to empower or see unfold in your life, so long as it is within Divine Will. It is like making a prayer for support to flow to what you believe is your highest path in life.

- *Wishing Well Elixir*: the water into which the Wishing Coin is tossed is used as an energy elixir to attune the Journeyer to the happy outcomes requested, such that personal vibrations attract those outcomes, so long as they are within Divine Will.
- Listed intentions reaffirmed as part of the Cooperative Contract already signed over.
- Engagement of this activity, if a Cooperative Contract has not yet been signed, an affirmation of acceptance of these intentions, corrected in perfection, and brought within Divine Will.

Action Statement:
"I request to make a wish at the Wishing Well, now please."

Note: *Skip to step 2 if you are coming immediately from the previous activity.*

Step-by-Step Activity Instructions:

1. Enter *Angelscape* at the Lotus Pool. Complete the spouting Water Breath Cleanse, sip your Lotus Nectar Elixir, and put on your Work Wrap to prepare for your journey. When you feel ready, you may continue.
2. A helper escorts you to the Garden of the Little Ones. A Little One greets you with a big smile, takes your hand, and walks (or skips) you to the Sacred Well in the back of the garden.
3. Imagine a spout of water streaming out of the carved lion's mouth from the stone wall. The clear pure water falls into the fountain just below it. The bottom of the fountain is dotted with glittery coins that sparkle in the sunlight.
4. Your Little One begins to remind you of the dreams you had as a child. You may have flashes of insight, a memory, or your Little One may speak or draw you a picture. You may be directed to watch the water of the fountain to see visions of your childhood dreams.
5. Your Little One pulls out a bag of golden coins and tosses a coin into the fountain. The water responds to the coin, as if it has an enthusiasm that matches the wish. Your Little One reaches for the drinking cup on the wall of the fountain,

drinks some of the wishing water and then hands you the bag of coins.

6. It is your turn to make wishes. Your Little One smiles in encouragement. Imagine the biggest, most joyful vision of your personal future. This would be one where you are walking your Path of Light. It is a vision where you are positively contributing to your family and your world while applying your God-given talents, skills, passions, and abilities. What would your life look like if you were able to follow your brightest and most joyful path? Imagine it, talk it out with your Little One--then toss the coin into the Wishing Well.
7. Imagine as the coin hits the water, that you feel a wave of energy move outward from the ripple. The water responds to the energy of your wish. Colors or sparkles swirl in the water and you may hear music or hear humming vibrations of sound. A vision of your brightest future may begin to show up on the surface of the water, like a snippet of a movie of your own future life. In this vision, you are happy and peaceful. What has unfolded in your life?
8. When the vision begins to fade and sparkle back into the clear water of the fountain, your Little One dips the drinking cup into the water and hands it to you. Imagine drinking down the cool, refreshing clear liquid. It may even taste a bit sweet and unexpected. The vibrational Wishing Well Elixir hums into every cell of your body, tuning you like an instrument to follow your Path of Light. Imagine feeling waves of hope moving though you. Your Little One says, "*It is going to be okay.*"
9. When you are ready, say good-by to your Little One and express your gratitude for reconnecting to the power of hope. You can come back anytime you need to infuse yourself with the energies of a bright future.
10. Your Divine Advocate escorts you to the adult TLC Bath where you will coat yourself in the soothing energies, sip your Graceful Integration Elixir, and then wrap yourself in the Resiliency Comfort Wrap. Do not drive, operate heavy machinery, or do any activities that are dangerous, or that require you to be fully attentive, until you feel fully shifted

back to a normal waking state. Take some time to journal or take notes before your memory of the experience fades.

Continuing Thoughts

The Wishing Well is an area to help empower you to create a bright future for yourself. Follow up on the insight that you received while in this activity. You can get yourself a real table sized water fountain that you can use as a special tool to connect to your wishing well.

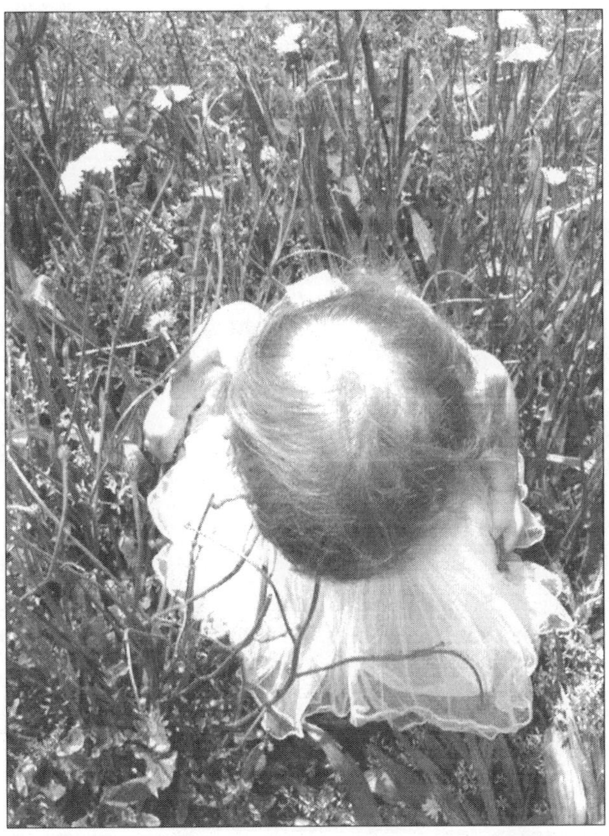

To reflect upon the child within, you must remember how to marvel in the smallest things.

Photograph 72184
by morguefile.com
user: anitapatterson

Summary and Wrap Up

Complementary Activities

- Emotional release therapies, such as, Emotional Freedom Technique (see resource list for free manual on-line).
- Inner child work of any kind with a qualified therapist.
- Do something fun, joyful, and spontaneous.
- Go to a water park, the beach, or a pool to frolic in the water.
- Research any job or career paths inspired by the Wishing Well.
- Take a skills and talents assessment evaluation that can give feedback as to what jobs would be a good match for you.
- Artwork or creative work of any kind is especially good as follow up.

Project Ideas

Make a scrapbook of the brightest future you can imagine. Create supportive affirmations to engage you in the momentum of walking the path that will take you to your brightest future. Collect pamphlets for new training, or whatever you need to do to prepare for your future. Begin to write a plan to achieve it. What do you need to do? What steps do you need to take? What support do you need? What parts of your plan need work or revision? What is the *first* step?

Reflection Questions

1. Describe how you were feeling before and after the activities.
2. What were the most vivid details of your imagery during the activities?
3. Describe your helpers, the tools, and their assistance.
4. What surprised you the most about your experiences?
5. What was your favorite activity in Section 3?
6. What was your least favorite activity in Section 3?
7. Can you integrate your new skills into your more familiar practices?
8. Were there any details that seemed highlighted to you that you might want to think about?
9. Do you feel inspired to do any research in any other related area? If so, what is it?

10. How many Little Ones seemed to need a lot of attention?
11. What were some of the main distortions that you know have caused trouble for you as an adult?
12. How did your Little Ones respond to the Baby Pool Double Dip?
13. What childhood dreams or visions did your Little One show you?
14. How do the childhood dreams correspond to your vision of a bright future?
15. What are some of your unique skills, talents, and abilities?
16. How do your unique talents play into a vision of a bright future?
17. What is the first thing you need to do or learn, or the first step you have to take to move forward on your Path of Light?
18. What tools or gifts did you give to or receive from your Little Ones?
19. What did the Little Ones enjoy the most and least about the work?

Don't forget to rest along your journey when you feel the need to regroup and recharge.

Photograph 212936
by morguefile.com
user: blondieb38

Focus Group Feedback

Sharon

Little One Healing and Restoration

I went to the Garden of the Little Ones for the healing and restoration activity. The gong was rung by Blessed Mother. All my teams were assembled around the amphitheatre. As the children were assembling, I notice the wide variance in ages. There were "children" there from very young through adults. I also noticed that as they were passing the pieces of paper up that some of them were pretty nasty, smelly, dirty and moldy. As Blessed Mother began to read the distortions, there is a sudden feeling of anticipation, of a "new day", a "new start". The crowd gleefully and purposefully shouts back to her, almost like the vibrations of the sound of their voices will shake loose all the negative energy and feelings so they can be lifted off the children. The volume of their voices together surprised me.

I reach to the person sitting in front of me and place my hands on her shoulders as each distortion is declared. When they have all been read, the person turns around, the person is me at the same age I am now, looking right at myself. I tell her (me) that I am loved, whole, perfect and totally lovable. I tell her that I love her for who she is now. That's a pretty bold statement coming from me to me. It's a tough statement to digest and I'm going to have to keep working on that. I kiss each one of the children's foreheads as I help my team of advocates tuck them into their resting place, wishing them peace and healing. Then Blessed Mother comes up to me, kisses me on the forehead, and says that I am well cared for and every need is met, that I am protected and all is secure.

Baby Double Dip

My (deceased) grandmother meets me at the baby lotus pool. After giving me a big hug and kiss, she gives me the bottle of scrubbing bubbles and I enter the pool and ask her to go get the "kids". Five little ones walk forward and enter into the pool. There is a small toddler about one year old and a five-, nine-, twelve-, and fifteen-year-old girls. Hiding behind a large tree not far from the pool is a small boy about seven-years-old with sandy blond hair and blue eyes peeking out timidly, very uncertain, and somewhat afraid. My grandma tries to guide him over but he resists. I get out of the pool, go over, and kneel down in front of him. I ask him if he would like to come with me to play with the other children in the pool. I explain that he doesn't have to get in if he doesn't want to. I put my arm around him and lead him toward the pool. He is very apprehensive, but at the same times wants very much to “belong”.

The other children are playing happily, laughing and splashing one another. The fifteen- year old is tentative but is splashing the younger children, which make them squeal in delight. I re-enter the pool and ask him if he wants to join us. At first, he shakes his head no, but with a little more prompting, he slowly steps into the water. I hold his hand and tell him everything is going to be fine and that he's not alone. I pour the bottle of bubbles into the water and immediately there are lovely bubbles everywhere of all different sizes and colors. They smell like a candy store, sweet and delicious. The other children are really having a lot of fun laughing, joking and giggling.

The twelve-year-old girl playfully splashes the little boy “inviting” him to join in on the fun. He smiles. The other children then call to him to come in and play. A little unsure, he goes farther into the pool and begins to timidly splash the other children. At last, everyone is laughing and having a great time. I call to all of them to watch and see what I can do with the water breath. I teach them how to breathe the water in and out, and how much fun it is to have the “silly squiggly thing” vacuum stuff out, and if they listen, they can hear the clinking and clanking as it goes into the tube. They all think it is hilarious. When I show them how to blow the water out the top of their heads, they erupt into laughter thinking this is awesome.

We continue to “blow our tops”. They all are enthralled by the whole process. After we are all done I give all my “kids” a big hug and a butterfly, telling them that they are all like butterflies and soon they will fly free from doubt, worry, guilt or whatever is keeping them from stretching their wings. I tell them that we will be together again very soon. My little boy then hands me a beautiful white and blue flower and kisses me on the cheeks with a smile. My grandma then takes them all back to the healing place so they can rest, be at peace, and heal with the other children.

Wishing Well

As I enter into the garden of the little ones, I am greeted by two little girls about seven years old. They take my hands and lead me back to the Lion fountain. I love the sound of the water falling into the base; it’s so soothing and peaceful. As we stand there and look at the sparkling clear water, my blonde little girl reminds me that when I was young I wanted to be a forest ranger in Yosemite National Park. I wanted to ride a horse and be totally one with nature, with the plants, animals, water and sky. She reminded me that I wanted to help people see what I saw; the beauty, majesty the sacredness of mother earth. She reminded me that I wanted to discover the secrets stored in the rocks and plants, and to hear her voice in the wind.

They reminded me that I loved houseplants and that I had so many in my room when I was young that my sister would complain to my mom that I had to stop getting more. I was reminded that I knew all their scientific names and what kind of care they needed, and that I loved each and everyone one of them, and had given each a name How in the end, I was made to give it up because it invaded my sisters “space”. They reminded me that I have always been connected, and still am connected, to my friends in nature, and that they are still there waiting for me.

Then my other little girl gave me the gold coin to make a wish. I make my private wish, which is a long list of things I would like to accomplish and become. I throw the coin into the fountain and thc water starts to bubble like its boiling. Out of the water raises up a spear with feathers and beads on it (the kind a Native American would use), then a “medicine bag” comes up out of the water, then a dogwood branch with pink flowers, and a hooded green velvet cape lined in gold fabric and beautiful cording around the edges. Then a gorgeous angel appears with a perfect quartz crystal ball about the size of a cantaloupe. It has rainbows inside and the angel said that all I need to know is inside, to look inside to see. The water settles and I drink from the cup. It tasted a lot like the lotus flower nectar. I thank my angel and the girls for the gifts of the wishing well. I kiss and hug them both.

Laura

Little One Healing and Restoration

The spiritual helper using the gong on stage was Archangel Raphael. I wasn't aware of that many children gathering, but I flashed on a few school pictures of myself as they came in, like there were key ages that each child who showed up were there to represent.

Some of the replacement phrases I was hearing them yell out were, “capable”, “strong”, “wise”, “intuitively guided”, and “successful”. They were more than happy to tear up old programming with great gusto. I had to smile because the thought in my mind as I watched this was, “At last. About time. Watch this. Alright!”

I felt curious as to where this would take my mind and heart before I started. The most vivid details involved my emotions and feeling of “wistfulness”. As to helpers, I didn't see them this time so much as felt their presence. After Archangel Raphael, it was all formless sensing of the presence of them. My favorite part of this activity was the redefining of distortions.

Baby Lotus Pool

Moving to the baby pool, I was laughing with the Little Ones and felt very maternal toward them, protective of them. I can't explain that one, since in this life I didn't have any children. We played and enjoyed the water, then I lay on my back and just completely relaxed, again, like the adult-sized lotus pool, it was as though I became part of the water. I couldn't tell where I stopped and the water started. It was very healing and peaceful.

Wishing Well

The wishing well made me pretty teary eyed. I spontaneously "wished" that "I knew in my heart, and not just my head, that everything would be alright". Boy, for some reason that hit a nerve. I've been challenged on a lot of levels the last year or two and a profound sense of how exhausting it has been trying to "soldier through". I have to acknowledge the difficulty was pretty emotional. This is really an issue ripe for healing right now. The water was sweet, a sense of it's purity. "Simplicity" came to mind, as in a message like "it's simple"--but I make it hard. The ladle felt cold from the "Ice Mountain" sense of the water's source! I didn't want to go from this place. All was well there; that sense of timelessness with all cares and concerns at bay. I wished time could stop like that a while longer, like a time "oasis" where I could forget my responsibilities for a while. Hard to go, I wish it could be brought into my own reality.

Lourdes

Little One Healing and Restoration

This was a very powerful meditation for me. The garden amphitheater is smaller than usual for me today. The only children that showed up were a toddler, a six-year-old boy, a six-year-old little girl, a ten-year-old little girl, a thirteen- year old, and a sixteen- year old. Each had their guardian angels with them. When the distortions were released, there was a lot of crying.

All of the children, except the three year old, were distraught. They were blessed by wonderful angels that helped ease their discomfort. As the butterflies were released, the youngest tried to catch the butterflies, and all were in awe as the dust spread out over the theater. Clapping ensued at the end. The kids were led to be cleansed and tucked away.

I knew this one was going to be tough, because I have a lot of distortions. I felt as if I could have cried on for days. Lack of sleep and a stressful job did not help the crying situation either. I decided to go into the cleansing pool for a while and couldn't wait to be done with my day so I could go to bed and bury myself under blankets. My toddler and six-year-old little boy loved this exercise! The rest of my kids were not ready for it yet. Above all, my adult self needed this more than the kids.

Baby Lotus Pool

After the healing exercise, I was more than ready for the pool. I jumped in so fast, you would have thought that I was part fish. As I sat in the pool, the first one to approach was the toddler. She wasn't too thrilled until she saw the water coming out of my feet as bubbles. That was pure delight for her and all she did was laugh and giggle as she tried to imitate me. The peals of laughter brought in my six-year-old boy, who was delighted that he could blow bubbles out of his feet too! This made the three-year-old even happier. There were bubbles and rainbows all over the pool in all shapes and sizes. Although they didn't want to get suctioned off, they were pleasantly tired after the pool. They ate a snack and went off to take a nap. I was upset that I had to come back to this reality. The pool accomplished a great deal under the gentlest of ways.

Wishing Well

I had little angels meet me on the beach and we went up the winding path up to the garden. As I received my coin, I saw that there was a rainbow on one side, and the word “dream” on the other. As I tossed the coin into the fountain, the water turned a sparkly shade of gold with many bright colored flecks in it. I made my wish and was filled with hope. I didn't get a chance to drink the water, but the littlest angel kissed my cheek and told me that my dream was already set into motion. I kissed the top of her head and went back down the path home. Although I didn't take a sip of water that day, I went back the next day and took a sip then. The water tasted pure and sweet. The Wishing Well will be seeing me a lot!

Lori

Special Interaction with single Little One/Baby Lotus Pool

When I entered the very protective area, I saw lots of children everywhere, but I noticed in a corner, where the swings were, that there was one little girl with pigtails swinging alone. She had her hands under her chin staring at the ground, obviously not enjoying herself. I knew in my heart that the little girl was me. I had neglected my inner child for a long time. I think that it was because my childhood was very stressful and negative, with a not-so-forgiving mother, and issues that even exist with her today. I had gone through counseling for the issues that I had, and it helped--I do not see myself as a victim, yet I also didn't want to go back there either. But seeing my Little One so sad and neglected, I knew it was painfully obvious that I had neglected a part of myself, a critical part of myself, sadly, for a very, very long time.

I walked over to her. She raised her head so quickly and gave me a big smile and reached for a hug. I was glad to see her also. She sat back down in her swing and I sat down beside her. We talked a lot and revisited painful events, but I explained them to her, to myself, as not being her fault regardless of what was told to her before. I told her that big people are sometimes mean, but that is only because at some level they also are in pain and don't have the means to deal with it.

I went through all the painful things from a really strange "third person" point of view, which allowed the emotions to kind of fade away. I was explaining to her, and to myself as well, and found it to be extremely non-confrontational. I explained every bad memory and tried to also remember the good memories. We talked for a long time (we did the "Tag, Refuse, Rescript" here) and by the end, she was sitting on my lap and we began to swing together. It was a lot of fun and I felt *so free.* Free from a lot of misunderstanding, and actually happy that Spirit is the reason why I am able to heal from those awful experiences. We swung for a long time and then she jumped off and waited for me to stop.

She grabbed my hand and we went over to the baby pool. Before we got there, she stopped and picked up some really sparkly pink sand. She told me to hold out my hand and put a pile of it in my hand. She took hers and blew it. I also did the same. A second afterward, I felt really giggly. I am guessing this was my way of clearing some crap for good, maybe not all of it, but a great majority of it. We played and played in the water shower but for some reason I did not go into the pool. Maybe because I wasn't ready too, I don't know, but it also could be because you mentioned to be careful with these detailed exercises if you had a lot of childhood trauma. Instead, I just followed my Little One where ever she went, and just like children do, we darted everywhere. As I ran through the sprinklers, I saw the rainbows from the sun and felt how warm and wonderful it was to be a child again--when things were *simple*--when happiness seemed so *simple.*

Wishing Well

I then was pulled to the lion fountain and to the Wishing Well. During all of this, I did not feel that there were adults there, except some Grandmotherly looking angels with clear sparkling wings. Everything was sparkly to me; like a kid, I was really enjoying this. At the

Wishing Well, I thought about all the things I used to do as a child that made sense to me now. I use to go and pick weeds and build a little "pharmacy" using a pile of cinderblocks as my counter, and the holes in the cinderblock as my herb cabinets. I had great fun doing that. Now that I am a big girl, I am very much into herbs and make my own teas and such. I never really thought about it until I took the time to remember. I also use to collect all kinds of rocks and talk to them. Once again, I also love stones and have tons of them in my current home. I thought about my hopes and dreams for the future and had great fun talking about them with lots of hope and excitement.

As I threw the coin in, I asked that any latent talents come forth and that I have all the support I need for all the future endeavors I hoped to come. I also talked about all the things I was grateful for. I even recall yelling in the well just to hear myself echo. There was one more thing I really, really wanted to do, and I whispered it into my Little One's ear, I wanted to *color.* Oh, how I miss that. I loved to color and cherished my crayons with a vengeance when I was little. My little brother use to break them to make me mad. I treated them like they were gold and if one was getting smaller, I stopped using it because I wanted the pretty colors to last forever. We went to a table where there were other kids drawing, painting, coloring, and we colored rainbows, horses, stick figures. Oh, I will be coming back to do this again!

I felt like it was time to go, so I hugged my child self and promised to not forget, to visit again, and to sometimes do something fun that makes me feel like a kid, something like playing in the dirt or coloring. I promised to never neglect that part of myself and I told her/me that I loved her very, very much.

Little One Healing and Restoration

I arrived there and saw Archangel Gabriel standing on a huge stage, and for some reason, there were purple curtains. He hit the gong and all the Little Ones came out. I saw *lots* of them, some looked really haggard and bad, others pretty normal. They were all different ages, but all of them had brown hair. I remember thinking that these were all me at one time or another.

When the time came for the pieces of paper, I started crying. While I thought I released a lot on the swing with my child self, I realized there was still more, and I was more than ready to let go of it. I saw some really torn up pieces of paper. When they got to the front, I started thinking of all the really horrible things my mother had said to me, things that maybe consciously I don't believe anymore, but still may be floating around my subconscious. I felt really, really sad, but then relived too. I was in the bathtub when I did this, and I remember actually yelling some "*No's*" out when some were read. That felt so *good.* I was alone, so no one was here to think I was losing my mind. I actually got goose bumps afterwards.

The papers did turn into butterflies, and then to really cool sparkly pink stuff. I took some of that pink stuff to keep. It was given to me by Archangel Gabriel and I was told to use it on things that were no longer true to me. For example, if someone said something that hurt me, I could visualize the pink sparkles being put on those words, and it would neutralize them so they couldn't hurt me. I thought that was kinda cool.

Afterwards the children got sleepy; most had the most precious smiles of peace on their faces. These grandmotherly looking people came out, scooped each one up lovingly in blankets (fluffy glowing green and pink blankets), and took them off to nap. At this point, I left and went back out by the baby pool and saw my 'child self' playing and having fun. She came running and I gave her a great big hug. I reminded her that I told her I would be back, and that I kept my word. I told her I had something for her and I gave her a teddy bear and some of the pink sparkles Archangel Gabriel gave me. I told *her* how to use it. That seemed really important that I give her some and help her feel empowered to use it. Afterwards, I gave her a hug, but before I left, she yelled for me, ran away behind the hedge, and came back with a yellow daisy. That was so cool! That night I slept with thoughts of being wrapped up in a nice healing cocoon. It was the best night I have had in a long time!

Section 4
Healing Realignment & Rectification

Activities Introduction

Section 4 begins to define the imagery and protocols for healing the distortions and misalignments in our systems. This section of the work unfolds entirely in a spa-like setting that is set in a cavern of a cave. Caves symbolically represent a womb of the earth. Much of what is done in the *Angelscape* Spa will be like "rebirthing" our substance to be in alignment with the pure and primal design intended for us by God. This original and pure template of who we are, or who we are supposed to be, is called the Sacred Self Template. This section seeks to assess in what ways the fabric of your system has been pushed out of alignment with your Sacred Self Template. The purpose is that you can begin to imagine healing those issues and bringing yourself into increasingly better alignment. The Sacred Self Template is visualized as a file, such as a medical history file that doctors might use to treat you properly.

Once your Healing Team "identifies" the distortions from your Sacred Self Template, you can imagine a plan of action being established. As a continuing process of the activities throughout the book, you are brought through visualizations in which the distortions are systematically purged and the system is progressively realigned to the Sacred Self Template. The Diagnostic Healing Session is the first meditation session that sets the healing process in motion, but is seen as a *first* step, and not a one-time event. You are expected to continue working with your Healing Team to maintain the progression of healing, address new and emergent issues, and to support efforts that you initiate on behalf of your health and wellness. In this instance, the more exposure you have to healing session visualizations and protocols, the better. Each healing event that your mind observes (imagery counts) may add another pebble in the pond of actual healing and wholeness. Remember that human beings have amazing potential for self-healing, that is an indisputable and observable fact, but the biggest key is to *believe* it. If the mind believes, the body follows.

We use the same model of "Tag, Refuse, Rescript" in this section of the work. The Healing Team first "tags" the distorted patterns in your system, then you refuse the distortions, and then the distortions are rescripted and replaced with original pure patterns from your Sacred Self Template. Various healing activities are used to help you to imagine engaging the process once the initial diagnostic is facilitated. As with the Double Dip, this section utilizes the "Dip, Drink, Wrap" process, with which you are already familiar.

Most people find this area in *Angelscape* very relaxing and enjoyable. If, for whatever reason, you do not like the setting to be in a large cave cavern, you may create and design a spa environment that suits you. While writing, I tried to imagine the spa in an airy and outdoor place, but I could not create the imagery in my mind for it. It always went back to the cavern setting, which was quite easy for me to see and experience. My own bias is that I find caves and caverns to be especially powerful sacred places on earth. My parents took me to Luray Caverns when I was a small child and I thought it was the most magical and special place I had ever seen. Since healing the body and consciousness is something we want to manifest at the physical level, I think the cave setting helps to think in more primordial and "earthly" terms. If we were "made by mud and clay" by God, it makes sense to me that we imagine fixing and resetting ourselves in a setting that is of the earth.

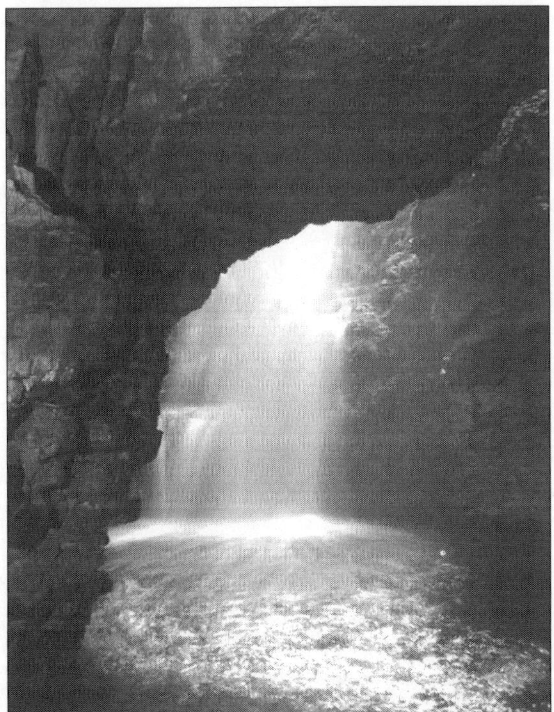

This reminds me of the entrance to the cave-like spa.

Photograph 59068
by morguefile.com
user: ariadna

Direct Route Activity #4
Diagnostic Healing Session

Environment Setting: The *Angelscape* Spa

Complementary Scenic Route Activities
SR 4 A: All Element Mud Bath
SR 4 B: The Mineral Bath

Purpose: The Diagnostic Healing Session is the primary healing assessment that tags the inconsistencies in your system from your original Sacred Self Template. This is done so that the original pure patterns can be re-established and anchored.

Usage Suggestions: The Diagnostic Healing Session is used as the primary assessment to see what your status is as compared to your Sacred Self Template. You may go back to this activity for follow up assessment sessions when you are prompted to do so. For example, after six months of progress, follow up assessments to imagine and sense how you have progressed may be helpful.

Activity Props: Since this work is done in a spa setting, you can integrate an actual trip to a spa or the steam room of your local gym. If you are lucky enough to live near an actual cavern, you might consider a trip to refresh your connection to that kind of a setting.

Summary: You will go to the *Angelscape* Spa to be greeted by one of your Healing Team members. You go directly to the Healing Room section of the spa where the rest of the Healing Team is waiting for you and ready to go. You will imagine lying down on the table in the room and then your Healing Team begins the scanning and assessment process. You imagine a gentle scanning sensation moving through you, moving in sections throughout your system. The diagnostic sessions may last longer than you expect. You are encouraged to recline on a bed or couch so that you can fall asleep if the session is long. Once the diagnostic session is done, your helpers will present you with a list of system distortions for your refusal. As the rest of the book unfolds, you will imagine rescripting your system to the Sacred Self Template.

The diagnostic is followed up by a soak in the All Element Mud Bath and the Mineral Bath. You can go directly to the Scenic Route activities if you have the time. The mud bath symbolizes the sum of all elements and materials available in the natural world; the pure primal raw material that God used to create us. We are essentially going to soak in it to imagine having access to all possible healing substances we need to properly heal and mend ourselves. The Mineral Bath is used as a way to imagine being revitalized. Rocks and crystals are used to imagine a physical representation of color, sound, and energy.

Helpers: Your Healing Team members are the primary workers in the spa. Other helpers who are dedicated spa workers may also be seen, but you do not have to place your attention on them.

New Concepts: Sacred Self Template, Sacred Self Elixir.

Intentions Supporting Activity

- Intentions added from anywhere else in the book that are relevant to this work.
- All Assistance, as appropriate, for any matter that needs attention.
- Diagnostic assessment of Journeyer's current status as compared to the Sacred Self Template.
- Tagging and identifying of all discrepancies and distortions from original Sacred Self Template.
- Journeyer refuses and releases all distortions from the original Sacred Self Template and gives full permission for them to be cleansed from the system.
- Slating of distortions for immediate refusal, release, and cleansing from the system in the order of most critical and urgent issues first.
- Remedies and "medicine" for distortions identified and slated for activation in the system in the most appropriate way.
- Support for active, empowered, and responsible participation of the Journeyer with his/her own healing process.
- Support to research and investigate actual healing protocols beneficial to wellbeing (vitamins, therapies, and so on).
- Interactive and dynamic support from Healing Team to back up conventional healing processes, as needed.
- Support and guidance for behavioral shifts to support the Journeyer to take the best care of him/herself for wellness.

- Healing session that can be initiated through active imagery or passive requests for healing sessions to commence at bedtime.
- Soul lessons, which involve learning through health issues, to be offered in more graceful ways, when possible.
- Support for soul lessons to be learned with greater speed and grace that cannot be shifted to something easier to experience.
- Enhanced integrity and strength to any portion of the self that requires it to successfully meet healing challenges.
- All preparation necessary for Whole Self Synchronization and reintroduction of Little Ones.
- Immediate urgent or emergency care with or without the guided imagery session, when required.
- Healing Team allowed to proactively address emergent issues and to establish guidance for preventative care, wellness affirming life habits, routines, and protocols.
- Healing assistance to relevant networks of connection within Divine Will, when appropriate and possible.
- Activation of sacred space and a supportive healing environment within the home, hospital, or any actual space the Journeyer visits for healing care.
- Support to all actual health care practitioners of any kind that serve the Journeyer to be as compassionate, effective, insightful, intuitive, and competent, as possible.
- Candles lit for each discrepancy/distortion in the system for perfected rectification and realignment with Sacred Self Template.
- Resiliency, vitality, enhanced strength, and courage, as needed.
- *Sacred Self Template*: a file that is a symbolic representation of the pure template of the self that God intended, the best you that you can be that is in a state of perfected alignment with God.
- *Sacred Self Elixir*: energy drink tool used as a way to tune the Whole Self to the pure patterns and vibrations of the Sacred Self, such as an instrument is tuned. It is used to enhance and maximize all healing work by preparing the system to be as receptive as possible to alignment with the Sacred Self Template.

- Listed intentions reaffirmed as part of the Cooperative Contract already signed over.
- Engagement of this activity, if a Cooperative Contract has not yet been signed, an affirmation of acceptance of these intentions, corrected in perfection, and brought within Divine Will.

Action Statement:
"I request to initiate the Diagnostic Healing Session, now please."

Step-by-Step Activity Instructions:

1. Enter *Angelscape* at the Lotus Pool. Complete the spouting Water Breath Cleanse, sip your Lotus Nectar Elixir, and put on your Work Wrap to prepare for your journey. When you feel ready, you may continue.
2. A helper escorts you to *Angelscape* Spa, which is located behind a waterfall and inside of a large cave. One of the members of your Healing Team meets you at the entrance and walks you through the main gallery of the large cavern and into the hallway that leads to the Healing Room. All of the other Healing Team members are present and at different stations in the room. They are all ready to get to work.
3. You are led to the comfortable table in the center of the room. Imagine that there is an indentation in the shape of a human figure on it. You get on the table and align your body to match the indentations. It is warm and comfortable on the table. The indentations seem to match your body like a glove. One of your helpers puts a cover on you that has a silky metallic sheen. Scanning equipment is lowered from above the table and your Healing Team members are busy in front of equipment that reminds you of diagnostic computers.
4. You are told that the scanning process will take a little while and that you may feel some sensations while it is going on. They further explain that the movement of energies will run through different systems in your body, such as your DNA, circulatory system, organs, energy system, and so on. You are told that your muscles may involuntarily twitch, you may feel humming or vibrations in your body, some fleeting mild discomfort or pressure, changes in temperature, or you may

just feel sleepy and begin to nap your way through the session. You may feel nothing at all.

5. The main helper who greeted you at the entrance gives the signal that the Diagnostic Healing Session is to begin. You hear a slight whir of action, the lights in the room dim, and the scanning equipment beams light into your system. The colors of the light may change, the section of the body where it focuses will gradually move, and different helpers may move from their stations in the perimeter of the room to tend to you by the table. They may turn knobs and adjust the equipment to check on various data that has been produced. Everyone seems to have a specific job and the teamwork is excellent. You feel relaxed and a little sleepy. You may drift off while the scanning is going on.
6. When the scanning and diagnostic process is completed, a member of your Healing Team gently touches your shoulder to bring you back to awareness in the Healing Room. If you have actually napped, you may pick up the session right here. You feel refreshed and happy to move your body a little. One of the helpers assists you to sit up and gives you a small glass of the Graceful Integration Elixir energy drink. You are allowed to reorient in a peaceful way.
7. When you are ready, one of the helpers comes to your side with your special file. A report is pulled out that has a detailed diagnostic breakdown of the departures your system has made from your Sacred Self Template. The list looks long and your helper smiles while it is explained that *everyone's* list is long. You are allowed to look at it and read it, if you can. You do not have to read it if you cannot see or experience it.
8. You are told that this list of distortions from your Sacred Self Template needs your official refusal and release, so that your Healing Team can begin to help you to heal these issues. You are given a pen to sign a refusal of the list of distortions. You sign it and say, *"I refuse these distortions. I request to be realigned with my Sacred Self Template. Amen."* Your helpers echo with their own *"Amen."*
9. When you feel ready to hop off the table, your helper walks you back down the hallway to the main gallery area of the cavern. Your helper has the list of distortions you have

signed in hand. You both walk over to the large fireplace built into the wall of the gallery. It is a functioning representative of the Eternal Flame of God's Grace and Love. Your helper hands you the papers and you release them over to God by putting them in the loving flames. You may feel an immediate shift, as if things are already beginning to rearrange within your system.

10. An attendant with a platter comes up to you while you are standing by the fire with your helper. There is a drink on the platter called the *Sacred Self Elixir*, which is an energy drink to prime your system to be receptive to the healing work. The attendant explains it is something like doing warm up and stretching exercises before a full workout. You drink the Sacred Self Elixir and your helper and the attendant walk you to a comfortable lounging chair in the gallery so that you can sit down and rest.
11. When you are finished, you may continue with the Scenic Route activities, or your main Divine Advocate escorts you to the TLC Bath. Once at the TLC Bath, you will coat yourself in the soothing energies, sip your Graceful Integration Elixir, and then wrap yourself in the Resiliency Comfort Wrap. Do not drive, operate heavy machinery, or do any activities that are dangerous, or that require you to be fully attentive, until you feel fully shifted back to a normal waking state. Take some time to journal or take notes before your memory of the experience fades.

Continuing Thoughts

Healing Sessions

Your Healing Team has an entire wing of the spa available for healing sessions. You may have particular types of healing that you enjoy, which you may ask to receive from your Healing Team. Examples of this are, Reiki sessions, acupuncture, meridian work, energy body work, chakra balancing, and so on. Since the work is theoretically done from the spiritual level by Divine Advocates, you may find that your sessions are more powerful and useful than you might expect. You do not have to request a specific healing session, but you can go to the spa in your imagination before you go to bed, connect with your Healing Team, and simply request to initiate an appropriate healing session. They know what to do, so you do not need to detail a list of things you want addressed, but you can go to them for specific issues as well.

Initiating Healing Sessions

- Connect with your Healing Team (with or without *Angelscape* imagery), especially before sleep. *"I request to connect to my Healing Team, now please."*
- Request to initiate a healing session, which can be completed while you are sleeping, *"I request to initiate a healing session, now please."*
- If you have a specific modality you would like them to use, you may request it. *"I would like to initiate a Reiki session (or whatever), if it is appropriate, during this healing session please."*
- If you have specific concerns, address those concerns to your team before going to sleep. *"I would like for you to address my abdominal discomfort and carpal tunnel inflammation (or whatever) during this session please."*
- It is good to ask if your Healing Team has any suggestions for you to assist your healing process or to address your concerns. You may get flashes of insight, be drawn to research a topic, see images of supplements, herbs, or healing foods, and so on. Please keep a note pad by your bed in case you have a spark of inspiration. *"I request to receive guidance on what I can do to help my healing process on this end please."*

Guided imagery is a powerful way to create actual physiological shifts in the brain and body for healing. There are many good books, audio tapes, and other resources on the market that can help you to create and experience medically therapeutic healing imagery. Cancer patients, for example, are encouraged to imagine that the substances in their bodies that fight infection are sharks eating up the cancer cells, and so on. You can custom create healing imagery to address specific ailments and integrate that into your Angelscape healing sessions, or ask your Healing Team to empower the process so that it is as powerful as it can be for you.

Cleansing the system can be both energetic and physical. Many people experience extremely powerful shifts in their physical health when they address detoxification of the body. There are many different ways to engage a detoxification process, all of which should be approved by your doctor. Everything runs better when the sludge is removed. This is true for our energetic systems, but it is especially true for our physical systems.

You don't necessarily have to go to a spa to get muddy. You can do it yourself.

Photograph 101136
by morguefile.com
user: clarita

Scenic Route Activity #4 A
All Element Mud Bath

Environment Setting: *Angelscape* Spa, Healing Baths Section

Purpose: The All Element Mud Bath activity provides an opportunity to imagine that every possible healing substance in creation is accessible to you, and will be introduced to your system to initiate healing sessions that bring you into alignment with your Sacred Self Template.

Usage Suggestions: The All Element Mud Bath is designed to be used often. If you have pressing physical healing needs, this would be an excellent activity to imagine before requesting a healing sleep session with your Healing Team.

Activity Props: You can do this activity in the bathtub, as the Lotus Pool, but you might enjoy adding sea salt and a little bit of detoxifying bath clay. You can do a mud treatment in your own home using spa grade clays relatively cheaply. There are dietary supplements that use bentonite clay that you can use when you imagine drinking the All Element Mud Elixir (follow directions on package). Obviously, if you are lucky enough to be able to take an actual mud bath, that would be ideal.

Summary: You go to the healing baths area of the spa and select the area that has the mud bath. You get into the All Element Mud Bath and imagine breathing the mud up through your body, as in the Lotus Pool Water Breath Cleanse. You do not have to push the mud back out of your feet, like in the cleansing activity, but rather just pull it up and then push it out the top of your head. A helper brings you the All Element Mud Elixir, which you drink like any energy drink. Once you are fully saturated with the healing mud, you receive an Emerald Healing Wrap to seal it in.

Helpers: Members of your Healing Team and other spa help may be present for this activity, though much of it is done on your own until the Emerald Healing Wrap.

New Concepts: All Element Mud, All Element Mud Elixir, Emerald Healing Wrap.

Intentions Supporting Activity

- Intentions added from anywhere else in the book that are relevant to this work.
- All Assistance, as appropriate, for any matter that needs attention.
- All rectification and healing necessary to bring Whole Self into alignment with Sacred Self Template with grace and ease.
- Support to feel empowered to engage a healing path and to treat all parts of the Whole Self with care and nurturing.
- Support and guidance to engage complementary healing protocols that are beneficial, such as guided imagery.
- Support to enhance any other treatment for health and wellbeing, such as healing sessions with practitioners, surgery, or other healing procedures.
- Support to effectively utilize, activate, and synergize healing substances of any kind introduced to the system.
- *All Element Mud Bath*: healing bath that represents all elements, raw material, and resources available in all creation that are needed for healing.
- *All Element Mud Elixir*: energy drink of All Element Mud that is ingested like a medicine drink to initiate healing shifts within the system.
- *Emerald Healing Wrap*: used to imagine the activation of all healing substances from the All Element Mud in order to correct all departures from the original Sacred Self Template.
- Listed intentions reaffirmed as part of the Cooperative Contract already signed over.
- Engagement of this activity, if a Cooperative Contract has not yet been signed, an affirmation of acceptance of these intentions, corrected in perfection, and brought within Divine Will.

Action Statement:
"I request to initiate the All Element Mud Bath, now please."

Note: *Skip to step 3 if you are coming immediately from the previous activity.*

Step-by-Step Activity Instructions:

1. Enter *Angelscape* at the Lotus Pool. Complete the spouting Water Breath Cleanse, sip your Lotus Nectar Elixir, and put on your Work Wrap to prepare for your journey. When you feel ready, you may continue.
2. A helper meets you at the Lotus Pool and escorts you to the spa. At the entrance, you are greeted by a member of your Healing Team. You are lead through the main gallery of the cavern where you are given a Sacred Self Elixir to drink. You gulp it down and allow the preparatory shifts to unfold.
3. You are brought into the Healing Baths section of the spa. It is steamy and warmer in this hallway. You go into the room that contains the All Element Mud Bath. Your helper explains that you are going to get into the mud bath and breathe the mud up your body, filling every inch of you with the healing substances. Imagine stepping into the healing mud and settling down for a good soak.
4. An attendant enters the room and hands you the tall glass of the All Element Mud Elixir, which looks like a thick chocolate shake. It is explained to you that the All Element Mud is the main resource material from which all cures are fashioned. It will intelligently replace distortions by using your Sacred Self Template as its guide. Drink it slowly. Notice where the sensations are in your body as you finish the All Element Mud Elixir. When have finished the elixir, you may begin breathing the mud into your body.
5. Imagine slowly breathing the mud up your legs from your feet. Feel it filling up your whole body, filling in all the cracks and crevices, slipping into all the places where the distortions were removed. Imagine that the mud feels silky and rich. It is thick and takes more effort to move up into your body than the water in the Lotus Pool. You breathe more deeply and more fully to compensate for the difference in thickness. Imagine feeling whole and complete, as if nothing is missing from your system, and nothing is out of place. (You may use this time to engage in guided imagery of healing processes relevant to ailments that you have. Soak until you feel you are finished.) When you are finished, call for your helper.

6. Imagine that your helper assists to pull you out of the mud bath. You are heavy and saturated with the healing mud on the inside and out. Your helper brings you to a table next to the mud bath. A large emerald green sheet is on the table. You are instructed to lie down on top of the sheet.
7. The emerald colored sheet is wrapped tightly around you, just as a swaddling blanket. It reminds you of being wrapped up like a sushi roll. Your helper takes out his/her Sword of Light and taps on the swaddling three times. The emerald sheet begins to brightly glow a living color of emerald green. You feel warm and relaxed and you sense much activity within your system.
8. The mud activation through the Emerald Healing Wrap begins to wind down and the glow begins to fade. When the process is fully complete, you will have soaked in the Emerald Healing Wrap and the mud will appear gone. What you need from the mud has been taken and used.
9. When you are finished, you may continue with the next Scenic Route activity, or your main Divine Advocate escorts you to the TLC Bath where you will coat yourself in the soothing energies, sip your Graceful Integration Elixir, and then wrap yourself in the Resiliency Comfort Wrap. Do not drive, operate heavy machinery, or do any activities that are dangerous, or that require you to be fully attentive, until you feel fully shifted back to a normal waking state. Take some time to journal or take notes before your memory of the experience fades.

Continuing Thoughts

The All Element Mud Bath is an excellent imagery activity to engage during any other healing process. You can imagine soaking in the mud bath during a healing session with a practitioner, or as a preparation for surgery, chemotherapy, and so on. You may also use the imagery after you take medicine, drink herbal tea, or take any healing substance. The overall intention is to pull the most useful healing materials from anything that you are taking, and for that material to be efficiently put to use.

Scenic Route #4 B
Mineral Bath Tune Up

Environment Setting: *Angelscape* Spa, Healing Baths Section

Purpose: The mineral spring bath is used to imagine healing energies from the mineral kingdom being introduced to the system. It is primarily an energy body vitalizing and balancing activity.

Usage Suggestions: This is an alternate healing bath option for those who enjoy crystalline energies, or who like color, sound, or vibrational healing. It is meant to enliven and vitalize the energy centers of the body and increase the power, flow, and strength of the system. It can be used as a "pick me up" session whenever you feel depleted, ill, or would like to maintain high levels of personal energy.

Activity Props: You can take a bath with added sea salt, bath salts, or bring your favorite rocks and crystals into the tub with you. I would also recommend playing healing music, using flower essences, gem elixirs, or any other "vibrational" tools of your choice.

Summary: You go to the healing baths area of the spa and select the area that has the hot mineral spring. The walls and ceiling of the room look like the inside of a crystalline geode. The crystals growing on the sides of the wall and ceiling seem to be lit from behind the wall, as if it were something like a giant light board with colored pegs in it. You go into the mineral bath and a colored light sequence with corresponding tones will begin. The minerals, colored lights, and tonal sounds initiate a full "tune up" of your energy body system. Some crystals or minerals may be placed within your body by the helpers to tune up areas in your energy body that need additional assistance. The minerals dissolve and soak in when the area is brought into balance with the system.

Helpers: Members of your Healing Team remain present for this activity to oversee the tune up session. They may place some of the minerals or crystals within your body for areas that need more attention.

New Concepts: All Mineral Bath, Mineral Water Elixir, Crystalline Vitality Wrap.

Intentions Supporting Activity

- Intentions added from anywhere else in the book that are relevant to this work.
- All Assistance, as appropriate, for any matter that needs attention.
- Full tune up of the energy system, energy body, energy centers, and energy circulation systems within the Whole Self.
- Energy body synchronization, alignment, harmony, and balance.
- Vitalization and strengthening of the energy system.
- Removal of discordant issues from energy system.
- Enhancement of the flow of Divine Light through system.
- Pathways and channels of energy movement, cleared, strengthened, and stabilized.
- Support to become more aware of the energy system, movement of energy, and the quality of the energies within the system.
- Support to become more aware of the sensation of harmonious or discordant energies within the Whole Self, ones environment, or from outside sources.
- Support to be able to use energetic sense as a way to assess information about the quality, intent, benefit, or lack of benefit of something in relation to the self.
- *All Mineral Bath*: used to imagine a healing bath with sound, color, and vibrational remedies to enliven and align the energy body system, to bring vitalization, and increased strength and potency to the system.
- *Mineral Water Elixir*: All Mineral Water in energy drink format, used to imagine ingesting whatever vibrational assistance is necessary to initiate healing shifts.
- *Crystalline Vitality Wrap*: used to imagine the activation of all useful vibrations introduced in the Mineral Bath and for those energies to be sustained to bring continuing vitality and strength to the system.
- Listed intentions reaffirmed as part of the Cooperative Contract already signed over.
- Engagement of this activity, if a Cooperative Contract has not yet been signed, an affirmation of acceptance of these

intentions, corrected in perfection, and brought within Divine Will.

Action Statement:
"I request to initiate the Mineral Bath, now please."

Note: *Skip to step 3 if you are coming immediately from the previous activity.*

Step-by-Step Activity Instructions:

1. Enter *Angelscape* at the Lotus Pool. Complete the spouting Water Breath Cleanse, sip your Lotus Nectar Elixir, and put on your Work Wrap to prepare for your journey. When you feel ready, you may continue.
2. A helper escorts you to the spa. At the entrance, you are greeted by a member of your Healing Team. You are led through the main gallery of the cavern where you are given a Sacred Self Elixir to drink. You gulp it down and allow the preparatory shifts to unfold.
3. Imagine that you are brought into a room that looks like a crystalline geode with a whirlpool tub within it. The crystals on the walls and ceiling are of every imaginable color and appear to be lit from within, as if the wall and ceiling were a light box with colored pegs in it.
4. You settle into the mineral bath. The water is warm, very fizzy and energetic. Your body feels as if it is buzzing. Your helper pushes on one of the crystals on the wall that causes the chamber to transform into something that reminds you of a disco club. Colored lights begin to dance around the room and tonal music begins to play, causing a symphony of vibrations in your whole system.
5. An attendant enters the room and hands you an energy drink that looks a large glass of clear water with a rock candy stirring stick. You are told to stir the stick of crystals around in your water until the crystals dissolve, and then you can drink it. You stir the drink and watch how the colors swirl around in your glass and then sparkle into the drink. Imagine drinking the gem-infused water and allowing the humming sensations to enliven every cell in your body. Imagine

breathing the mineral water from the warm tub up into your body as well.

6. Once the light and sound session has calmed, your helper moves next to the mineral bath and places colored gems into various places in your body. They look like glittery jewels, very pretty. You are given the Crystalline Vitality Wrap, that seems something like a plastic wrap, but your helper explains that it is clear quartz in fabric form. Your helper finishes up and stands up by the foot of the mineral bath. S/he takes out his/her Sword of Light and places the tip of it into the water, and says, *"Activate"*. The sparkly gemstones within your system begin to gently vibrate and hum, like tuning forks. The Crystalline Vitality Wrap melts onto your skin, like a clear shiny candy coating, and then slowly fades from view.
7. When you are finished, your main Divine Advocate escorts you to the TLC Bath where you will coat yourself in the soothing energies, sip your Graceful Integration Elixir, and then wrap yourself in the Resiliency Comfort Wrap. Do not drive, operate heavy machinery, or do any activities that are dangerous, or that require you to be fully attentive, until you feel fully shifted back to a normal waking state. Take some time to journal or take notes before your memory of the experience fades.

Continuing Thoughts

You may wear gemstone jewelry that you love while doing this activity to imagine your jewelry being infused with spiritual energies. Wearing the jewelry can be a nice way to reaffirm the work done in this activity and to begin cultivating a more tangible energy sense. All things have an energetic vibration of some sort, just as colors and sounds correspond to light waves and frequencies.

You can practice sensing the difference in the vibrations of things by holding them, or concentrating upon them. As you hold them, visualize the "hum" that they make within your system. One of the best places to practice sensing different energy is in a jewelry or rock shop. Stones have a steady vibration and are often amplified in intensity in comparison to other things. In other words, they are easier to sense than most physical objects, which is why many people like working with stones for energy healing.

Hold the object one at a time and observe the subtle energy hum each one emits, or where in your body the hum seems focused.

The Mineral Spring Bath is set inside a large crystal geode. Imagine the walls looking like this photo.

Photograph 194757 by morguefile.com user: ricorocks

Summary and Wrap Up

Complementary Activities

- Research natural healing.
- Go to a naturopathic doctor for a second opinion and alternative options.
- Research supportive nutritional and dietary changes.
- Engage in actual healing sessions with a practitioner.
- Go to a spa for a mud bath or wrap.
- Do some form of physical detoxification.
- Read about using Guided Imagery for healing.
- Buy or find jewelry or rocks that were predominantly featured in mineral bath.
- Find subliminal or Guided Imagery audio tapes for healing.
- Go to a sauna or steam bath.

Project Ideas

Some of us have handfuls of supplements that we take each day to support our well being or healing. We can ask for our substances, whatever they are, to be blessed and empowered to be the most beneficial to us as they can be within Divine Will. You may imagine lighting a candle on behalf of empowering your substances, or you can imagine a member of your Healing Team touching it with a Sword of Light, symbolizing the infusion of God's Grace and Love into the substance. You may simply pray for the substances to be blessed by God in whatever way you are familiar.

Action Statement:

"I request to bless and empower my vitamins (or whatever), now please."

Reflection Questions

1. Describe how you were feeling before and after the activities.
2. What were the most vivid details of your imagery during the activities?
3. Describe your helpers, the tools, and their assistance.
4. What surprised you the most about your experiences?
5. What was your favorite activity in Section 4?
6. What was your least favorite activity in Section 4?
7. Can you integrate your new skills into your more familiar practices?
8. Were there any details that seemed highlighted to you that you might want to think about?
9. Do you feel inspired to do any research in any other related area? If so, what is it?
10. What methods have you used to heal yourself?
11. Did you notice any particular healing substances being shown to you repeatedly? If so, what were they?
12. Could you identify any of the gems that were placed within your body? If so, what were they?

"March on, and fear not the thorns, or the sharp stones on life's path."

Kahlil Gibran

Focus Group Feedback

Sharon

Diagnostic Healing Session

I am guided back to the Healing Room. I lie on the table and get ready for the scanning. My healing team warmly welcomes me, but is very serious and mindful that they have work to do, so we get started. From the very start, there is a low buzzing. There is a lot of movement or concentration in my head and solar plexus. There is actually a great amount of pressure in both of those areas, like a pushing down and pulling up. My head is in constant motion, twitching and moving back and forth. About half way through the scanning, I am asked to turn my hands palms up. They put, what felt like a heavy vibrational blanket, across my body. It has a low voltage buzzing. As the scanning session comes to completion, the buzzing gets lower and slower until is stops all together. The blanket is lifted off and I am told the session is complete.

I am helped to sit up. They then come and show me my list, which was very long. I couldn't read it even if I had wanted to. I *gladly* sign the list of distortions and throw them into the fire. Yeah for me! I am then given my Sacred Self Elixir that tasted more like mint chocolate and felt warm and "burny" as it went down, like cough medicine does. I was then given the All Element Mud drink, which I actually enjoyed very much. After I was finished, I left the spa and went to bed. Ever since I completed this session, I try to initiate the healing session every night before I go to bed. I like knowing I'm being "worked" on, even while I'm sleeping.

All Element Mud Bath

I really liked this activity very much. I enjoyed the warm feeling of the mud, both on the out and inside, the sensation of a full cleansing. It was like a leaching out of the unwanted and the absorption of what is needed. I felt a kind of suspended, supported feeling the mud gives by almost "holding" me up. I liked the feeling of oneness with the earth. It was very organic and "grounding". No pun intended. The Emerald Healing Wrap was a great finish to an already wonderful session.

Mineral Bath

Okay this activity "rocks". This one is so up my alley between the crystals, the lights and the tonal music…Yeehaw. Oh, I will be doing this one again!

Laura

Diagnostic Healing Session

The diagnostic room was beautiful, light and the table slightly contoured, made of clear quartz and warmed to skin temperature for comfort. Refracted light passed over the place where you would be lying down. Before doing so, I put my hand on the file and immediately a dialog began, explaining that I came to this incarnation with a perfect body, I did not come here to be ill. The physical challenges I have manifested were designed by me to help with the adjustments that were needed to successfully complete this lifetime. On that happy note, I lay down on the table.

I was physically lying down as I did this, and for the next forty-five minutes went in and out of being aware of my body and not. There was intense energy around the heart center as well as the belly energy center, and a dialog about certain conditions being "adjusted" within the physical body. I felt really detached from my physical body as this was done, but wasn't "out of body" in the classic sense. Very relaxed, however, like "have at it!" I took the list and had absolutely no interest in reading it; it was a feeling of "old news", and just signed off and gladly pitched it unceremoniously into the fire. That act left me with a feeling of relief, like, "Thank God!"

All Element Mud Bath and Mineral Bath

I thanked everyone at its conclusion--but went directly to the mud bath. It was a real target destination for me--that and the mineral water. Before hand, I did the Sacred Self Elixir (which reminded me of chocolate milk) and the tall drink, which I can only say felt, looked and tasted like thin chocolate pudding (All Element Mud Elixir). Of course, this was fine and dandy, because chocolate is one of my personal favorites. It felt filling and smooth. The idea that it was some kind of "mud" wasn't very appealing, but as chocolate pudding, it was great. It just sort of settled into my solar plexus area and I was aware of a comfortable stillness. It felt like the body drinking it in to each molecule--just sucking it up--reminded me of a plant when you water it and the soil makes little sounds as the water is absorbed.

Finally, into the mud bath, and wow, that was a comfortable, thick warmth. I didn't stay long, though, I sort of rubbed my skin under the surface of the mud, as though I were making sure it got into my pores and such. Then I got out and under a shower of warm water to rinse off and then into the mineral water--which was apparently my favorite--you couldn't get me out of there! I felt the bubbly warmth, just floated in there--not the "thick water" I felt in the lotus pool, more like warm club soda.

While the mud bath area was in a dimly lit area with candlelight, the mineral bath was bright and flower-surrounded. There were big pots of flowers that smelled wonderfully--freesia comes to mind now, but at the time I didn't really look closely to see what they were.

By now I was getting hungry, so I finally brought the meditation to a close with thanks and hugs for my healing team. I do remember saying I loved coming here.

Lourdes

Diagnostic Healing Session

I did not want to do this exercise. I felt it was too long (my ego was fighting this one tooth and nail). In order to do this exercise, I divided it into a couple of nights. When it came time to see the filc, I only saw a couple of the distortions for the first round. I know it will take a while for me to get this one done, but it will get accomplished. I felt very tired on the second night after the refuting of all the distortions. I used the healing session for two nights and requested Reiki. This felt right for me.

All Element Mud Bath

I did this exercise while I covered myself in mud physically. Although I couldn't do a mud bath, the covering of my body in mud was helpful. Before starting the meditation, I covered myself in the clay. It felt better than I expected. I thought it would be very uncomfortable, but it wasn't (very messy though). As I did the meditation, the mud did feel sluggish in my system. It took longer than I planned to let everything out. I did want to nap afterwards. I also felt a relief in the back pain I had been experiencing.

Mineral Bath

For this treatment, I went down on the ground and put crystals on myself. I gave myself a Reiki healing attunement. I felt very at peace and the crystals tingled when I first put them on. The sensations felt wonderful on my back.

Section 5
Synchronization in Angelscape

Activities Introduction

In this section, you will visualize that each piece of the self is cleansed, protected, healed, and brought into synchronization with the Whole Self. The Little Ones will be reintroduced back into the system of the self, having been fully healed and restored to happy, well-adjusted children. In the synchronization process, all of the things that no longer serve the Whole Self will be brought through a gradual and graceful release process that allows for the positive qualities of the Sacred Self to take root and grow within the system.

All of the various layers, levels, and aspects of the Whole Self will be imagined in this process, whether they are known and understood, or not. Every part will be brought into alignment, such as being brought onto the same page as the rest of the system. Some parts, which seem more like past lives or out of context, will be moved into the Light, as appropriate. The synchronization process brings the system into greater and growing alignment with the Sacred Self, such that the divine qualities of the Sacred Self can eventually replace the qualities that no longer serve the self, or which prevent you from living a sacred life that is a blessing to the world.

The first Scenic Route activity further explores the concept of the Sacred Self and how we can develop this idea to make it more concrete. We will dig a little deeper into what s/he looks like, acts like, and what blessings the Sacred Self has to offer the world. In order to begin replacing what is not authentically us with what is authentically us, we need to be able to define and construct a model of what the ideal version looks like. In short, we need to be able to recognize our Sacred Selves in order to invite them in.

The second Scenic Route activity provides a platform for us to observe and deal with the issues we have about ourselves that we need to transform in order to become our Sacred Selves. God made us the way we are. Even in our imperfection, there is probably a plan. The "warts" we are given have something to tell us about what we need to learn to love and accept before we can transform our hearts into vessels of unconditional love. The warts are like a map of places we need to visit, tour, and then choose not to live. We all have them. They must be there for a reason. This activity explores the perceptions of our flaws, what they teach us, and how to gracefully break the patterns that bind us to the narrow limits of what we consider ugly within us. Each ugly duckling is also a beautiful swan.

The nature of this work addresses aspects of yourself that are hidden and out of view. Sometimes those aspects are reluctant or resistant to be seen, cleaned up, or to become a part of a larger unified whole. It is a fascinating process to observe because this is precisely how unconscious motivations, patterns, and prompts to dysfunctional behavior express in our lives. When we are not on the same page *within*, it is difficult to get a coherent plan of action that serves our best interest. It is like having too many cooks in the kitchen, each putting into the pot what they think should be there without telling anyone else. *You*, your primary waking consciousness, should be Head Cook and should be aware of and have full authority over what influences your personal soup. Ask and pray for help if you feel resistance to the work.

Direct Route Activity #5
Whole Self Synchronization

Environment Setting: Chamber of Light

Complementary Scenic Route Activities
SR 5 A: Sacred Self Portrait
SR 5 B: Warts and All

Purpose: Whole Self Synchronization is the process used to bring all of the pieces, layers, levels, and aspects of the self into alignment, harmony, and balance as a unified single system under the primary waking consciousness as the appropriate free will agent in alignment with Divine Will.

Usage Suggestions: This activity is used as a leap into wholeness and balanced integration of the many aspects of the self. All parts, regardless of your awareness, are included in this activity, so the facilitation of additional Whole Self Synchronization is not necessary. However, you may wish to facilitate it as a ceremonial way to acknowledge and honor newly discovered parts of yourself as you grow and blossom.

Activity Props: You may use Chamber of Light props for this activity, pictures of flowers, yourself, or interesting mandalas. If you have one of those funky drawing gizmo's from the 70's, the Spirograph, you might find that a nice meditative preparation for this work. You might be able to find a puzzle of a flower that would be interesting to do as an active meditation during this activity if you cannot visualize the process itself.

Summary: The Whole Self Synchronization is similar to the synchronization process that was facilitated with the Divine Advocates during the guide assignment activity. Synchronization is a Divine Alignment process, which takes all pieces of a system and places them in balance with and through God as the centering unifying force. Again, this can be visualized as creating a "flower" with each piece representing a petal, distinct but connected, with God as the center.

Your Divine Advocates will call in all of the parts of your Whole Self. They will be arranged in concentric circles around the Eternal Flame of God's Grace and Love. If there are any aspects that look like they are from past-lives, or are obviously not from your immediate life reference point, they will be placed closest to the Eternal Flame so that they can be moved into the Light, where they belong. All other authentic aspects of the Whole Self, including the Little Ones, who have all completed their Butterfly Sleep at this time, will be arranged by the Divine Advocates in their most appropriate places. The synchronization process will begin, similar to the experience of synchronizing with All Assistance. When it is completed, you will imagine that all participants have a chance to hug and greet you, exchange forgiveness (if necessary), and then will "walk into you" to symbolize your Whole Self being unified under the umbrella of your main consciousness. Your main consciousness is your aware waking consciousness that has volunteered to be in alignment with Divine Will.

Helpers: Any or all of your Divine Advocates may be present at this activity.

New Concepts: Whole Self Wrap.

Intentions Supporting Activity

- Intentions added from anywhere else in the book that are relevant to this work.
- All Assistance, as appropriate, for any matter that needs attention.
- Full cleansing, clearing, purification, protection, healing, coherence, and rectification of Whole Self in perfection.
- Synchronization, integration, and harmonization of all relevant and appropriate layers, levels, and aspects of the Whole Self in perfection.
- Continuing care and healing to any aspect not ready for synchronization, with perfected replacement infill in system, until such time that aspect is fully healed and able to synchronize with Whole Self.
- Any aspects of Whole Self under continuing care to be sequestered, such that the capacity to exact inappropriate influence on any other part of the self is removed or mitigated.
- Automatic perfected upgrading and synchronization of newly healed aspects to be included in the Whole Self when they are ready, throughout life.

- Bringing of free will authority of Whole Self under the main holistic aware consciousness/personality that has volunteered to be in alignment with God/Divine Will.
- Any use of free will, other than through the main holistic aware consciousness that is in alignment with Divine Will to be immediately vacated, nullified, and misuse of authority rectified.
- Divine Alignment of Whole Self with God, and with All Assistance through God.
- Whole Self fully functional, grounded, and filled with God's Grace and Love.
- All parts of larger Soul Self, outside of a reference point with current life, to go immediately "to the Light", and back to God (aka: past-life clean up).
- All inappropriate bleed through influence from "past-life" experiences to be removed and rectified.
- All relevant and helpful wisdom from the soul level, or past-lives, to be integrated with grace, as appropriate within Divine Will.
- Self-forgiveness and requests for God's forgiveness, as needed.
- Support to unconditionally love the Whole Self.
- Support for development of Left to Right Brain Hemisphere synchronization, or Whole Brain thinking, as appropriate.
- System enhancement and strengthening to have perfected resiliency.
- *Whole Self Wrap*: a tool used to bring continuing and sustained integrity to aspects of Whole Self, such that all aspects can be gracefully integrated as a Whole Self consciousness capable of anchoring the Sacred Self when ready.
- Listed intentions reaffirmed as part of the Cooperative Contract already signed over.
- Engagement of this activity, if a Cooperative Contract has not yet been signed, an affirmation of acceptance of these intentions, corrected in perfection, and brought within Divine Will.

Action Statement:
"I request to initiate Whole Self Synchronization, now please."

Step-by-Step Activity Instructions:

1. Enter *Angelscape* at the Lotus Pool. Complete the spouting Water Breath Cleanse, sip your Lotus Nectar Elixir, and put on your Work Wrap to prepare for your journey. When you feel ready, you may continue.
2. A helper escorts you to the Chamber of Light. Light a candle for your Whole Self Synchronization. Request a Sacred Self Elixir energy drink from one of your helpers. Drink your elixir and allow yourself to feel the shifting energies preparing you for the work ahead. A large gong is sounded, summoning all relevant parts, layers, levels, and aspects of your Whole Self for synchronization.
3. Imagine the Chamber of Light as it begins to fill with symbolic parts of your Whole Self. The Little Ones from the Garden of the Little Ones are skipping in, happy and bright. You may see parts of the Whole Self coming into the chamber wearing clothing from other time periods, other genders, or other ethnicities. Allow the experience to be what it is.
4. The Divine Advocates arrange all of the Whole Self participants in different layered rings around the Eternal Flame of God's Grace and Love, making many circles radiating out from the center. Each part is placed according to its appropriate alignment within the Whole Self. The participants that look like they are from other time periods are placed closest to the Eternal Flame.
5. Imagine that the Divine Advocates and other helpers have finished arranging the rings around the Eternal Flame. They then nod to your main Divine Advocate. Your main Divine Advocate stands next to the Eternal Flame and says, *"We ask God for the Eternal Flame to cleanse, clear, and purify all parts of the Whole Self, now please."* Holy Fire from the Eternal Flame begins to whip around all of the rings of participants. You can hear the children giggle, as if the wind and fire tickles. You can hear sizzling and popping, as if other things are being consumed in the Eternal Flames.

6. Your main Divine Advocate waits for the flames to run to completion and then says, *"We ask God to place all parts of the Whole Self under Divine Care and Protection, now please."* Balls of fire from the Eternal Flame spread out over the crowd and engulf all participants within their own Guardian Angel Shield. The Divine Advocates spread out within the rings of the crowd and tap each shield three times to fully activate them. The Little Ones are so excited to be inside a big bubble of their own. They feel safe and cozy.
7. Your main Divine Advocate waits for all of the Guardian Angel Shields to be activated and then says, *"We ask God to call Home, all parts within the Soul Self that are outside of this current life reference, now please."* The ring of participants closest to the Eternal Flame, who are dressed from other time periods, are escorted by the Divine Advocates into the Eternal Flame and into the Light. They vanish from view. There is a sense of deep joy and relief that they have found their way Home.
8. Your Divine Advocates instruct you that it is appropriate for all participants to ask God for forgiveness for anything that they have done that has been out of alignment with Divine Will. You are told that you should forgive all parts of *yourself* for being out of alignment with Divine Will and for any instance of falling short of your own Sacred Self qualities, self-sabotage, and self-destructive behavior. Allow this to be what it is and to take however long it requires.
9. When you have completed the forgiveness process, the main Divine Advocate smiles and says, *"We ask God to initiate the Whole Self Synchronization process, now please."* You feel the swirl of energies pick up and move in a spiral around all of the remaining rings and individuals.
10. When the energies of the Whole Self Synchronization have completed, the Divine Advocates put a Whole Self Wrap around each participant of the synchronization. It will add strength to all layers, levels, and aspects of the Whole Self, such that it has coherency, cohesion, balance, and full integrity. The Whole Self Wraps absorb into the bodies of each participant.
11. Your main Divine Advocate lines everyone up in a single file line, facing you. When you are ready, each one is presented

to you. You tell each one that you love them, thank them, forgive them, embrace them, and hold them as sacred through God. Imagine hugging and embracing each one. Allow the precious pieces of yourself to melt back inside of you, perfectly healed, protected, and nurtured, and placed where they belong.

12. When all of the different parts of your Whole Self have been reintegrated, your Divine Advocates say a blessing for your Wholeness.
13. When you are finished, you may continue with the Scenic Route activities, or your main Divine Advocate escorts you to the TLC Bath where you will coat yourself in the soothing energies, sip your Graceful Integration Elixir, and then wrap yourself in the Resiliency Comfort Wrap. Do not drive, operate heavy machinery, or do any activities that are dangerous, or that require you to be fully attentive, until you feel fully shifted back to a normal waking state. Take some time to journal or take notes before your memory of the experience fades.

Continuing Thoughts

Whole Self Synchronization asks to unify a house within that may have been divided. The main part of any journey in expressing your Sacred Self is to get all of the pieces that make up your Whole Self into a coherent system with the free will authority placed squarely in the hands of the *conscious you*, instead of the unconscious you. Spiritually and energetically speaking, this work has been completed. However, you will be brought through a process of self-awareness in which you will be shown how hidden influence has affected your life so that you develop the skills and tools to competently deal with and triumph over inappropriate influence. There is no use fixing something that does not also come with higher functioning, or else, there is nothing to prevent the reversal of gains made. So, buckle up and put on your hip boots. You are going to be brought to higher functioning by practicing your skills and seeing how they work.

Develop an interest and mindfulness about what "makes you tick" and what motivates your behavior. Reflect upon your actions, dig deeper to find why you feel the way you do, act the way you do, or think the way you do. When you find that how you feel, think, act, or believe are at odds, it is your responsibility to find out if there are distortions, self-sabotage, interference, or unconscious patterns expressing themselves and asking to be healed. If your conscious waking self is to continue to be master of your house, you cannot fall asleep at the wheel and slip back into automatic pilot. If you abdicate your awareness, you are at the mercy of unconscious and hidden influences, most of which suffer under distortions and are not particularly self-loving.

The work in this book will help you to become more aware of these hidden influences. You will become more aware of your "inner critic" and negative mental mind talk that seeks to keep you down and subjugated by distortion and falsehoods. It is your job to "Tag, Refuse, and Rescript" these internal conversations. Do not ignore them. Do not allow the negative mental mind talk to subjugate you to doubt, absurdity, or falsehood. The conscious you is the appropriate authority in your life; co-authority, since you have also volunteered to be in alignment with Divine Will. (It makes the bumper sticker that says, "God is my Co-pilot" particularly meaningful!) Do not abdicate your authority. The Sacred Self is an Aware and Awakened Self.

Every large undertaking requires you to take one piece at a time until it all fits.

Photograph 38710
by mrguefile.com
user: calgrin

Scenic Route #5 A
Sacred Self Portrait

Environment Setting: Your choice

Purpose: The purpose of this activity is to introduce you to the evolving vision of the ideal you, also known as the Sacred Self.

Usage Suggestions: This activity begins to introduce the idea of the Sacred Self to you through the medium of a portrait. The portrait may change and evolve many times before you feel that it is complete. You may visit with your master artist any time you feel prompted to make adjustments to your Sacred Self Portrait, or you can simply ask to see how it is evolving from time to time.

Activity Props: You can use art books from your favorite master artist or sculptor, your favorite masterpiece, a photo album of yourself, examples of favorite items or activities, or pictures of anything about which you are passionate that you consider "a part of who you are".

Summary: In this activity, you will imagine that one of the world's greatest master artists is commissioned to create your Sacred Self Portrait. The portrait will be a vision of your ideal self doing what you were put on this planet to accomplish. Your greatest compassion, beauty, grace, and inner purpose will be drawn in loving detail. It will be considered a work in progress until later. This is just the beginning of truly seeing the beauty of your Sacred Self.

Helpers: Your favorite master artist is a helper here, as well as any other Divine Advocate of your choosing. One of your Divine Advocates may show up in costume as the master painter.

New Concepts: Sacred Self Portrait.

Intentions Supporting Activity

- Intentions added from anywhere else in the book that are relevant to this work.
- All Assistance, as appropriate, for any matter that needs attention.
- Support to build a tangible working image of the Sacred Self.

- Increasing joy, peace, sense of well-being, sense of accomplishment, and perception of self-competency.
- Support to define and recognize Sacred Self qualities.
- Support to discover and define life's purpose and work.
- Support to embrace the Sacred Self.
- Support to discover hidden talents, dreams, skills, and abilities.
- Support to see the beauty within.
- Support to view the self as a work in progress.
- *Sacred Self Portrait*: used as a way to define and identify the Sacred Self, such that those qualities can be integrated into life with purpose, grace, and ease.
- Listed intentions reaffirmed as part of the Cooperative Contract already signed over.
- Engagement of this activity, if a Cooperative Contract has not yet been signed, an affirmation of acceptance of these intentions, corrected in perfection, and brought within Divine Will.

Action Statement:
"I request to initiate my Sacred Self Portrait, now please."

Note: *Skip to step 2 if you are coming immediately from the previous activity.*

Step-by-Step Activity Instructions:

1. Enter *Angelscape* at the Lotus Pool. Complete the spouting Water Breath Cleanse, sip your Lotus Nectar Elixir, and put on your Work Wrap to prepare for your journey. When you feel ready, you may continue.
2. A helper escorts you to the waterfall in front of the spa. Your Divine Advocate gives you a Sacred Self Elixir energy drink. It tastes especially good today. Imagine that another figure steps from behind the waterfall to greet you. It is your favorite master artist. S/he has just been with your teams, looking at your personal Sacred Self file, and is delighted to finally meet you.
3. The master artist has been commissioned by God to create a masterpiece. The masterpiece is your Sacred Self Portrait.

You get to select, perhaps from templates of your favorite figural paintings or sculptures, what setting you get to visit, what activity you wish to be engaging, and any details you wish to include.

4. Your Divine Advocate touches you and the master artist on the shoulder and asks you to close your eyes to envision a scene that most accurately describes the qualities and purpose of your Sacred Self. When you open your eyes, you and the artist are in the scene you envisioned, or you will receive a little bit of help to begin to define your Sacred Self. Start somewhere, even if you think you may need to update it later.
5. Imagine standing in the intended art scene and look around. Ask to feel your Sacred Self as a preview of your growth and evolution. Imagine seeing through your Sacred Eyes, feeling through your Sacred Heart, touching through your Sacred Body, and thinking through your Sacred Mind. Begin to describe your Sacred Self, such as the qualities that you embody, the talents you possess, the passion of your life's work just waiting to be uncovered, and so on. Take in all the sensations and allow the master artist to see beyond the rock to the polished and gleaming jewel within you.
6. The master artist will need time to complete this work of art. You may look at the progression that the artist is making any time you wish. The art piece will be presented to you later. You may model for your artist as long as you wish as a way to get in touch with your Sacred Self.
7. When you are finished, you may continue with the next Scenic Route activity, or your main Divine Advocate escorts you to the TLC Bath where you will coat yourself in the soothing energies, sip your Graceful Integration Elixir, and then wrap yourself in the Resiliency Comfort Wrap. Do not drive, operate heavy machinery, or do any activities that are dangerous, or that require you to be fully attentive, until you feel fully shifted back to a normal waking state. Take some time to journal or take notes before your memory of the experience fades.

Continuing Thoughts

If you could be the very best person you could be, what qualities would you exhibit? Make a list of the positive qualities that you consider sacred. What qualities do you already exhibit that you consider beautiful or sacred? These sacred qualities are the ones that will replace the old ones that you have volunteered to refuse. What old qualities are the easiest to replace with the sacred qualities? What are the steps you have to take to make those shifts? Begin to describe having those traits in the present tense. Allow them to manifest as soon as possible.

Ideally, what kind of work would you be doing (volunteer or career) that you think would nurture your soul? How do your natural talents and abilities correspond to this kind of work? What are the first things you would need to do to begin walking in the direction of what would nurture your soul?

If you had trouble with this activity, I suggest that you look at art reference books and begin to tag the art pieces that move you the most. Imagine placing yourself in the scene and adding details that are relevant to you. Allow your Sacred Self portrait to adapt, grow, and even change as you uncover more about yourself and the beauty within you.

If you do not know what kind of work would nourish your soul, I recommend doing some research on careers. Imagine your dream job where you feel like you are contributing to the world, or where you are a blessing to the world. Imagine doing something that would make your heart sing and add to the happiness around you. This too, may be a work in progress.

"You cannot dream yourself into character: you must hammer and forge yourself into one."

Henry Thoreau

Photograph 221179
by morguefile.com
user: CarolinaJG

Scenic Route #5 B
Warts and All

Environment Setting: *Angelscape* Spa

Purpose: The purpose of the Warts and All activity is to learn to honor and love yourself, "warts and all" and to provide a method for you to counteract negative and critical self-judgment and assessment.

Usage Suggestions: You can use this as a strategy to address and counteract self-judgment any time you feel you need a refresher.

Activity Props: You can do this activity in front of a mirror if you would like. You might imagine using an eyeliner pencil to draw in your "warts" and then wipe them off when you have removed them. You can use old light bulbs wrapped in a towel to "break" the perception, such as in a Jewish wedding, instead of breaking a real glass (glass is sharp, please use caution). Hard candies are also good props to use as the follow up support candies.

Summary: In this activity, you will be prompted to address what you consider your biggest personal flaws, to see the patterns behind the flaws, to shatter and overcome them. You are brought to the spa where you are prepared and supported to uncover and view your personal flaws, or what you think are your personal flaws (distortions). These flaws will appear as warts on your face to correspond with the popular phrase that says, "We should love ourselves, warts and all." Your Divine Advocates stand by and beam unconditional love to you as you move through plucking off your warts, putting them into a golden bowl. The warts are transformed into glass knick-knacks that you toss into the Eternal Flames (the fireplace). They then become little hard candies that you can imagine eating when you need the support to move through doubt, self-criticism, bad habits, or negative self-talk.

Helpers: The helpers that show up here are generally the ones that are grandmotherly, nurturing, or who show up in the Garden of the Little Ones, but any of your Divine Advocates can assist you according to your own needs.

New Concepts: Show Me the Ugly Elixir, Warts, Golden Bowl, Flaw Breakers.

Intentions Supporting Activity

- Intentions added from anywhere else in the book that are relevant to this work.
- All Assistance, as appropriate, for any matter that needs attention.
- Support to embrace, learn from, and triumph over personal flaws and failures.
- Support to view self as a "work in progress".
- Support for self-forgiveness and self-acceptance.
- Support to see your own flaws and love yourself anyway, to foster unconditional self-love.
- Support to gracefully and positively resolve dichotomy, duality, and opposing qualities within the Whole Self.
- Support to "Tag, Refuse/Break, and Rescript" dysfunctional patterns, or what no longer serves the self, without shame, guilt, or blame.
- Support to release patterns of shame and guilt.
- Support to remove the power from "inner critic" and judgmental thoughts.
- Support to use effective strategies to refuse and rescript negative influence.
- Support to extract wisdom and higher functioning from previous flaws and failures.
- Support to break flaws, behaviors, and patterns which no longer serve the self.
- Support to allow yourself to be loved in an authentic way, and to hold high standards for how others are allowed to treat you.
- Support to see the self as able to handle challenges effectively and successfully.
- Support to use tools to accomplish your personal goals of self-improvement.
- Support to change your perceptions to those which are in alignment with your Sacred Self qualities.
- *Show Me the Ugly Elixir*: energy drink used as a transition activity to reveal and uncover what the Journeyer considers to

be personal flaws and inner "ugliness", shown as warts that grow on the face.

- *Warts*: the warts symbolize each individual judgment or perception of a flaw and inner ugliness, such as with the ugly Scripts used in the amphitheater in the Garden of the Little Ones.
- *Golden Bowl*: used as a chalice of transformation by the Divine Advocates.
- *Flaw Breakers*: used to symbolize the energetic support needed to overcome a flaw, habit, or perception that needs to be changed through effort and consistent attention.
- Listed intentions reaffirmed as part of the Cooperative Contract already signed over.
- Engagement of this activity, if a Cooperative Contract has not yet been signed, an affirmation of acceptance of these intentions, corrected in perfection, and brought within Divine Will.

Action Statement:
"I request to learn to love myself Warts and All, now please."

Note: Skip to step 2 if you are coming immediately from the previous activity.

Step-by-Step Activity Instructions:

1. Enter *Angelscape* at the Lotus Pool. Complete the spouting Water Breath Cleanse, sip your Lotus Nectar Elixir, and put on your Work Wrap to prepare for your journey. When you feel ready, you may continue.
2. Your Divine Advocate escorts you into the spa. You are lead through the main gallery of the cavern to a sitting area in front of the large fireplace. An attendant brings you the Show Me the Ugly Elixir drink. Imagine taking a sip and wrinkling your nose. This energy drink tastes strongly of bitter medicine. You gulp it down and sit down on the sofa in front of the fireplace.
3. Your sweetest and most nurturing Divine Advocate sits next to you, pats your hand, and then hands you a mirror. You are told that the energy drink you took reveals all of the ways

that you find yourself flawed. These are the characteristics that you judge and that are used to keep you in a state of distorted self-worth, shame, and guilt. Your Divine Advocate explains that the flaws themselves are not the problem; in fact, they are powerful teachers of transformation. The condemnation and continuing cycle of self-abuse for feeling flawed and imperfect is the problem.

4. Imagine you can feel the structure of your face changing, and you do not want to look, but the kind and gentle eyes of your helper gives you the courage to continue. Your helper is charged with beaming unconditional love to you, even as your biggest flaws are revealed. You will witness that the flaws have no power to crush authentic and unconditional love. Imagine picking up the mirror and looking at your face. How many warts do you have on your face? How distorted is your image of yourself? You quickly give the mirror back to the helper, who is still smiling warmly and lovingly at you.
5. Next, imagine that your helper pulls out a golden bowl and sits it on a small table in front of the sofa. Your helper leans over, pulls off one of your warts, and tosses it into the golden bowl. It does not hurt, but you can hear a "pop" sound when it comes off. You are instructed to pop off the rest of the warts and to put them into the golden bowl. You are more than happy to do this. Imagine hearing the pop, pop, pop.
6. When the warts are all off your face, you are given the instructions to stand in front of the fireplace with the golden bowl of warts easy to reach. You are instructed to pick up a wart, which symbolically represents a flaw that you perceive in yourself. Imagine that your helper taps your hand, like a magic trick, and that you feel the wart grow and change into a small glass sculpture that represents the flaw. It is an ugly, mangled little knick-knack.
7. You are instructed to say, *"I see you and love you anyway. You had something to teach me and I am grateful. I forgive and release you."* Close your eyes and imagine beaming unconditional love toward the knick-knack. When you open your eyes, the mangled little knick knack does not look as ugly to you as it did before you made the statements. Imagine that it has begun to take on a quirky charm that you can appreciate.

8. Your helper instructs you to throw the knick-knack into the fireplace of the Eternal Flame of Gods Grace and Love. You hesitate for a moment, but are willing to release it into the Hands of God. Imagine throwing this flaw into the fireplace with the very satisfying sound of breaking glass. The pattern of this flaw is shattered.
9. Your helper reaches into the fire and retrieves a bag of hard candies created from the transformed substance of the flaw. They are called *Flaw Breakers.* You place one of the Flaw Breakers into your mouth and feel the warm tingly sensation it brings to your body. You follow up the Flaw Breaker with a wink and smile into the mirror and a gentle well-earned self-hug. The Flaw Breakers that remain are pocketed for continuing support. Use them as needed.
10. Your helper instructs you to repeat this exercise for each wart that is in the bowl. You should have a large bag of Flaw Breakers by the time you are finished. Just ask for them when you need them from now on.
11. When you are finished, your main Divine Advocate escorts you to the TLC Bath where you will coat yourself in the soothing energies, sip your Graceful Integration Elixir, and then wrap yourself in the Resiliency Comfort Wrap. Do not drive, operate heavy machinery, or do any activities that are dangerous, or that require you to be fully attentive, until you feel fully shifted back to a normal waking state. Take some time to journal or take notes before your memory of the experience fades.

Continuing Thoughts

The Flaw Breakers are symbolic of perfected medicine and support that you can use to gracefully transition away from the previous patterns. When you feel the temptation to judge yourself, or engage in the patterns of the shattered flaw/habit, imagine popping a Flaw Breaker into your mouth. This method can be used to break a bad habit and to help you to engage in improving acceptance of yourself.

You can substitute the Flaw Breakers candies with any other substance, if you want. You can ask God to empower actual hard candies, sugar free is fine, so that the supportive energies to help you release those patterns are at your fingertips all the time. If you feel you would like to hear the sound of shattering glass as symbolic of the patterns breaking, you may ask to see a recording of the original shattering you performed in front of the fireplace. Do not imagine 're-shattering' it again, because that indicates that you have reformed the pattern in order to break it again, which is counter-productive. You may just say, *"I reaffirm this pattern is shattered"* in order to "hear" the sound again.

When you notice your "inner critic" coming to take a swing at you, you may use the same phrase as you did with the glass knick-knack. *"I see you and love you anyway. You had something to teach me and I am grateful. I forgive and release you."*

You decide who you are every time you wake up to a new day and every time you make a choice. There may be days or choices that you make that do not reflect your best qualities. There will be days that do. Your job is to do the very best you can do, and when you can do better, do better. It is important to practice the art of self-love and appreciation with as little judgment as possible. It is important to shift judgmental thinking in general, not just about yourself, but pay attention when you are thinking judgmental thoughts about *others* as well. Some firmly believe that what we judge in others is what we fear is true about ourselves. We reveal a lot about ourselves within our private judgmental thoughts.

We can apply the "Tag, Refuse, Rescript" model on judgmental thoughts. If you catch yourself in a negative, judgmental, self-righteous, or inappropriate thought about yourself or someone else, immediately go into the Tag-Refuse-Rescript model. One of the easiest ways to short circuit the judgment train of thought is by actively "loving" whatever is in front of you with awareness before the unconscious negativity even begins to play. You can light candles everywhere you go, or some other simple form of acknowledging that you prefer to see them "through God".

Remember, this awareness goes on *within your own head*, not as a conversation with others (unless you like padded cells).

When you notice the judgmental thought:

- Tag it. "Dang, I was just thinking the cashier was ugly."
- Refuse it. "This is unkind and I refuse it. I am sorry."
- Rescript it. "The cashier is a beautiful child of God and I ask to light a candle for her (or whatever works here)."

Suggestions for proactive method of "loving" first:

- Light a candle by imagining a candle superimposed on the person, or by thinking, *"I request to light a candle for this person…(or myself)… (or this situation)… (whatever)."*

- Ask God to bless the person, event, situation, and so on.
- Imagine a beautiful golden or pink bubble of loving energies around the person, event, situation, and so on.
- Say in your mind (or else you will be carted away), to people with whom you interact, *"I love you."*
- When you encounter someone who is behaving badly, say in your head, *"I see you and love you anyway. You have something to teach me and I am grateful. I forgive and release you."*
- Smile and look people in the eye when you interact with them. Compliment them on something authentically wonderful that you can acknowledge.

Be gracious, grateful, and kind. You choose who you are with each interaction you share with another person. Have no regrets. Choose well. If you have regrets, or make a mistake, be the kind of person who can apologize and then learn from whatever mistakes you have made. Be willing to forgive those who have been unkind to you. Being human is complicated. Sometimes we mess up, sometimes they do. We are them. Just clean it up. Tomorrow is another day.

Summary and Wrap Up

Complementary Activities

- Engage any self-esteem boosting activity.
- Create positive self-affirmations.
- Gaze into the mirror and smile at yourself, tell yourself that you love you.
- Be as kind to yourself as you are to others.
- If you smoke, quit smoking, or make forward progress to prepare for it.
- If you have any bad habits, take steps to overcome them.
- Buy yourself a new outfit that shows your inner confidence.
- Pamper yourself, or get a make over.

Project Ideas

Create a collage of you as your Sacred Self. Use photographs, drawings, raw materials of any kind to create a collage or work of art that symbolizes your Sacred Self and what kinds of activities and passions that nurture your soul. Any time you find a new aspect of your Sacred Self, add it to the collage in progress.

Spend a day trying to tag all of the judgmental thoughts that you spontaneously have. You may be surprised how many of them you have when you place your awareness on it. This is a good homework assignment to help you to become aware of the unconscious ways we constantly cut ourselves or other people down. Tag, Refuse, and Rescript as many as possible.

Spend a day proactively loving all those with whom you interact, as described in the Direct Route Continuing Thoughts section. How did you feel about yourself, other people, and the world? How did it change your perceptions?

Reflection Questions

1. Describe how you were feeling before and after the activities.
2. What were the most vivid details of your imagery during the activities?
3. Describe your helpers, the tools, and their assistance.
4. What surprised you the most about your experiences?
5. What was your favorite activity in Section 5?
6. What was your least favorite activity in Section 5?
7. Can you integrate your new skills into your more familiar practices?
8. Were there any details that seemed highlighted to you that you might want to think about?
9. Do you feel inspired to do any research in any other related area? If so, what is it?
10. How do you feel about the Whole Self Synchronization?
11. What did your art piece in progress look like?
12. What were the Sacred Self qualities that you discovered in this activity?
13. What were the flaws that you dealt with in this activity?
14. How often do you find yourself entertaining negative or judgmental thoughts?
15. Now that you are aware of this undercurrent of inner criticism, are you surprised at how much of it there is?
16. How do you encourage yourself to be the best person you can be?

Focus Group Feedback

Sharon

Whole Self Synchronization

Let me say up front I was very apprehensive and uneasy about doing this activity. I kept putting it off and making excuses. I really couldn't tell you why. I still don't know. However, I did do it and am glad that I did. Much of it was very weird and I'm not sure how to interpret or understand some of the "parts" that showed up. Perhaps they were symbolic and I'm not supposed to take them literally.

I enter the Chamber of Light. I am given a Sacred Self Elixir by an attendant waiting at the door. My beautiful angel meets me and takes my hand. He leads me down to the Eternal Flame where I light a candle for myself and the process that lies ahead. I am a bit uneasy and I sit down and gaze at the Eternal Flame for a moment to center myself and connect with the brilliance of the flame. I love to watch the beautiful gold and white flames dancing and glowing. Its radiance is all consuming. I notice that I have on a beautiful Grecian or Roman style long, flowing, white dress with gold braided trim that criss-crosses my chest. It is quite lovely and etheric. My hair is pulled up with gold ribbon weaving in and out.

My angel leans from behind me and says, "You have to move forward." Indeed I do. Archangel Michael sounds the gong and the Chamber of Light starts to fill with symbolic parts of my Whole Self. Frolicking down the aisle are my Little Ones, as happy and carefree as ever. Some run over to greet me with a kiss and hug. There are many people, and to my amazement, there are also animals; a lion, wolf, deer, rabbit, cougar, fox, a horse, dog and butterflies. Some of the people were dressed in rags, were very poor looking, or have leprosy. Some are very old and crippled over in pain. There were some dressed quite royally. There was a marvelous Egyptian lady dressed in silver lamé, as well as a doctor, teacher, a person from India, a friar and a nun. The person that stood out the most was an oriental woman dressed in a magnificent floral sarong of red and gold accented in black. She was very prominent but not "up front" during the whole process.

My team arranges all the Whole Self participants in the different layers. Around the front of the circle was a woman from the 1800's, a peasant from the 1600's, another very timid woman whom seemed that she had been extremely abused, and a beautiful woman from the 1700's dressed in the finest clothes from Paris. She was wearing a grand hat with feathers and a lovely lace dress and parasol. She is very refined and knows it. Archangel Michael activates the Eternal Flame, it encircles the group with purple and gold streaks of fire swirling, and twisting faster and faster until it dissipates.

The Guardian Angel Shield is then activated. Archangel Michael calls home all the parts outside of the current life reference. The outside-of-time people are led home by my team with the refined lady in the feather hat in the front, of course. Archangel Michael then initiates the Whole Self Synchronization process. The fire swirls around the circles like a tornado. The wind actually goes "through" us, somewhat like a cleansing or spring-cleaning. I ask God for forgiveness for all past and present transgressions against others as well as myself. The wind continues for some time, but it is glorious and freeing being in the middle of such intense wind/energy. After the wind has subsided, we are put into our wraps, which is very nice and quite beautiful. Archangel Michael then lines up all the participants. I greet each with one with love, forgiveness, appreciation and acceptance. The last "person" in line was a beautiful, luminescent angel. She floated up, kissed me, and then dissolved within me.

Sacred Self Portrait

My Sacred Self Portrait is of a beautiful, slender and strong Native American woman. She is standing in the mist of a magnificent forest that edges a large lake surrounded by soaring mountains. She is holding up in her hands an offering of incense that is burning in a large seashell. In fact, I am told that the name of the portrait is, "The Offering". She is resolute in her posture, and is looking reverently, loving, and longingly up to the heavens. There in the distant sky are a hawk and eagle circling. Hiding within the forest foliage are deer, rabbits, and other animals. The colors are glorious. They are so rich and deep that they are hard to describe.

Warts and All

Let me start out by saying that I tried to do this activity twice, and both times I ended up having a full allergy attack with sneezing, swollen eyes, runny nose and itching. I gave up the first time, but pushed through the symptoms the second time armed with a box of tissues and some Irish Catholic stubbornness. Ironically, at the end of the activity, I was fine other then a couple red eyes. I was drained and tired. I'm going to take a shower and go to bed. This was one of the tougher of the activities. I'm glad my Divine Advocates were around me.

I was met by my Divine Advocate and led over to the sofa. I requested at that time that all my helpers be present. I felt I needed the entire team's support for this one, they all assembled in the area around me, and we began. Blessed Mother sat on my right and another nurturing helper was on my left. Needless to say, it got pretty ugly and took quite a bit of time to pull off the warts and to throw them in the fire. At times during the activity, I felt shaky and a bit "wobbly", but my team supported me the whole way. After collecting all my candy, which tasted like hot cinnamon, I sat on the sofa a while with my team and watched the fire. It was quite an experience and I'm grateful and happy I pushed through it, but it was terribly exhausting.

Laura

Whole Self Synchronization

Entering the chamber, I was instantly carried back to the peaceful sense of calm I got the last time I was here. My inner guidance had said, "just go with it", when I was wondering how this would unfold, so I did just that. I lit the candle, and as I was watching the flame and repeating my intention, in came my guardian angels with the energy drink. The taste was the flavor of a Yerba Mate tea that I've been drinking a lot of lately. I felt it seep through my being with a nice warmth.

Then the gong sounded as Archangels' Raphael and Michael materialized to "ride herd" on the crew that began to assemble. I was immediately drawn to, not only the children who were happily approaching, but another little one who was still a bit shy--but as we saw each other eyeball to eyeball, she smiled and ran up for a hug. I felt especially close to this one!

The others who really caught my attention were dressed as anything from a Priest to a U.S. Cavalry officer, a nun, a frontier-looking woman, an elaborately dressed lady I wanted to identify as a "Courtesan" (whatever that is--I'll have to look it up!) and several others I felt were almost "incomplete" forms and just partially visible. They seemed perhaps like thought forms, instead of fully defined beings. Anyhow, as they gathered around the flame, spontaneously we all had in our hands a goblet of gold and someone heartily cried out, "To Life!" as we all raised our goblets and toasted the situation/each other/the opportunity to work on this. The mood was joyous.

As the flame worked its way through the middle part of the exercise, the individuals became more like orbs of light that I reabsorbed. Some definitely aligned with certain energy centers and some just merged with my own aura, which was quite bright around me. I mentally was speaking to the ones who became a part of me, but it was a "merging" rather than a sense that a physical being was entering my physical being. Each one that entered made me feel really good--in an indescribable way. Complete, maybe? There was a sense as it finished of the phrase, “And so it is…” I turned and left the chamber feeling really amazing.

Lourdes

Whole Self Synchronization

I felt warmth as flames went around the circle. What was surprising were the parts that seemed to be from past lives. I found I had an old woman, a young man in medieval attire, a Spanish Conquistador, and even a blond little girl. The amount of inner children was large too. It seems that every time I go past the kiddie pool area, more kids show up. For this exercise, more teenagers showed up. I feel as if I opened up a Pandora's Box. I knew I needed a lot of healing, but never realized how much until I began these exercises. It felt good to welcome everyone in.

Sacred Self Portrait

This was possibly the easiest assignment yet. The end result of my portrait will be of my Higher Self, who I can envision and who usually accompanies me to *Angelscape*. For this activity, I imagined going into *Angelscape* with my Higher Self. I danced around the grass barefoot before reaching the waterfalls. I was very happy and didn’t even know why. When I got to the waterfall, the angel helper was Gabriel. She was there to help me communicate with the master painter about who I was and who I am to become. The Sacred Self Elixir was a strawberry cream flavored drink. It was a pink color and was appropriate since my portrait ended up having a soft pink glow. Before beginning, AA Gabriel put her hands on my shoulders and I told the artist that the end result would be a portrait of my Higher Self. She said that it would take time, but that it was okay.

The master painter sat down and asked what I wanted. My Sacred Self Portrait is a portrait of me looking out from a balcony looking out onto the ocean. It's really odd, but I have seen this portrait in dreams since I was a teenager. At the end of the session, Archangel Gabriel kissed the top of my head. Another Divine Advocate came, kissed the tips of her fingers, and then touched them to the middle of my forehead. She told me that the way I looked at myself would be softened. I was beginning to feel hopeful. My higher self is a softer, more “alive” version of myself. I can’t wait for the transformation!

“The world is a looking glass and gives back to every man the reflection of his own face.”

William Thackeray

Section 6
Turning up the Light

Activities Introduction

Section 6 is about opening ourselves up to the flow of incredible resources available through the spiritual level. The Direct Route activity, the Healing Heart and Hands Activation, is initiated as a way to imagine the "plumbing" through which spiritual and earthly healing energies can move into and through you. Once the channels are established, you may call upon healing energies for self-healing or as a way to assist moving healing energies where needed in larger systems. This visualization essentially plugs you more fully into the spiritual and physical levels in such a way that a conduit, or bridge, is imagined and created.

The Scenic Route activities build upon the opening up to resources and effectively utilizing them. The Expansion Attunements are generally regarded as "energy fitness" sessions. Each time you engage one of these sessions, you imagine that you are provided with the next layer or level of vibrations that can flow through your heart and hands. The more you attune, the stronger you can imagine your healing channels becoming. It is similar to building muscles, except the expansion attunements are much more fun. It can be viewed as a way to imagine cultivating strength, stamina, and core system integrity.

The process of receiving an attunement is similar to using a tuning fork to help you tune an instrument, but in most instances, it is also like adding a *new* string to the instrument (and then tuning it) so that you have more notes to work with. The more you add, theoretically, the better your system will be for moving energy.

The second Scenic Route activity, the Team Self-Treatment, provides a way for you to imagine being an active participant in healings initiated for you. In this activity, you allow your healing team to use your own hands as a tool to direct energy where it is needed in your body. You will be giving yourself a self-treatment, but you will be imagining that your healing team is placing their hands within yours and giving you directions on what to do next. This is both a skills building activity and a conceptual healing session. The more you do this kind of session with your Healing Team, the better you will get at responding to your own healing needs.

Section 6 activities are about empowerment. You are asked to begin seeing yourself as a useful link in the chain of blessings that extend to this level of being. When you agree to be in Divine Alignment, you can imagine that you are positioned to be a conduit of God's Grace and Love flowing to the world. There is a saying, "Your life is God's gift to you. What you do with it is your gift back to God." In activating your healing heart and hands, you can imagine feeling empowered that you have volunteered to be in service as a conduit for the Eternal Flame to glow brightly wherever you go. You can imagine being a blessing by simply allowing the embers of the Eternal Flame to radiate through you.

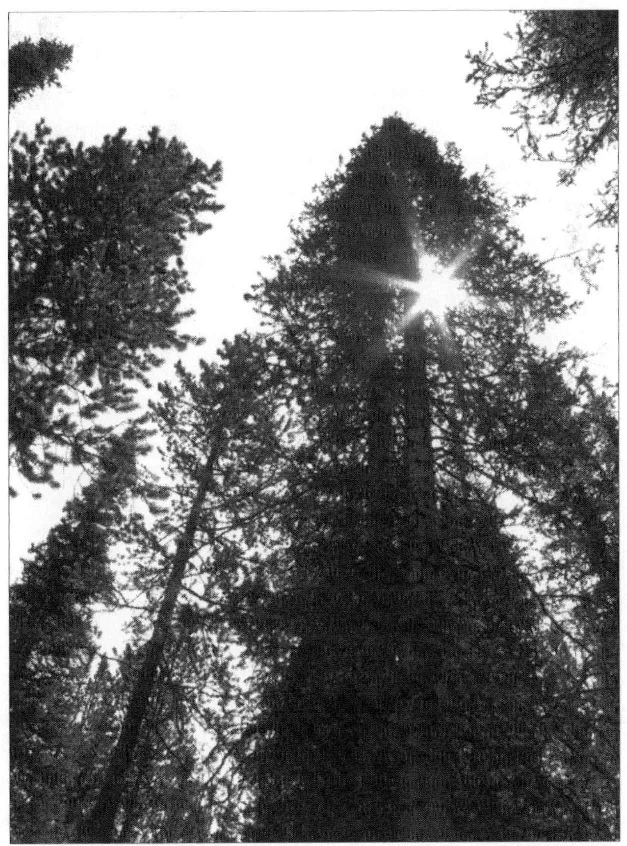

You use imagery of a giant tree reaching for the light in this section of the book.

Photograph 68408
by morguefile.com
user: skeletoyz

Direct Route Activity #6
Healing Heart and Hands Activation

Environment Setting: Chamber of Light

Complementary Scenic Route Activities
SR 6 A: Expansion Attunement
SR 6 B: Team Self-Treatment

Purpose: This activity is used as an opportunity to open channels of healing light, and to provide a system of moving, grounding, and directing healing light in a safe, comfortable, and balanced way.

Usage Suggestions: You may do this activity as often as you like, but once the embers are imbedded, they are permanent. The Expansion Attunement Scenic Route activity is designed to provide ongoing building, strengthening, and refreshing of healing energy channels. It is more appropriate for you to use that activity to keep your energy channels clear and strong.

Activity Props: You may use a picture of your favorite tree, or do this guided meditation while sitting under your favorite tree or on a stump where a tree used to be. It may be helpful to do this barefooted and outside with your feet on the ground.

Summary: In this activity, you will go to the Chamber of Light to open up to a flow of healing light. Your Divine Advocate will use his/her Sword of Light to clear the energetic pathways and then you will receive embers from the Eternal Flame of God's Grace and Love within your system. These embers are used to symbolize healing energy anchored to you and moving through your heart and hands, as needed. You will use the imagery of a tree to visualize the circuitry that moves heavenly energies to a physical level. You will imagine branches reaching for the sun (spiritual energies) and roots growing deep into the earth. Appropriate grounding is necessary for the efficient manifestation of spiritual energy and assistance at this level. The Breath of God is used to imagine activating, fanning, and enkindling of the sacred embers within your system.

Helpers: Your main Divine Advocate will likely be the one who uses his/her Sword of Light to clear your pathways and channels. Additional helpers may show up, as needed.

New Concepts: Eternal Flame Embers, Breath of God.

Intentions Supporting Activity

- Intentions added from anywhere else in the book that are relevant to this work.
- All Assistance, as appropriate, for any matter that needs attention.
- Establishing self (aka Whole Self) as bridge and conduit for divine healing energies, resources, and blessings to flow to the self and outward to others, as appropriate.
- Increasing sense of connection between the self and God, spiritual energies, and spiritual resources.
- Increasing sense of connection to the earth, natural earth energies, and natural resources.
- Establishing of deep rootedness to the earth and the physical level, such that higher spiritual energies can be manifested at the physical level.
- Establishing of self as an instrument of God's Grace and Love, such that the self is holding space for light to shine and flow into this level of being.
- Support to perceive oneself as an instrument of God's Grace and Love, and as a blessing to the world.
- Increasing ability to consciously direct healing light as prompted and called.
- Increasing capacity to maintain higher personal levels of light as a process of growth and spiritual evolution.
- Expansion of energy channels, or movement of energy, moderated by Divine Advocates to support personal healing, growth, and evolution in a comfortable and stable way.
- Increasing integrity and strength to the Whole Self as broader and higher bandwidths of healing light are activated in the system.
- Reparations and rectification to any part of the Whole Self which requires healing in order to establish appropriate channels of energy movement, anchoring, or flow.

- Establishment of the structure of channels of healing light to be considered a part of the Whole Self, and as such, subject to all protections, care, and upkeep as necessary.
- *Eternal Flame Ember*: symbolizes the seeding and enkindling of the Eternal Flame of God's Grace and Love within you, establishing you as a conduit for God's Grace and Love on earth within Divine Will.
- *Breath of God:* an action symbolizing the activation and empowerment of something by God directly, imagined as a wind that blows through the scene in some way.
- Listed intentions reaffirmed as part of the Cooperative Contract already signed over.
- Engagement of this activity, if a Cooperative Contract has not yet been signed, an affirmation of acceptance of these intentions, corrected in perfection, and brought within Divine Will.

Action Statement:

"I request to initiate the Healing Heart and Hands Activation, now please."

Step-by-Step Activity Instructions:

1. Enter *Angelscape* at the Lotus Pool. Complete the spouting Water Breath Cleanse, sip your Lotus Nectar Elixir, and put on your Work Wrap to prepare for your journey. When you feel ready, you may continue.
2. A helper escorts you to the Chamber of Light. Light a candle for the Healing Heart and Hands Activation. Light a candle for your family. Light a candle for humanity. Light a candle for all creation. Light candles for any other issues, as you wish, to prepare for your work.
3. One or more of your Divine Advocates steps through the Eternal Flame of God's Grace and Love. You are asked to stand near to the Eternal Flame, within the warmth of the sunlight streaming down from the circular opening in the ceiling. It is a glorious sunny day and the sun's position is at high noon, directly overhead.
4. One of the Divine Advocates steps forward, draws his/her Sword of Light, and sticks it into the Eternal Flame. Seven

apple-sized embers are retrieved from the Eternal Flames and placed within a vessel next to you. These embers will be placed within your body and activated in order to create channels of healing light through your system.

5. Imagine that the first two embers are placed within the soles of your feet. You have to lift your feet in order for your Divine Advocate to anchor them there. The next ember is placed gently at the base of your spine. Your heart is the location of the fourth ember. Your hands receive the fifth and sixth embers. The very top of your head, where your soft spot grew together as an infant, is the site of the seventh ember. You can feel the embers warming your body and you relax into the sensations. Your Divine Advocate may take the opportunity to place additional embers anywhere else in your body that is beneficial.
6. Your Divine Advocate takes out his/her Sword of Light and gently pushes the beam of light down into your head, down through your spine, and down through the bottoms of your feet into the earth (the beam splits into two beams at your legs). The Divine Advocate gives the Sword of Light a twirl, as if it were a spinning top. A whirl of energy moves gracefully through your body and deeply down into the earth. The channels of light are being established and connected.
7. You are asked to hold your arms up to the light shining through the circular open ceiling as if they are branches of a tree reaching toward the sky. Imagine holding the sunlight between your hands and breathing it down through your body and into the earth. Your Divine Advocate may adjust your energy field as you do this. Continue visualizing the sunlight streaming into and through your body until your Divine Advocate has made all necessary adjustments. You may lower your arms once this part is completed.
8. Next, you are asked to imagine that your legs and body are the trunk and roots of a mighty tree. Imagine a strong and sturdy root system moving from your feet deep into the center of the earth. Allow the roots of your energy channels to fully anchor in this sacred space. Your Divine Advocate may make further adjustments to the energy channels connecting you to the earth.

9. Imagine that your Divine Advocate finishes establishing and adjusting the channels of light. You are asked to hold your arms up to the sky and stand with your feet apart and solidly placed. Two helpers come to approach you on both sides to help steady you for the activation process. Your Divine Advocate says, *"We request to initiate the Breath of God, now please."*
10. A great wind begins to swirl down through the circular opening in the Chamber of Light. Your helpers hold onto you firmly. The whirlwind moves down into the chamber and connects with your head. It moves swiftly down through your body, activating and enkindling all of the embers. You can feel the Breath of God move all the way through you and into the earth, as if you were a flute through which the wind passes. The whirlwind subsides and your helpers gently let you go to stand on your own. You feel refreshed and enlivened. You are given a moment to reorient to the chamber.
11. Imagine that your Divine Advocate smiles at you and asks you to hold out your hands. You look at the palms of your hands and perceive the ember and a small flame contained within your hands. You are asked to imagine breathing in, down through your head, into your heart, and then to exhale out of your hands. When you do this, a radiant light moves from your heart and hands in waves. You can feel the movement of energy all through your body.
12. Your Divine Advocate says a blessing for your newly established healing heart and hands. You are asked to light the same candles that you lit at the beginning of this activity. You may light more candles on behalf of any issue, subject, or concern that you wish. When you light the candles, intentionally allow the newly established pathways to move healing energies through your heart and hands to the subject of the prayer.
13. When you are finished, you may continue with the Scenic Route activities, or your main Divine Advocate escorts you to the TLC Bath where you will coat yourself in the soothing energies, sip your Graceful Integration Elixir, and then wrap yourself in the Resiliency Comfort Wrap. Do not drive, operate heavy machinery, or do any activities that are

dangerous, or that require you to be fully attentive, until you feel fully shifted back to a normal waking state. Take some time to journal or take notes before your memory of the experience fades.

Continuing Thoughts

This section is designed to help empower you to advocate for yourself and others using your own heart and hands as tools of God's Grace and Love. No matter where you go, you take your heart and hands with you. When we agree to be in Divine Alignment, theoretically, we have access to and can help to distribute enormous assistance and resources. Keep in mind, however, that the hose is just an instrument of the Gardener to flow water where it is needed. It is not your job to worry about the details, to feel responsible, or to attach your sense of worth to the process or outcome. It has *nothing* to do with you beyond your agreeing to be an instrument for the movement of healing energies to pass, and a volunteer to direct it when you see that something is "dry".

Practice moving healing energy through your hands and outward to other subjects, such as your children, pets, plants, spouse, willing friends, and so on. You may notice your hands getting warmer, or they may tingle. If you hold them up in front of you in dim light, you may see what looks like waves of heat coming from them. All of that is normal. You may feel and see nothing at all. Be patient, it may take time to establish a strong healing flow that you can observe. Placing your hands between the back shoulder blades of a volunteer is often the best place to start because it is at the back of the heart center. Always ask permission before putting your hands on anyone, or before moving positions from one spot to another during a session.

There may be times when your hands spontaneously flow with healing energy. There is likely someone in the immediate environment that has the need of healing energy. You *do not* have to offer to help in an obvious way, especially if it is inappropriate to do so, but you *can* intend for the healing energies to flow to whoever requires it. You can follow up by lighting a candle, or saying a prayer, for whomever it is that needed the help, even if you are not sure who exactly it is. You do not have to have physical contact in order to direct the healing energy. You can imagine concentric ripples of healing light waves rolling out of your heart, going wherever needed.

Scenic Route Activity #6 A
Expansion Attunements

Environment Setting: *Angelscape* Spa, Healing Rooms Section

Purpose: The expansion attunement process is designed as a way for you to imagine a regular tune up that introduces another level of vibrational healing energies into your system. As you do so, you will be able to move larger bandwidths of healing light through your system, to connect with a particular type of energy that is beneficial to you, or to empower positive re-scripted pathways.

Usage Suggestion: Expansion Attunements are meant to be refreshers and "energy muscle building" exercises. Once you are finished with the main *Angelscape* journey, you can request to receive an Expansion Attunement on a consistent basis, when you feel prompted, when you have a new healing need (for yourself or others), or when you feel ready to pump up to the next level. It would be ideal to ask for a general Expansion Attunement once every month or so.

You can ask for specific attunements (flavors of energy), which your Divine Advocates can modify and provide for your best interest, if you are prompted. Be sure to follow up with the TLC Bath and plenty of rest. Overworking your energy system can be as uncomfortable as overdoing it at the gym. In order to build "good muscles" you have to pace yourself. It will all come in good time.

Activity Props: You can use the same props as you used for the Direct Route activity. For future Expansion Attunements, in which you request a specific flavor of energy, you may use pictures or props of whatever you wish to attune to if the energy has a physical counterpart, such as a crystal, symbol, Divine Advocate, color, flower, or healing substance of any kind.

Summary: Expansion Attunements can be directed by your Divine Advocates, such as whatever is the most appropriate next healing pathway to establish for you, or you can request for a particular healing attunement to something specific. In this first activity, you will allow the Divine Advocates to simply provide you with exposure and attunement to the next most appropriate level of healing energy.

You will go to the spa for the Expansion Attunements since they are seen as a way to build up your energy fitness and healing flow. Your Divine Advocate will use the Sword of Light attunement process, such as during the Direct Route activity, but the details may change according to the attunement specifics. The Expansion Attunement may be as simple as your Divine Advocate doing the Sword of Light spinning technique; it may involve color, sound, or vibrations. Just let it be whatever it is. You do not have to imagine implanting the Eternal Flame Embers again, as they have already been permanently placed in your system and fully activated. If you are requesting a particular attunement, allow your Divine Advocates to provide the proper protocol.

Helpers: Any of your Divine Advocates can do the Expansion Attunements. They may rotate duty according to your needs and their area of expertise.

New Concepts: Expansion Wrap, Attunement, Happy Trails Attunement (see Continuing Thoughts).

Intentions Supporting Activity

- Intentions added from anywhere else in the book that are relevant to this work.
- All Assistance, as appropriate, for any matter that needs attention.
- Attunement, exposure, and resonance to new or beneficial energies to the system, such that those energies can freely be used and moved through the healing light channels.
- Correction, rectification, moderation, or modulation of any requested attunement, such that it is in Divine Alignment and supports the wellbeing of the self.
- Perfected graduation and progression of attunements, such that an orderly, systematic, efficient, and supportive expansion process is maintained.
- Correction and perfection of any previous attunements, as needed.
- Support for the Journeyer to seek God to receive direct spiritual assistance, gifting of blessings, attunements, and movement of resources.

- Support for the Journeyer to be patient and compassionate to the self, such that s/he moves forward with ease and grace.
- *Expansion Wrap*: used to provide consistent and ongoing support through the establishment, anchoring, and graceful integration of new energy streams, as provided through the Expansion Attunement process.
- *Attunement:* the process of synchronizing with unique resources, energies, Divine Advocates, or to empower an expansion of functioning, ability to move energy, or growth.
- *Happy Trails Attunement:* an Expansion Attunement option, used to provide support and assistance for transitioning spirit from the physical to the spiritual worlds, or to assist lingering/lost spirits, such as ghosts, to be called to the Light, aka: called Home to God, with as much ease and grace as possible under Divine Will.
- Listed intentions reaffirmed as part of the Cooperative Contract already signed over.
- Engagement of this activity, if a Cooperative Contract has not yet been signed, an affirmation of acceptance of these intentions, corrected in perfection, and brought within Divine Will.

Action Statement:
"I request to initiate the Expansion Attunement, now please."

Note: *Skip to step 2 if you are coming immediately from the previous activity.*

Step-by-Step Activity Instructions:

1. Enter *Angelscape* at the Lotus Pool. Complete the spouting Water Breath Cleanse, sip your Lotus Nectar Elixir, and put on your Work Wrap to prepare for your journey. When you feel ready, you may continue.
2. A helper escorts you to the spa. You are led through the main gallery of the cavern where you are given a Sacred Self Elixir to prepare for the Expansion Attunement. You drink it down and continue down the hall into the healing rooms section. You select a room with a comfortable chair.

3. Your Divine Advocates enter the room with your Sacred Self file. After consulting the file, a new layer of energy is selected for your Expansion attunement. Your Divine Advocate may take out his/her Sword of Light and adjust the light, tone, or vibration of it to select the proper setting for the process.
4. Your Divine Advocate stands behind your chair and gently inserts his/her Sword of Light down through your head and down through the length of your spine. S/he spins the Sword of Light like a top. S/he allows the sword to spin on its own and moves in front of you. Your Divine Advocate may use any other tools, symbols, objects, sounds, colors, or glowing orbs to place within your system to initiate the rest of the Expansion Attunement. It may be different from one attunement to the next.
5. When your Divine Advocate has finished the attunement, you will be given an Expansion Wrap. It will continue to provide support as your system integrates the new energies.
6. When you are finished, you may continue with the next Scenic Route activity, or your main Divine Advocate escorts you to the TLC Bath where you will coat yourself in the soothing energies, sip your Graceful Integration Elixir, and then wrap yourself in the Resiliency Comfort Wrap. Do not drive, operate heavy machinery, or do any activities that are dangerous, or that require you to be fully attentive, until you feel fully shifted back to a normal waking state. Take some time to journal or take notes before your memory of the experience fades.

Continuing Thoughts

You can use the Expansion Attunements to request a specific kind of energy, such as Cherry Vanilla Reiki (not an actual energy), or whatever the newest bandwidth of energy is called that day. You may also ask to attune to the energies or qualities of a favorite Divine Advocate, a crystal, sacred site, color, flower, healing herb, personality characteristic (kindness, patience, and so on), emotion (love, happiness, passion, and so on), or you can ask to attune to a quality that is in alignment with something you wish to manifest in your life (abundance, good luck, opportunity, and so on). Have fun with it. Your Divine Advocates are in charge of what you actually receive, so if you ask for something irrelevant, foolish, or inappropriate, they will simply edit your request to be something that is good for you.

You can ask to attune to anything you wish, whether you have a physical representation of it or not. You *can* be holding the physical object, but you do not *have* to. You can be creative with your requests and use the Expansion Attunements often, though it is best to wait until you have integrated one before requesting another. This process is the best way to expand your ability to move energy, and often enjoyable and exciting.

There are some tips to follow for attunement requests. Ask for just one type of energy at a time and keep it simple at first. You may need multiple passes or sessions for a requested energy until you are fully attuned to it. If in doubt, attune at least three times to the same energy over the course of a month. Remember, it is like building muscles. You do not go to the gym, work out one time on a particular machine, and have instant results. The same is true here.

Action Statement:
"I request to initiate an Expansion Attunement to the energies of ______________, now please."

Note: *Using the Expansion Attunement process is not the same as becoming a practitioner with official training. The energy is free. Training, however, is not free. For example, if you ask for "Chocolate Flame Reiki" (not a real energy stream) in an Expansion Attunement, and you receive the "Chocolate Flame" from your Divine Advocates, it does not give you the right or authority to call yourself a Chocolate Flame Reiki "practitioner". If you want to be an official Chocolate Flame Reiki practitioner, presuming that it is a healing "system" named and developed by some other human being, you have to find yourself a Chocolate Flame Reiki Master teacher to attune and train you. Divine Advocates do not issue certification.*

Authors Note: *"Happy Trails" Non-Traditional Reiki Symbol*
Back in the late 1990's, I was just learning about spiritual energy work, Reiki, and the use of symbols in healing work as a way to direct intention. My father, at the time, was dying of cancer and my main concern was helping him in any way that I could. I went to several Reiki Masters (fancy title for "teacher") to seek a protocol for helping the process of death to be as graceful and supported as possible. I could not find one already on the books, so I prayed and asked for a symbol to be given directly to me so that I could help my father.

In 1998, I was inspired to doodle a symbol that looked like a spirit taking flight from within a Star of David. I used this symbol to support my father (and myself to not feel helpless) and found it useful. I promptly posted it on my website, free of charge, for anyone who was in a similar situation of the imminent death of a loved one. The Happy Trails information has since circulated, without my knowledge, on various "pay for" sites that sell attunements like a commodity.

Since the late 1990's, the way I do things has certainly changed. I do not use symbols as a focal point anymore, but it was a good system for me to start understanding energy work concepts and it helped to provide a logical progression from a tangible focal point, such as a symbol, to the intention itself being the focal point. Some of you may enjoy the Happy Trails attunement, especially if you work with those who are very ill, aged, or if you are a paranormal ghost hunter hobbyist. I will try to write up instructions that are more detailed to post on my website for those of you who are interested.

If you would like to attune to *Happy Trails*, just use the Action Statement.

Action Statement:

"I request to initiate an Expansion Attunement to the energies of Happy Trails, now please."

Your hands are powerful tools of the heart.

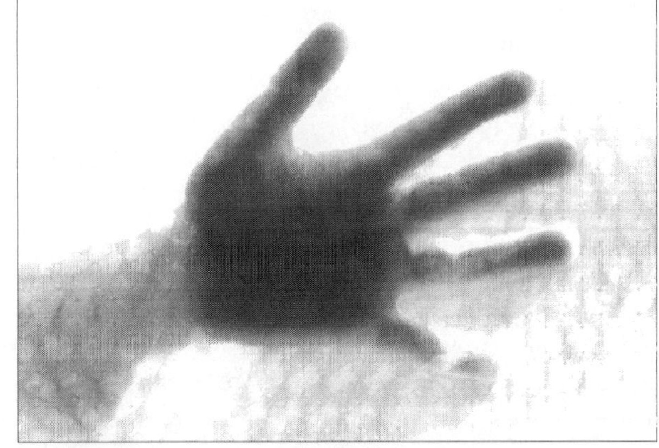

Photograph 173865 by morguefile.com user: ali110

Scenic Route Activity #6 B
Team Self-Treatment

Environment Setting: *Angelscape* Spa, Healing Rooms Section

Purpose: The Team Self-Treatment is used as a way to imagine collaborating with your Healing Team in order to initiate active healing sessions on behalf of your wellbeing.

Usage Suggestions: Team Self-Treatments can be initiated as often as you feel you need them. If you are sick, healing from surgery, or have a chronic illness, you may want to initiate a Team Self-Treatment once a day as a way to meditate on your wellness and healing process. If you are well and feeling good, weekly or even monthly Team Self-Treatments are fine. This is different from asking a healing session to initiate when you go to sleep because you are awake and participating in the session.

Note: *The Team Self-Treatment is not a substitute for authentic medical care. The activities in this book work with the Mind/Body/Spirit theory of interconnection and healing. A theory (however good) is a theory, not a fact. Go to your doctor if you think you have a medical issue.*

Activity Props: This activity is best initiated while you are lying comfortably in bed or on a couch. You can use fuzzy gloves if you wish to help you imagine your Divine Advocate's hands superimposed over your own.

Summary: The Team Self-Treatment is a healing session that you are asked to actively attend, listen to guidance, and use your own hands as tools for your Divine Advocates to move healing energy into your system. You go to the spa and select a healing room with a comfortable table; you can even use the diagnostic room, if you wish. Once you are settled in, your Healing Team will ask you to put your hands on your body in progressive stages from your head to your feet. You will linger at each position from five to ten minutes while you imagine your Divine Advocates placing their hands *within* your own to supply you with the appropriate healing energies. You do not need to have a working knowledge of the human energy system, but if you do, you will be a little easier to guide. Your Healing Team will let you know what to do, but likely, you will just need to put your hands on yourself and let them work.

Helpers: Your Healing Team will be present for this activity.

New Concepts: Using Your Hands as Tools.

Intentions Supporting Activity

- Intentions added from anywhere else in the book that are relevant to this work.
- All Assistance, as appropriate, for any matter that needs attention.
- Active progressive healing session in cooperation with Healing Team, such that the Sacred Body can be manifested.
- Cultivation of tactile energy sensing for practical healing work purposes and scanning.
- Cultivation of healing intuition with spiritual guidance.
- Support to perceive the self as a competent advocate for healing.
- Vitalization and strengthening of the energy system.
- Enhancement of the flow of Divine Light through system.
- Pathways and channels of energy movement, cleared, strengthened, and stabilized.
- Support to become more aware of the energy system, movement of energy, and the quality of the energies within the system.
- Support to be able to use energetic sense as a way to assess information about the quality, intent, benefit, or lack of benefit of something in relation to the self.
- Support to feel empowered to positively and proactively impact personal health and wellbeing.
- Support to feel optimistic, hopeful, and to maintain a positive mental/emotional outlook for personal health and wellness.
- Support for the growing belief and faith in spontaneous miraculous healing.
- *Using Your Hands as Tools:* a technique where you use your own hands as tools for your Divine Advocates to use during a visualized session. You physically use your hands in whatever way you can while engaging the imagery of assistance by your Divine Advocates.
- Listed intentions reaffirmed as part of the Cooperative Contract already signed over.

- Engagement of this activity, if a Cooperative Contract has not yet been signed, an affirmation of acceptance of these intentions, corrected in perfection, and brought within Divine Will.

Action Statement:
"I request to initiate the Team Self-Treatment, now please."

Note: *Skip to step 2 if you are coming immediately from the previous activity.*

Step-by-Step Activity Instructions:

1. Enter *Angelscape* at the Lotus Pool. Complete the spouting Water Breath Cleanse, sip your Lotus Nectar Elixir, and put on your Work Wrap to prepare for your journey. When you feel ready, you may continue.
2. A helper escorts you to the spa. You are led through the main gallery of the cavern where you are given a Sacred Self Elixir to drink. You drink it down and continue down the hall into the healing rooms section. You select a room with a comfortable table and lie down.
3. Members of your Healing Team enter into the room once you are comfortable. You are asked to place your hands on your head. A member of your healing team superimposes his/her hands within your own. You may be instructed to move your hands into different positions around your head.
4. Continue putting your hands on your body in small segments at a time and then allowing your Healing Team members to "work through" them. Follow the prompts you have to move your hands to various places and allow the energies to move freely through them without doubt. Just allow yourself to respond to the subtle ideas that come to you as you go through the session.
5. When you are finished, your main Divine Advocate escorts you to the TLC Bath where you will coat yourself in the soothing energies, sip your Graceful Integration Elixir, and then wrap yourself in the Resiliency Comfort Wrap. Do not drive, operate heavy machinery, or do any activities that are dangerous, or that require you to be fully attentive, until you feel fully shifted back to a normal waking state. Take some

time to journal or take notes before your memory of the experience fades.

Continuing Thoughts

This kind of healing session is one that places you as an empowered partner in your own wellbeing. You can integrate whatever kind of healing practices that interest you. Intuition often comes as sudden prompts to do something, but it can also come as a natural interest or fascination in some topic or idea. If you get an image of a certain flower, for example, it would make sense for you to look up the flower and then do research on the medicinal properties or the flower essence properties. You do not have to officially go into a deep meditation to initiate this kind of session. You can simply put your hands where it hurts and reaffirm that your Healing Team can place their hands on or within yours to boost your efficiency.

Summary and Wrap Up

Complementary Activities

- Book an appointment with an energy healing practitioner.
- Research topics about the human energy field, energy healing, hands-on-healing, Reiki.
- Research topics on the importance of spirituality on belief and healing.
- Research topics on the use of prayer in healing.
- Research whatever ideas pop into your head while doing the Team Self-Healing.
- Get a check up at your doctors, or visit a naturopathic doctor.

Project Ideas

Create a language system with your Healing Team to help you to respond to their prompts. For example, you can use the color green as a prompt to research herbal remedies, the color blue to represent breath work, pink to represent emotional healing, and so on. These are just a few examples. What "words" you need to communicate will depend on your own needs and will likely build and grow the longer you work with your Healing Team and allow yourself to surrender to the process.

Reflection Questions

1. Describe how you were feeling before and after the activities.
2. What were the most vivid details of your imagery during the activities?
3. Describe your helpers, the tools, and their assistance.
4. What surprised you the most about your experiences?
5. What was your favorite activity in Section 6?
6. What was your least favorite activity in Section 6?
7. Can you integrate your new skills into your more familiar practices?
8. Were there any details that seemed highlighted to you that you might want to think about?
9. Do you feel inspired to do any research in any other related area? If so, what is it?
10. If you have had a Reiki attunement before, how was this activation the same or different? Is the flow of energy through your hands stronger or the same?
11. What were the effects of placing your hands on other subjects? Did they feel anything?
12. Did you request a specific flavor attunement? What, if anything, happened?

"If we all did the things we are capable of, we would astound ourselves."

Thomas Edison

Focus Group Feedback

Sharon

Healing Hearts and Hands Activation

As I entered into the Chamber of Light I am met by my beautiful angel. He guides me down to light my candles. Out of the Eternal Flame step Archangels' Michael and Raphael. The sun streaming down from the dome feels warm and so very welcoming. Another angel is standing behind me. Both Archangel Michael and Archangel Raphael retrieve the embers out of the flame. It is an odd combination of the two. The embers glow red/orange/white but are encased in a green glowing light. In addition to the seven embers placed, one is put in my forehead, both shoulders, hips, and a very large one in my solar plexus.

When it was time for the Sword of Light to push down the beam of light, once again, Archangel Michael and Archangel Raphael used both their swords, one on top of the other, so the white light that goes through my spine is wrapped in a green glow. As I held my arms up to the ceiling, I could see streams of light or small lightning bolts come out of my fingertips connecting to the great light above. I "planted" my roots deep within the earth and attach them to the glowing golden orb. I feel very grounded and one with mother earth. I also feel at this time that my lower energy centers where being adjusted, opened and merged together like a tube. It was as if one color were running into the next, red merging into orange, and orange merging into yellow, like a rainbow.

One of the angels stood behind me as the Breath of God was activated. I felt as if there where two spirals of energy spinning in opposite directions pushing down through me and deep within the earth. I am humbled by this activity. I ask for guidance, clarity and wisdom that I may remain open as an effective and efficient instrument of God's healing power.

Expansion Attunement

As I entered into the spa, I was greeted by my Native American spirit guide. I was led to a warm comfortable room with a beautiful over-stuffed brown leather chair. Several other Native American guides entered the room. One took out a spear decorated with feathers, beads and shells, and inserted it through my head and down my spine. It actually hurt a little as it passed through my shoulder blade area. He then spun it and walked around in front of me. Two large drums adorned with an eagle and a hawk feather appeared on either side of the chair. I was told to place my hands on each of them. When I did this, a deep vibration ran up my hands and arms into my head and sat just above my ears. There was no sound coming from the drums, just intense vibrations. There was a lot of pressure inside my head and "ears". I could hear Native American chanting from behind me and drumming began; my hands and arms started to feel like pins and needles. I got the impression this was an attunement to the voices of nature. The chanting, drumming and vibration continued for a while and then slowly faded away. I thanked and hugged my Divine Advocates and then left the spa. This was a very interesting and fulfilling exercise. I'll be doing this every week and adding it to my "exercise" routine. My ears are still humming and are really sensitive to noise right now. I'm very excited to see (or hear as the case may be) where this will take me.

Laura

Healing Hearts and Hands Activation

As I entered the chamber and began lighting candles, a beautiful golden aura filled the room. I lit several for various situations, and had the sense that each was being flooded with this golden aura just as the room was. Through the flame came Archangel Michael on my left and Raphael on my right. Michael used his blue sword to remove the embers. They formed a very significant "Tree of Life pattern" superimposed over my body--there were two extras at the level of the belly energy center, one on each hip. As they were put in place, I was moved to a reclining position, but just suspended in air --no La-Z-Boy needed here! Then I was returned to the upright position and could clearly see energy lines connecting embers and forming this "Tree of Life" pattern. I heard faintly something about "sacred geometry", but no explanation--just like someone labeled (gave a name to) the Tree of Life pattern for me.

When I held up my arms, I was immediately aware of waves of warmth coming over me--my eyes involuntarily went upwards toward the light/warmth source--and I felt every atom opening to receive the energy and warmth into itself in my body. It was amazing! As soon as I began incorporating the "root system" that same narrator told me I had now "completed the circuit".

The two archangels placed their hands on my shoulders and hips as the Breath of God began. I was surprised to see the name of this exercise, because for many years I have used the term "Breath of God" as part of my healing meditations--I also use the term as I blow breath on crystals to cleanse them. As the breath, or wind, blew, I could feel a swelling in my heart and solar plexus. Some slight pulsing in my middle forehead, but not nearly as powerful as the heart and solar plexus where I had issues--I was aware. Then the pressure equalized after about thirty or more seconds--

seemed like a timeless moment, though. As I held out my hands for the ember and flame I was aware of a profound peace come over me.

Michael said the benediction. When he asked me to light candles, I went to town! In positions that roughly related to the numbers on a clock face, I lit candles for a host of issues I wanted to be flooded with this healing and cleansing. Many were duplicates of the ones I lit in the beginning, but I had the feeling they were now only "residuals" of those issues that still needed clearing. A couple were new.

I left feeling like I had really done some "ground-breaking" work, a term I heard, felt, and smiled about. I still felt quite a bit of healing energy in my hands, so when the cat jumped in my lap, I put them on her and she promptly chilled out and purred. This is a young cat who loves to bounce around and "cuddling" is very low on her priority list! Not this time--she turned into a melted lump in no time. It was very cute.

When I began, I was slightly scattered and anxious about getting caught up, since the after effects from my surgical experience had me really behind. After it was finished, I knew I was "right on time" according to Divine Order for me and due to the personal nature of the next few exercises, it had to wait until now. Not entirely sure why, but I've learned to trust the universe on such matters. It was a very easy and efficient exercise. I enjoyed the process a lot. I was surprised at the importance of my understanding the "Tree of Life" symbolism; the "completing of the circuit" and how I felt physically as a result.

Expansion Attunement

After drinking the Sacred Self Elixir, I was prompted to go get an angelite sphere I keep next to my bed, and hold it during this exercise. I felt it represented the presence of Archangel Michael, though I don't always think of him when working with angelite for other things.

Then, as the sword was working, I kept hearing the word "peace" chanted. I felt so relaxed, however, since I was trying to keep moving and not fall asleep, I asked that I be given some energy before I left, and did feel a burst from my feet upward. I became immediately focused again and was able to finish and move forward.

I think this would be a great thing to initiate before going to sleep for healing/balancing/adjusting conditions in the body overnight! I also will use this for attunement requests for Divine Order peace and prosperity. We need that around here! Good exercise for the State of Michigan, too, which is way out of whack at the moment, affecting all its citizens. It would be a good exercise for planetary peace, too. This is a key exercise I'll use often.

Lourdes

Healing Hearts and Hands Activation

I was as mildly apprehensive about starting this exercise. I knew it was going to affect me strongly in a good way. I walked up to *Angelscape* from the beach. It's a gorgeous day and everyone seems even happier than usual. I went to the chamber and found Archangel's Michael and Gabriel there. I lit quite a few candles since a lot of people I know need healing. Archangel Michael put his sword in the flame. It turned white (fire white) and then it turned purple and gold. He put the embers into me and I asked for additional ones for the rest of my energy centers, which Michael and Gabriel both thought I needed. I could feel the heat in the areas where the embers were placed. When Michael put the sword into me and twirled it, the colors turned into purple and gold. When I connected to the center of the earth, it was more of a tube going down from my spine into the center of the earth. My feet were also connected as if they were roots.

When the Breath of God was initiated, it felt as if fire were going through all my energy centers. The sound of the wind was there, but it moved like a fire through me and the energy turned all gold. When it finished, I could feel the heat as I exhaled through my hands. I felt very calm afterward, but a little dizzy. I forgot I hadn't eaten breakfast and had been up for hours. The Archangels did tell me to go eat something. I thanked everyone and felt unusually calm. What amazed me about this exercise is how quickly I went into the imagery. I'm not one to meditate easily, but being in *Angelscape* is getting easier and easier and I really don't like leaving.

Expansion Attunement

I just finished this exercise. I have some clients coming this weekend and know that I needed a little something extra to help them. I met up with Archangel Michael, Gabriel, Uriel and Raphael. All accompanied me to the session. As I sat in the chair, Archangel Michael asked me what I wanted. I told him I needed the next level of any Reiki attunement that would best help me help my clients. He put his sword in me and it spun out a clear light with many multi-colored specks. The other Archangels put their hands on top of my head, while another Divine Advocate came in and began shining a light into my heart. I felt the energy running through my hands and feet. The top of my head could feel the energy too.

My (deceased) grandmother also appeared. She came to hold my hands. As she held my hands, she told me she was proud of the work I was doing. Of course that made me cry, because although I know I have to do this work, my family doesn't understand it. They have not offered emotional support because it is too abstract for them. It felt wonderful for my grandmother to validate my work and to show love, pride and confidence in me. The session stopped, because I was getting dizzy. I thanked all of them and Archangel Michael brought me down to my body.

Team Self-Treatment

Archangel Michael came to take me to the spa for my treatment. I got to the spa, took my Sacred Self Elixir, which was a pink strawberry smoothie. I went into the room and Archangels Michael, Raphael, Gabriel and Uriel came to help me out. I felt the energy flow immediately and the heat was powerful. I started at my head and lingered on my ears, throat, and heart. I heard the word "hematite" (a shiny metallic stone of mostly iron). When the healing was over, I was calm, but very tired. When I got home from work, I went straight to bed. I had not realized how tired I was. I fell asleep in less than two minutes and woke up forty-five minutes later. I own a lot of hematite, so I will check if there is something else I need to know about this stone. I was wearing quite a bit of it today since I knew I was going to need grounding.

The path of service is beautiful.

"Our deeds determine us, as much as we determine our deeds."
George Elliot

Photograph 194697
by morguefile.com
user: Lisa Solonynko

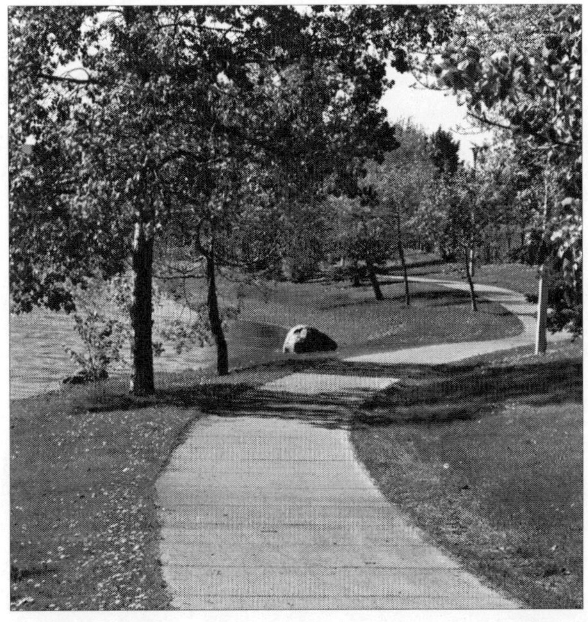

Section 7
Relationships & Interconnections

Activities Introduction

Section 7 reaches beyond the intense self-focus that is found in earlier chapters. The Journeyer is asked to imagine him/herself as a part of something larger. All of our loved ones are a part of us in some way through the myriad of energetic and emotional bonds that we forge through life. We all have a complex weave of connections that place us in relationships with others. These relationships are powerful and deep and they influence us, for better or worse, whether they are a thousand miles away or fifty years in the past.

If our voices, as some of us hope, are an actual part of the communal landscape of unfolding possibilities--our intimate relationships, family systems, and networks of personal connection are our local neighborhood. If we seek to apply assistance anywhere outside of ourselves, we should apply it closest to home *first*. The visualization activities in this section provide the opportunity to encourage gainful strides in interpersonal harmony and for care and assistance to flow to the entire family system. If it is possible for us to be of assistance and service to our family and friends in this way, it seems worthwhile to provide a space for that possibility to unfold. The activities in this section allow us to imagine those possibilities as being a real option and to conceptually work those options in a practical and positive way.

The Direct Route activity, the Family Care and Assistance Party, allows you to envision yourself as a volunteer conduit of God's Grace and Love (aka: Healing Light) to flow to your family and friends. Family, for purposes of this work, includes anyone (alive or deceased) who is a connection of personal consequence, by blood, emotional connection, marriage, or circumstance. The "party" is like a huge family reunion, long overdue, where everyone gets to reconnect and remember *how it should be* in a loving family. Connections are cleared and congestion purged.

The work initiated in the Scenic Route Relationship Rebalancing activity seeks to align and balance the energies of individual members of a relationship, to remove obstacles to peace and harmony, and to cleanse perceptual distortions that prevent the individuals in the relationship from "being on the same page". Our close relationships are of great consequence to our personal wellbeing and integrity. If there is drama, chaos, or imbalance close in our systems of connection, it is very difficult to maintain the focus needed to foster progressive movement toward personal wellness. This activity provides a platform to support individual relationships to stay in balance.

The goal of the Stage of Life Scenic Route activity is to begin understanding when unconscious dramas happen within our lives and relationships. We can learn to step away from the limits of those kinds of plays to live a life that is more authentic and less like a bad Hollywood script. The Stage of Life gives us a platform for working things out while being objective observers to our personal dilemmas. We may not always get the outcome we want, but we can be conscious, responsible participants in our own lives. We cannot help how people see us, what they are thinking, what conclusions they make, or what distortions they are using to view us through--but we can help what *we* do. We are masters of our own ship, and unless we abdicate that authority to unconscious dysfunctional patterns, we can decide to play, or *not* to play, depending on the quality the interaction brings to our lives. If we are *aware* of the play, we can write in our Sacred Selves in the starring roles. We can be who we have always wanted to be by being purposeful and selective with the kinds of roles and scripts we are willing to empower and play out.

You will imagine a large family reunion on the beach in this section. You can use a memory of a beach you used to visit as a child.

Photograph 221928
by morguefile.com
user: Nightwind23

Direct Route Activity #7
Family Care and Assistance Party

Environment Setting: *Angelscape* Beach

Complementary Scenic Route Activities
SR 7 A: Relationship Rebalancing
SR 7 B: Stage of Life

Purpose: This activity seeks to bring the self into greater alignment within larger systems of connection. It also establishes the self as a secured conduit of God's Grace and Love (aka: Healing Light) to flow to the systems of connection, as appropriate.

Usage Suggestions: The Family Care and Assistance Party can be initiated on a consistent schedule to help you imagine caring for your family system and networks of connection. The wellbeing of your family system is important to the wellbeing of your own system. I recommend initiating the Family Care and Assistance Party at least once a month--more often if there is discord in the family.

Activity Props: If you live close to the ocean, that would be a fantastic place to go to initiate this work. If not, you can use photos of the ocean, photos of family reunions, or photo albums of friends and family to help you imagine the scene. If you can get some of your family members to do this meditation with you, you can use an actual beach ball to toss back and forth to one another.

Summary: This activity will be imagined and initiated at the beach, as an enormous party reunion of family and friends. The ocean will stand in as a giant Lotus Pool to bring cleansing and purification to the system. Other fun activities will be initiated to cleanse specific connections between members. People have free will, but as much assistance as possible will be established for every individual within the system. If there is a family member that is too difficult for you to visualize, you do not have to visualize them--they will be included in the process regardless. Use imagery that you feel safe creating when structuring this experience for yourself.

Often, even family and friends who have died will show up at the party. You can use this activity as a way to imagine connecting with your crossed over loved ones, if you feel that is appropriate. You can establish *Angelscape* as a conceptual platform between dimensions, if you so choose. Some find this very comforting and reassuring, as well as intensely emotional and touching.

Helpers: Any or all of your Divine Advocates may be present at this activity, among others who may be working on behalf of the family system.

New Concepts: Blessed Beach Balls.

Intentions Supporting Activity

- Intentions added from anywhere else in the book that are relevant to this work.
- All Assistance, as appropriate, for any matter that needs attention.
- Establishing of the self as a secured conduit for All Care and Assistance to flow into relevant relational systems of connection.
- Perfected boundaries of personal self-integrity, such that personal integrity and healing are not influenced or disrupted by negative family system influences.
- Family system considered as part of the system of the self, as such, to be provided with Guardian Angel Shield protection, care, oversight, and upkeep, as appropriate.
- Containment and protection from disproportionate negative influence or destabilization of family from any individuals in the system.
- Family system to be defined and organized within Divine Will.
- All Care and Assistance to Little Ones, or dissociated aspects, within system.
- All Care and Assistance to any member of the system, alive or dead, or within ancestral matrix.
- Grief care support and communication enhancement to cultivate continuance of love, connection, and support through the veils between life and afterlife.
- Divine Alignment of family system; retrieval, rectification, and restoration of any aspect out of place or alignment.

- Appropriate vibrational infill or space holder in any position in the system that requires it in order to bring system into Divine Alignment.
- Establishment of Family Care Team of spiritual helpers to tend to the healing and restoration of the family system.
- Individuals in family system given opportunities to experience the patterns and vibrations of their own Sacred Selves.
- All Assistance to cleanse, balance, and to bring peace and Divine Alignment to relationships between the self and any member of the family system.
- Clearing the atmosphere of family system to support evolution, healing, wellness, and inner growth of system and members.
- Cleansing and purification of channels of connection between the self and members of the family system.
- Cleansing of dysfunctional relationship and drama patterns from the self and system.
- Cleansing and rectification of distorted perceptual filters impacting relationships such that an authentic shared reality supports the foundation of the relationship.
- Balancing of polarity and power within relationships, establishment of authentic equality, and respect for differing qualities and roles within the family and relationships.
- Support for the release of negative emotion and positive closure of challenges and learning opportunities between members of the family system.
- Support for the authentic reconnection and reconciliation between family members who have become estranged or distanced.
- Support for the self to forgive members of family system who require it, and to ask for forgiveness in whatever way is necessary.
- *Blessed Beach Balls*: orbs of light used to clean the connections of stagnant congestion and distorted perceptual filters between people in a relationship, such that an opportunity for a "clearing of the air" may occur within the relationship.
- Listed intentions reaffirmed as part of the Cooperative Contract already signed over.

- Engagement of this activity, if a Cooperative Contract has not yet been signed, an affirmation of acceptance of these intentions, corrected in perfection, and brought within Divine Will.

Action Statement:

"I request to initiate the Family Care and Assistance Party, now please."

Step-by-Step Activity Instructions:

1. Enter *Angelscape* at the Lotus Pool. Complete the spouting Water Breath Cleanse, sip your Lotus Nectar Elixir, and put on your Work Wrap to prepare for your journey. When you feel ready, you may continue.
2. A helper escorts you to the Chamber of Light. You are asked to light a candle on behalf of your Family Care and Assistance Party. Allow your own healing channels of light to fully flow. Reaffirm your connection to the Eternal Flame of God's Grace and Love. When you are finished, your Divine Advocates emerge from the fire dressed in beach attire and holding items in their arms for a party.
3. Imagine your Divine Advocates lead you to the *Angelscape* beach. A large gong is sounded three times, summoning the higher aspects of all members of your family and networks of connection. A large crowd begins to gather, greet, and enjoy themselves. Some of the people gathering are members of your family that have passed over, some are family you dearly love and know well, others are friends and acquaintances, and still others are only vaguely familiar. There may be hundreds of people gathered on the beach with you. Allow it to be what it is.
4. One of your Divine Advocates climbs onto a lifeguard stand with a megaphone and announces that it is time to take a cleansing dip in the ocean. Your Healing Team leads you and the others into the ocean water. You begin to do the cleansing water breath until you are spouting it firmly out of the top of your head, playfully splashing those near you. A large crew of spiritual helpers joins your party in the ocean to help everyone learn the cleansing water breathing activity. Soon

the entire beach has erupted in laughter and joyous water spouts.

5. Imagine dozens of glowing orbs of light, the Blessed Beach Balls, are tossed into the crowd. These balls cleanse and purify the energetic connections between members of a system. The glowing balls of light are tossed in every direction. You catch them and toss them back into the crowd. It reminds you of popcorn being popped. Sometimes you know who tossed you the ball and sometimes you do not. The Divine Advocates will make sure that all energy lines are fully cleansed between members by the time the beach balls are put away. Everyone is feeling lighter, brighter, and as if "this is how it is supposed to be".
6. The Divine Advocates pass out towels and wrap everyone up in Resiliency Comfort Wraps. Each person is also placed within his or her own Guardian Angel Shield. Every person on the beach is allowed to touch their own Sacred Self files and to experience the inner stirring of remembrance of who they are. They are told that they are loved and that All Assistance is available to them for the asking, whenever they so choose. They are given an invitation to visit the beach for care, cleansing, and comfort any time they choose.
7. Imagine that an official Family Care Team is established and introduced to the assembled crowd. These spiritual helpers will look after and maintain the integrity of the family system as strongly as they are allowed. All children are assigned at least one personal guardian.
8. All Little Ones belonging to unaware adults are provided with appropriate safe haven and care until such time that the adult is ready for their reintegration. You see butterflies landing on the heads of some of the young children. The children smile and begin to yawn. They are lovingly gathered up by the women who work in the Garden of the Little Ones to begin their Butterfly Sleep.
9. Some members of your family system may stay and linger at the beach after you have gone. Some are being tended by the Family Care Team. When you are finished, you may continue with the Scenic Route activities, or your main Divine Advocate escorts you to the TLC Bath where you will coat yourself in the soothing energies, sip your Graceful

Integration Elixir, and then wrap yourself in the Resiliency Comfort Wrap. Do not drive, operate heavy machinery, or do any activities that are dangerous, or that require you to be fully attentive, until you feel fully shifted back to a normal waking state. Take some time to journal or take notes before your memory of the experience fades.

Continuing Thoughts

Families and relationships are complex and always evolving. It is through our relationships that we learn the most about ourselves, others, and unconditional love. You serve as a blessing to your family system by tending to its cleansing and energetic health. We cannot choose on behalf of others to engage a healing path, but we can choose to keep the spaces we share with others as clear as we can. The Family Care and Assistance Party is something that you can do as an individual to foster a lightness of atmosphere within the energy of the family. This lightness allows others in the same space to enjoy a reprieve into clarity that they may not have otherwise. All things are easier when the congestion and muck is cleared away. You can use this activity as often as you are prompted to proactively tend your family and close connections.

Instead of being reactive in a situation with your loved ones, remember relating to them as you did on the beach. Intentionally seek out the best in them to help them manifest those qualities in real life. You can single out one member of your family, or a specific group, for a visit to the beach in your imagination to reconnect, cleanse energy lines, or simply to help your loved ones to “lighten up”.

If you do not have time to visualize this activity, you can simply use the action statement to move your Family Care Team into action.

Action Statement:

“I request to initiate the Family Care and Assistance Party, now please.”

Scenic Route Activity #7 A
Relationship Rebalancing

Environment Setting: Chamber of Light

Purpose: The Relationship Rebalancing activity provides an opportunity to bring a single relationship or a small system into energetic balance and alignment. This energetic alignment supports positive progress in the interpersonal dynamic between members.

Usage Suggestions: The Relationship Rebalancing activity is designed to give you a plan of action to bring your personal relationships into energetic harmony. Theoretically, it may support healing, shifting issues, challenges, and feelings of disconnection. You still have to do your front-end work of making things better, but the Relationship Rebalancing may help pave the way for a brighter interaction through the back door. Use it as often as you need to use it to keep the dynamics stabilized enough that you can make progress. Use the meditation before couples counseling, family counseling, or to assist in any plan to adjust and enhance group interactions and relationships.

Activity Props: You can use images of scales, a teeter-totter, or meditate on the infinity symbol, yin yang symbol, or any object or symbol that represents a perfect balance between parts in a system. You can also use a beach ball or any kind of ball to imagine tossing the cleansing orb of light (Blessed Beach Ball) to the other members of the activity.

Summary: The Relationship Rebalancing is initiated in the Chamber of Light and across the Eternal Flames of God's Grace and Love. Whoever is being called for the activity will sit on the Divine Scales, which looks like a teeter-totter type machine that has as many seats as needed for the rebalancing participants. The participants are seated, belted in, and the Blessed Beach Balls, as used in the Family Care and Assistance Party, are provided to clear the connections between people.

The machine is then set into motion after you beam love at your participants, spinning and adjusting itself, like a tilt-a-whirl at the county fair. Once the energies are balanced and harmonized, the wild ride will slow down and eventually cease. When the ride is over, the energy between participants are as balanced as they can get and it is an excellent time to follow up the meditation with the next Scenic Route activity, or to have an actual chat with the participants of your meditation. Your own perceptual shifts, if nothing else, can assist you to make progress in healing and strengthening the actual relationship(s).

Helpers: The helpers can be from your Healing Team, Family Care Team, or any other Divine Advocate that has wisdom to share.

New Concepts: The Divine Scales, the Balance and Harmony Elixir.

Intentions Supporting Activity

- Intentions added from anywhere else in the book that are relevant to this work.
- All Assistance, as appropriate, for any matter that needs attention.
- Rebalancing of relationship such that the members are in Divine Alignment within the system.
- Cleansing and rectification of distortions and dysfunctional relationship patterns.
- Support to identify when distortions are present, such that conscious awareness cultivates permanent, positive and lasting change.
- Support to forgive, accept, and unconditionally love other member(s) of relationship.
- Support to respect, cherish, and have gratitude for the presence and purpose of the self and other member(s) in relationship.
- Support to become aware when appropriate boundaries of self or others are being crossed.
- Support to become aware when resources or challenges of the system are disproportionately distributed, creating imbalance.
- Support for cohesiveness, unity, productivity, and graceful growth as individuals within a system or relationship.
- Support for equality, independence, and proportional responsibility between members such that balance is maintained.
- Graceful release and closure of relationship when time and appropriateness of relationship has concluded.

- *The Divine Scales*: used as a way to imagine the rebalancing of a relationship. It supports mutual understanding and communication that cultivates love and respect that sustains and nurtures each individual.
- *Balance and Harmony Elixir*: used as a way to sustain balance and centeredness within an individual, such that reactivity, drama, and perceptual distortions are minimized and objective clarity is enhanced.
- Listed intentions reaffirmed as part of the Cooperative Contract already signed over.
- Engagement of this activity, if a Cooperative Contract has not yet been signed, an affirmation of acceptance of these intentions, corrected in perfection, and brought within Divine Will.

Action Statement:
"I request to initiate Relationship Rebalancing, now please."

Note: *Skip to step 2 if you are coming immediately from the previous activity.*

Step-by-Step Activity Instructions:

1. Enter *Angelscape* at the Lotus Pool. Complete the spouting Water Breath Cleanse, sip your Lotus Nectar Elixir, and put on your Work Wrap to prepare for your journey. When you feel ready, you may continue.
2. Your Divine Advocate escorts you into the Chamber of Light. Light a candle on behalf of the Relationship Rebalancing work. Light a candle on behalf of all the individuals you will be including in the work. Light a candle for yourself. When you are finished, your Divine Advocates and teams emerge from the Eternal Flames of God's Grace and Love.
3. You are asked to name the relationship or small system (such as your immediate family) that you would like to bring into balance. A gong is sounded three times to call the higher aspects of all the individuals required to initiate the work. The individual(s) begin to enter the chamber.
4. Your Divine Advocates assemble a set of scales and balances across the Eternal Flame. It looks something like a large

scale of justice, or a multi-seat teeter-totter, depending on the number of members to balance. You and your attendees are asked to sit on your own seats upon the scales and to fasten your seat belts. Sometimes the ride is bumpy.

5. Imagine that you are given a large Blessed Beach Ball and are asked to toss this back and forth between you and the other(s), clearing your lines of connection of debris. Toss this back and forth until no congestion can be detected between you. You may need to discuss personal feelings or matters that are obstacles to a free flow of love. The energies are released as the ball is tossed through it. Your Divine Advocates may make adjustments as needed.
6. When the lines are clear, you are asked to flow healing light and love through your heart toward all other participants. As you do this, the seats begin to spin around the Eternal Flame, as if the scales have become a giant spinning top. You are asked to continue breathing and beaming love through your heart until the wobbles and bumps subside. Continue to beam love, releasing all else, clearing your mind of all else, until the rotation around the Eternal Flame is perfectly smooth. Your Divine Advocates will make adjustments as needed throughout this process. The spinning will slow down and eventually halt.
7. Each member participating in the rebalancing activity is given the Balance and Harmony Elixir energy drink to help stabilize and ground the patterns of balance and harmony within the relationship. Each individual is asked to give a spiritual gift of gratitude to the other.
8. When you are finished, you may continue with the next Scenic Route activity, or your main Divine Advocate escorts you to the TLC Bath where you will coat yourself in the soothing energies, sip your Graceful Integration Elixir, and then wrap yourself in the Resiliency Comfort Wrap. Do not drive, operate heavy machinery, or do any activities that are dangerous, or that require you to be fully attentive, until you feel fully shifted back to a normal waking state. Take some time to journal or take notes before your memory of the experience fades.

Continuing Thoughts

The Harmony and Balance work is just one tiny piece of a larger process. It can help you to imagine stabilizing the relationship between people for a time, but if you do not seek to change the cause of the imbalances--the system will fall into wobble again. Part of the energetic support is to assist you to become more aware of the nature of the imbalances so that you can begin to "Tag, Refuse, Rescript" the dynamics that are dysfunctional.

It may be a good idea to journal your thoughts or repetitive issues that come up. Some imbalances or challenges may actually intensify after doing this work in order that you gain greater insight and awareness. Remember that the point of the work is to learn and grow beyond the distortions that create disharmony within the relationship, not to just wave a magic wand and make them go away. You learn nothing by having your distortions removed without also gaining awareness and mastery over them. True balance and harmony begins within.

"After the game, the king and pawn go into the same box."

Italian Proverb

Scenic Route Activity #7 B
The Stage of Life

Environment Setting: Garden of the Little Ones, amphitheater stage, or dedicated indoor stage if you prefer.

Purpose: The Stage of Life is a platform for you to become aware of the inner dynamics of interaction so that you are not at the mercy of dysfunctional patterns or perceptual distortions. The stage is used to help you gain perspective, and to work through various choices and possible consequences, so that you can behave with mindful clarity in your decisions.

Usage Suggestions: The Stage of Life is a tool to use anytime you need to work through an issue, conflict, or need to establish a clear plan of action. It can be very useful in helping to shift your own perspectives and to gain wisdom and understanding of your own internal processes, as well as the ways that we interact with one another that are not authentic. Use it as often as the need emerges. The more practice you get using this technique, the better you will get at scripting your life to be something you enjoy instead of something you have to survive.

Activity Props: You can use theater costumes, funny glasses, sunglasses, hats, gloves, stage props, a puppet theater, or anything that helps you to play various parts within the same "scene". You can imagine your old high school theater or some other stage that you can easily visualize.

Summary: This activity will be like living in a dress rehearsal. You get to watch or participate, as you wish. You can have other actors (or your Divine Advocates) play a specific "drama" from your life, or you can pretend that you and those involved are actors playing the scene out with one another. You are to identify who is playing the victim, the bad guy, the rescuer, the dumb blonde, the angry loner, or whatever "roles" you can tag. Once you have identified and tagged the actors with their various characterizations, then you get to refuse those roles and rescript the interaction to be something more enjoyable. The goal is to rewrite a script that maximizes the good and minimizes the suffering of everyone involved. The best types of scripts you can recreate are those that allow the authentic Sacred Self of each participant to come to the surface--a scene where everyone is beautiful, compassionate, and full of love. "Tag, Refuse. Rescript."

The stage is meant to be playful, not stressful. It is *not* designed to be a space where you work through traumatic matters that are best left within the office of a professional therapist. The stage is a way for you to find creative solutions to cope with everyday kinds of dramas. This is where you learn that when you change your own role in a story, everything else changes with it. Your Guide Team will function as behind the scenes directors, makeup people, lighting, and so on. The director will be one of your Divine Advocates that you can imagine as being particularly dispassionate. This director will help you in the removal of emotional reactivity when you examine motivations, behavior, and characterizations. No blame--all game. Have fun with it and gain insight.

Helpers: Your entire Guide Team and various Divine Advocates may be present in this activity.

New Concepts: The Drama, Drama, Drama Elixir.

Intentions Supporting Activity

- Intentions added from anywhere else in the book that are relevant to this work.
- All Assistance, as appropriate, for any matter that needs attention.
- Support to tag the various unconscious roles that are played in day-to-day interactions in order to free oneself from those limits.
- Growing awareness of unconscious dysfunctional patterns of behavior.
- Cultivating the ability to refuse playing a role that is out of alignment with the qualities and characteristics of the Sacred Self.
- Cultivating the ability to refuse supporting others to continue playing roles with you that are out of alignment with their Sacred Selves.
- Support to change the dynamics of an interaction by changing the dynamics of personal choice and behavior.
- All Assistance to support the Highest Outcome for any situation, event, or interaction.

- Support to make decisions that allow the Sacred Self to star as often as possible in real life.
- Support to bring a sense of joy and adventure into the art of living.
- Support to find the path of ones highest potential with maximum joy and minimal suffering.
- *Drama, Drama, Drama Elixir*: energy drink used to reveal and uncover the hidden roles and dramas that are played out in interpersonal interactions, such that they can be easily and playfully Tagged, Refused, and Rescripted.
- Listed intentions reaffirmed as part of the Cooperative Contract already signed over.
- Engagement of this activity, if a Cooperative Contract has not yet been signed, an affirmation of acceptance of these intentions, corrected in perfection, and brought within Divine Will.

Action Statement:
"I request to initiate the Stage of Life, now please."

Note: *Skip to step 2 if you are coming immediately from the previous activity.*

Step-by-Step Activity Instructions:

1. Enter *Angelscape* at the Lotus Pool. Complete the spouting Water Breath Cleanse, sip your Lotus Nectar Elixir, and put on your Work Wrap to prepare for your journey. When you feel ready, you may continue.
2. A helper escorts you into the Garden of the Little Ones. You may proceed to the outdoor amphitheater, or to an indoor theater, if you prefer to be in a more "realistic" stage setting. Your Divine Advocates come dressed up as stagehands and crew. One of your Divine Advocates shows up dressed up like the director. You are given the Drama, Drama, Drama Elixir to support the process.
3. You are given the choice to be an actor in the scene or to view it from the audience. You are asked to bring up a current "drama" in your life that you would like to play out to provide insight and guide the energies to a desired

outcome. Make your selection and then decide whether you and the actual people will be the actors or whether you will be working with the director to cast other players for those roles. When you have decided, a gong is sounded three times and the actors begin to show up for the scene.

4. Imagine that the director begins telling the actors about the scene, what goes on in the scene, and the roles the various actors will play. What are the "tags" for each character? What are the inner motivations of each player? What circumstances or back stories contribute to the complexity of the motivations? What is the exact behavior or situation without an emotional element? What about the behavior or situation is being misinterpreted or being seen through distortions? Get into the meat of what the scene is founded upon. Where is the comedy? Where is the tragedy?
5. Play out the scene as you remember it, except with exaggerated details to heighten the sense of drama. The director stops at key points to observe, make characterizations, and to punctuate the moments of dramatic tension so that it can be objectively dissected. What are the roles being played? All of the actors are given nametags that define the role they are playing.
6. You are empowered to find the nametag with the title of the role you are playing in the drama, and toss it into the fireplace. Everyone else then rips up his or her nametags. The old script is given to the players and everyone gets to rip it to confetti. The shreds are placed in the fireplace. Imagine that each player now gets a nametag that simply says, "Sacred Self".
7. You and the other members of the drama are given the opportunity to creatively rewrite the drama in order that the maximum good unfolds, and that the Sacred Self of each individual is coaxed out of the background and into the light. Let the director give you advice on how you can construct this kind of scene. Play several options out and find the one that you feel the best about. Once you have found the best outcome you can think of, sign it, and hand it to the director or heave it into the fireplace to give it to God. Request that it be corrected in perfection for the Highest Possible Outcome.

8. Once you have handed over the best script you can, you release the outcome into Divine Hands and allow the appropriate changes to be made. Light a candle on behalf of the Highest Possible Outcome to unfold for all involved within Divine Will.
9. When you are finished, your main Divine Advocate escorts you to the TLC Bath where you will coat yourself in the soothing energies, sip your Graceful Integration Elixir, and then wrap yourself in the Resiliency Comfort Wrap. Do not drive, operate heavy machinery, or do any activities that are dangerous, or that require you to be fully attentive, until you feel fully shifted back to a normal waking state. Take some time to journal or take notes before your memory of the experience fades.

Continuing Thoughts

The stage is a way to examine possible outcomes or to reweave the dynamics of a drama that is in progress. We can also use the stage as a way to play out old dramas that require closure, or to examine repeating dramas/issues that we have not grown beyond yet. It can sometimes be difficult to examine our own limited motivations or flaws, but the stage gives us a way to do it in a playful and non-judgmental way. It is especially helpful to imagine that the people with whom you have trouble are actually good friends who are just playing roles of conflict with you. You can play the role in the scene, and then laugh and hug each other because it isn't "real". Change the dynamic and change the story. If you can change your perception of an enemy into a friend, you have actually changed an enemy into a friend. No one can be your enemy *without your consent.* You may not be able to change their perception of you, but you can change your perception of them and try to hold them in the best possible light. Change the dynamic from one angle and change the story. "Tag. Refuse. Rescript."

You can also combine the Stage of Life with the Wishing Well activity to play out things that you would like to manifest. It does not always have to be about fixing things that have gone wrong, but can also be about empowering things that are wonderful and in Divine Alignment that you would like to see happen in your life.

Summary and Wrap Up

Complementary Activities

- Organize a family reunion, or a family trip to the beach.
- Watch old home movies of family events and good times.
- Pull out the family albums and reminisce.
- Attend a play or a dress rehearsal.
- Join or attend an "improve" theater that uses spontaneous cues from the audience to set up a drama without a prewritten script.
- Smudge your home with incense, white sage, or other cleansing herbs.
- Create a picture collage of family members.
- Create a shelf of remembrance for passed over loved ones.
- Connect with old friends, forgive and release grudges.

Project Ideas

When you work with the family system, it can be helpful to actually clear the family home of clutter and debris. Set up a spring cleaning day with your family that culminates in a yard sale. Use the proceeds of the yard sale to do something fun and family related.

Reflection Questions

1. Describe how you were feeling before and after the activities.
2. What were the most vivid details of your imagery during the activities?
3. Describe your helpers, the tools, and their assistance.
4. What surprised you the most about your experiences?
5. What was your favorite activity in Section 7?
6. What was your least favorite activity in Section 7?
7. Can you integrate your new skills into your more familiar practices?
8. Were there any details that seemed highlighted to you that you might want to think about?
9. Do you feel inspired to do any research in any other related area? If so, what is it?
10. How do you encourage other people to be the best that they can be?

11. Did you find that you take on particular roles often, and if so, how can you proactively script your behavior to change that role?
12. Have you noticed that your interactions with others have changed after doing the work in this section? In what ways has it changed?

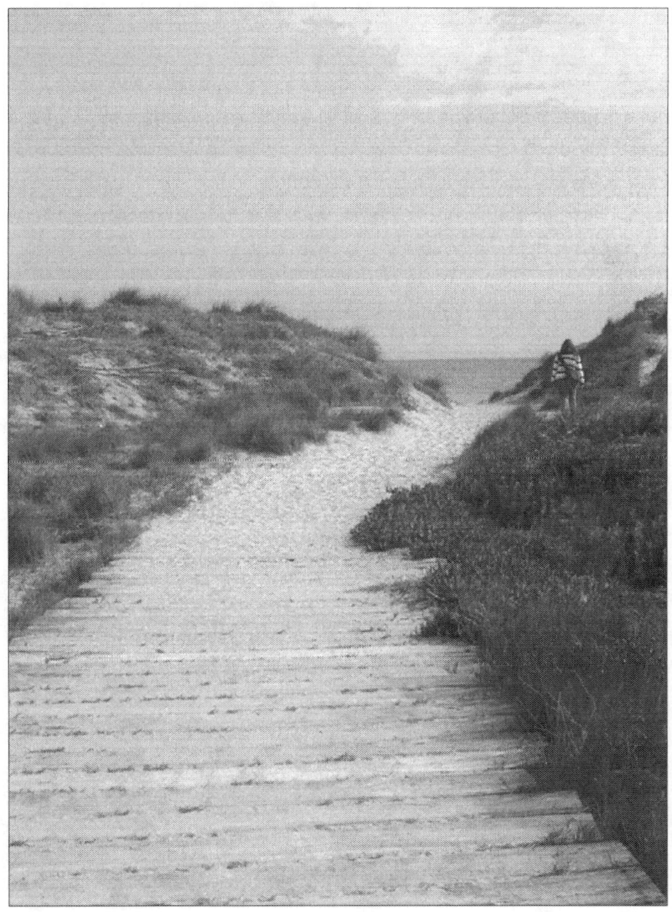

The reunion is never far away. Go back any time you wish.

Photograph 90914
by morguefile.com
user: ariadna

Focus Group Feedback

Sharon

Family Care and Assistance Party

I thought this was one of the most fun and nicest of all the activities so far. I *loved it*! Plus, it just made me laugh. I enter into the Chamber of Light with excitement. I feel it's going to be a fun day. I light my candles and walk down to the Eternal Flame. I am met by one of my angels dressed in a tank top and Bermuda shorts. Then, looking something like a rock star, wearing sunglasses and sunscreen on his nose, is Archangel Michael carrying a beach chair. Another Divine Advocate walks out next, and then Jesus, who is also dressed in beach attire carrying a beach ball under his arm.

Jesus claps his hands and says, "Let's go." We all laugh and walk down to the beach. There are many, many people there. Some are family and friends that are still alive and others that have passed. It is so marvelous to see them all so happy, talking, joking and enjoying themselves. I stand and take a minute to drink in the scene before me. How perfect, how simply perfect. There is music playing in the background. A volley ball game is in progress on the right end of the beach and others are playing a rowdy game of horseshoes. Laughter fills the air and it is magical. My (deceased) dad walks up and gives me a big, big hug. (*Nobody* gives better hugs than my dad and man do I miss them. He could make everything better with one of his hugs.) It was so good to see him again. I miss him so much.

My grandparents are here and so many more people. The more I look around, the more faces I see, the happier I feel that they have all come. It's an amazingly wonderful feeling of coming home. There are also many animals. My beloved dogs and cats that have passed over are there. The dogs are running in and out of the water chasing each other and my cats lying in the sun on cushioned chairs that have been placed along the beach. It is a perfectly beautiful, sunny day! I run and start to hug people, some I recognize, others I don't, but I feel I love them all deeply. There is lots of food, fun and barbecue.

Jesus announces that it's time to begin the cleansing. About half the people there join me happily in the water. The others stand on the beach watching, talking and laughing. Others are sitting by the edge of the water, just close enough to get their feet wet. The water feels good. It feels fabulous to be there in the water, to wash clean some of the debris that has lodged itself deep lately. It's a beautiful feeling of oneness sharing the light of God with all my loved ones--past, present and future. It excites me to be apart of this. The balls are released, hundreds of them. They are different sizes and colors that leave streaks of light as they are tossed like shooting stars, creating a matrix of lines interconnecting each person to the other. It's fabulous. Everyone is involved; the beach is alive with laughter and joy.

A radiant rainbow appears in the sky, as if to say that its time for the rainbow colored Resiliency Comfort Wrap. As I am wrapped, I reach out to touch my Sacred Self File, which is bound in beautiful brown leather with an embossed picture of the Celtic Tree of Life. My heart leaps a little as I touch it in recognition of my true self. Many people are still swimming playing and laughing as I make my way up to leave. What a beautiful day, what a beautiful feeling of oneness, of service, of gratitude for such a wonderful gift.

Relationship Rebalancing

I actually started to do this activity a few times, but always walked away. Not because I was afraid of it or apprehensive--I guess I felt I just needed to "prepare" for it. I feel in many ways I've been preparing for this particular activity for a long time now. I felt strong going into it and very protected, so it ended up being a very helpful healing activity. I know this is only the start, but it was a good start.

I enter into the Chamber of Light. I light candle for myself as well as each of my seven brothers and sisters that will take part in this activity. When I am done Jesus, Blessed Mother, Archangel Raphael and other helpers emerge out of the Eternal Flame. Jesus sounds the gong and in walks my four sisters and three brothers. To be honest, I'm surprised some of them show up, but I am very glad they do. We all take our seats on the "scale". Some are reluctant at first (kind of with a "this is stupid" attitude), but with some gentle nudging from my team they take their places.

The Blessed Beach Ball starts out in my hands. I toss it to my sister across the way, she tosses it back. I toss it to another sister, and she tosses it back. I toss the orb of light to each of my siblings and they toss it back to me. After the last of my siblings tosses the original orb of light back to me, three other orbs are tossed into the circle. With the extra balls, each one of us is an active participant in the activity, whether throwing or receiving. As the orbs continue to be passed back and forth and around, a circle of light is being created between all of us that grows larger and larger and until it encircles the group. There is laughter and peace, no tension, no airs just cooperation and love. It's nice for a change.

We then throw the orbs of light into the Eternal Flame where they explode into beautiful glimmers of light that fall softly upon each of us. As this happens, the scales begin to spin. The beams from our hearts connect in the center of the Eternal Fame, like spokes on a wheel--all connected but separate. The scales spin and we all hold on, laughing like we are on a carnival ride. Hair flying, hearts racing, joy-filled and gleeful. It is nice, happy and light. As the spinning starts to slow and stop, we all get off laughing and joking. We take the Harmony drink and clink glasses. We hug each other and say, “I love you.” They leave. I stay behind to thank my team. Jesus gives me a wink and a pat on the shoulder, “Good job.” On the way out, I light a candle for my mom and dad. I leave a white rose in front of the Blessed Mother Statue and a red rose in front of the statue of Jesus. Before I go, I turn around and blow my team a kiss of gratitude and leave.

Laura

Family Care and Assistance Party

I felt great power being called in upon the invocation of the term “Conduit of God's Grace and Love”. It was like I was really tapping into a limitless well of special energy available to anyone who can recognize it.

My helpers were my usual pair--Archangels Michael and Raphael; however this time they were joined by Archangel Gabriel. As I went to light the candle to begin, it became a massive ivory colored, three wick candle upon a golden candle stand. It was the first time I’d been given that visual. I knew I was calling in a tremendous energy when I saw it. I was led to reach into the candle flames and withdrew a basketball-sized ball of “liquid light”--sort of like looking at rain during a sun shower. I sort of melded into it--which seemed to establish the connection we were looking to establish here.

The beach was breath taking! The water was a beautiful blue-green and the sand made of clear quartz. I was taken to one of the Keys in Florida as a supporting visual. I heard crowd/party noises; seagulls and waves fill the air. I was aware of the three groups I had called in for this who were up and down the beach, spread comfortably out.

When we all hit the water, something that has happened each time I’ve gone into water in *Angelscape*, I became liquid energy instead of a body in water. I had no boundaries of physical form. I dissolved and the water flowed freely through/in/out/around my “essence” in the water. The healing didn’t wash over or through me, I just became the healing and cleansing. I love that feeling.

Here's a neat part--the orbs of light are the same ones I saw and handled back at the beginning of this exercise! Again, I heard the term "liquid light". I moved to each group, lightly batting the ball from person to person off our fingertips, as though handling something sacred. I felt a knitting together of our collective energies with one another and God, all at the same time.

Before being given a towel and/or wrap, I had a warm shower--then I put on the coverings. I was shown to a beach chaise for a nap in the comfortably warm sunshine.

Relationship Rebalancing

I actually did two of these relationships/small systems. The first was me, my husband, his business, a company he's in litigation with, and our lawyer. There's a cheery combo! The second was my husband and a government body he's negotiating with at the moment. I knew I was in for quite a ride with this cast of characters!

When group 1 sat on the scales/teeter-totter, at first they were taking the ball of light and heaving it at each other like dodge ball. It was adversarial, to say the least! I knew there were issues still to be cleared, but as I started to say to myself "this isn't good!", a warm shower of illuminated rain washed over all concerned. Right away, the orbs of light stopped being dodge balls and became a gentle thing flowing off our fingertips. I heard the terms, "peacefully, gently, amicably."

When group 2 sat down, it was the same deal. The orb of light became a missile! The illuminated shower began, along with a voice saying, "Divine Justice-Divine Healing." Again, the parties involved began lightly touching the orb of light with their fingertips instead of hurling it at each other.

When group 1 began the heart light exchange, out of the center of the teeter-totter came a maypole type pole with a golden ball on top. The ribbons of heart light came from the heart of one, to the top of the pole and then to the other parties. It was like the heart light was still being transmuted somehow, or adjusted in some way, on it's way to the other party. The whole experience felt light and cleansing. Like a celebration. Ditto with group 2. Then as both groups began the spinning, the aura around each became a vivid lavender color. I heard for group 2, that it was right action, Divine understanding-- and the rotation became the horizontal infinity sign. Group 1, where I was, stayed in the lavender light until everything sort of dissolved under us.

The energy drinks passed out to each group were used to toast one another. There was an amicable feeling in the circle. I was given a small box I knew to be a symbol of "I'm sorry". My husband got one meaning "Thank you". Our lawyer got one that symbolized "Well done". I didn't get a meaning for the company in litigation, but I can guess because I saw the classic brown envelope used in movies; fat with money, being slipped into a breast pocket of a suit coat worn by someone whose face I couldn't see.

In the other group of my husband and the government agency, there was a toast to "A perfect settlement". (Yippee!) My husband and the symbolic government agent actually hooked arms to drink their drinks! That's got to be a *good thing*, as Martha Stewart would say. Everyone left the chamber laughing and talking easily.

The Stage of Life

The title of this play was on the cover of the script and it was "The Office Has to Move". I have asked my husband to move his office out of the house because it's become too chaotic and the atmosphere in the house has suffered for it. He's agreed, but is being a bit passive-aggressive--doing nothing to move things along. The stage is set with boxes of stuff everywhere, piles of papers strewn around on every surface. There's a "Fibber McGee's Closet" prop (from an old radio show) which, every time the door opens, tons of stuff falls out and knocks over the hapless person who opened the door. You get the picture.

There is really only a couple of people in this play. I felt, and the director agreed, that I'd "let go" and allow Spirit to handle this mess, so I sat in the audience. My husband was played by a mule! Now don't get me wrong, I actually do like mules, but this was pretty perfect "typecasting"! His inner-motivation was instantaneous: *No!* If I ignore this, it's not happening! The comedy is obviously the mule, the tragedy is that the longer he waits, the more stuff piles up, and the more he hurts himself with the disorganization. He has already lost crucial documents in the piles of paper and only puts himself further and further behind the eight-ball. But I am determined to sit in the audience and just let this scenario play itself out. I am not the director, the producer, the damsel in distress under the piles of paper (my old job), or the heroine who saves the day. Today, I am just the observer.

As the scene begins, the mule is sitting on his haunches refusing to budge. The papers and boxes are piled all around, but on stage left we see a bulldozer coming slowly into view, pushing all the mess before it. Even when it reaches the mule, who is still reciting his lines about not budging, the bulldozer gently but firmly gathers it up with all the accumulated mess and pushes it off stage. I was impressed that the bulldozer is "Divine Order", as in, it's at work whether we can see it or not. There is a moment of silence. Nothing moves. Nobody says a word. From stage left comes a small man who looks exactly like M. Gandhi in a janitor's uniform, walking quietly along, sweeping the stage with a big push broom, and then exiting stage right. In the background, a window (I just notice as part of the scenery) fills with rising sun light. The sunlight fills the stage. I hear the term "rebirth".

All I had to do was step back and "Let God Work".

When we re-wrote the drama, the bulldozer was a moving van. The mule was once again my human husband. He's telling me, while I'm still sitting in the audience, that he's ready to get the stuff moved and that he's got someone to work for him part-time. He is putting boxes in the truck. The truck is full, he drives it off the stage to the right. Again, sunlight fills the stage, which this time doesn't need to be swept. It's clean. The audience behind me and I jump to our feet and clap wildly, yelling, "Bravo!" My husband comes out and takes a bow.

That is the script handed over-- I light three candles--for him, the company and his new secretary--but hear they also represent *thought* activating *principle* creating *results*-- something I teach all the time at church. As I close a door on the exercise, I see a sign on the door right in front of my eyes: *Let God work*. Amen to that!

Lourdes

Family Care and Assistance Party

This exercise took the longest for me to complete. I have been very stressed and once I got into the Chamber of light, I couldn't stop crying. I had the Archangels place their hands on my heart for a long time, before the candle lit well. Once on the beach, I found all my inner children. The only other family members there were my grandparents, who have passed. The cleansing in the water took a very long time. I had so much sludge coming out, I was afraid that I was never going to get it all out.

After finally getting the gunk out, the balls came and my little ones loved it. The teenagers played with the younger ones. I stayed on the edge of the beach for a while with my grandparents holding my hands. Eventually one or two of the balls came my way and I tossed them back to the younger children.

When it came time for the wrap, all my children needed a drink first. They all had smoothies in their favorite flavors. I had a strawberry milkshake, which was really odd for me, because I don't usually have milkshakes (except when I was pregnant) and strawberry is not my favorite flavor. I enjoyed this one and drank it all. Then when it came time for the wrap, I received a beautiful jewel toned wrap to help protect me. The angel shields were a crystal clear finish on all the wraps.

As the files were being given out, I realized that for the kids, they turned out to be books that opened to beautiful pages of bright colors swirling around. They brought pure enjoyment to all the kids. My file turned from the capiz shell to a beautiful lepidolite cover and all I did was hold it. It would have been too much for me to open it. I stayed there for a while and finally came back when it was time.

Relationship Rebalancing

I tried this exercise the first time, but was too tired to do it. When I went to *Angelscape*, I sat down in a lounge chair and slept. That was what I needed.

The second time, I went with my higher self to the cavern. [Lourdes has merged the spa and the Chamber of Light together as one work area, which works nicely for her.] My candles all had a pink flame, which was really nice and soothing. When it came time to play with the orb, my husband and two kids had a good time playing with it. It's been a while since we laughed as a family and it was nice to toss the ball around. When it was time to have a spin around the Eternal Flame, I asked that it go slowly since I had already felt dizzy. The flame was a lovely soft pink and it felt nice and warm. Afterwards we all had jeweled colored drinks, which were so nice. I stayed wrapped up in the blanket for the longest time and fell asleep.

Stage of Life

I was reluctant to do this one. I work at a performing arts center and the last thing I wanted to do, even in *Angelscape*, was to be reminded of work. I went up to the theater and had the Drama drink. Archangel Michael was the director. When the time came for the roles, I was the casting director. I asked for my real life family to take on their roles. My daughter and I were victims and my husband the silent hero. My son was a tall wooden soldier. None of us were communicating.

When the time came to tear apart our roles, we were all delighted and we all glowed when we became our Sacred Selves. Actually, we all were glowing a soft rose pink. What was nice was that when the play was being rewritten, we were all around a table discussing options and possibilities for the future. It felt like old times and I loved it. At the end, everyone went home. I stayed behind, took another soothing drink, and was wrapped up in a large medium pink blanket. I stayed in a chaise lounge chair for a while because I was too tired to move.

Section 8
Blooming Your Sacred Self

Activities Introduction

Section 8 Activities create a conceptual ceremony that anchors the Seed of the Sacred Self within and provides protocols to continue forward progress. The seed is used as the symbol of the Sacred Self because a seed is the start of new life. It is a *potential* that can unfold if the seed lands on fertile ground and is tended to take strong root. Human beings are constantly evolving. The Sacred Self is the symbol of the very best you can be and the highest potential you can achieve. It can only exist as an abstract because as soon as you reach higher levels of functioning, there are *always* higher levels to go. The journey and commitment to become a better person is the only thing we can make somewhat tangible.

The cultivation of the Sacred Self is a continuing process of nurturing the blossom that is unfolding within your heart. The flower is used as a metaphor of something you actively need to tend in order for it to express its highest beauty. The Planting of the Seed of the Sacred Self marks the beginning of your journey and commitment to express your very best self in the world. The ceremony will help you to feel released from the limits of who you *were* (warts and all), so that you can embrace the progression into the Sacred Self you are *becoming*. That kind of commitment has the potential to be monumental in the unfolding adventure of your life. How could it not?

The Scenic Route Masterpiece Theater activity assists you to learn more about the qualities of your Sacred Self and how you can listen to the inner guidance it provides. The Sacred Self, your spiritual aspect, has always been the "still small voice" inside your mind. You are brought through activities that remind you what the presence of your Sacred Self feels like as it expresses in your life. The Masterpiece Theater activity is a tool for you to explore the expression of the Sacred Self in practice runs of plausible real life scenarios. It is appropriate to start with the qualities that are closest to your current level of functioning and evolution. Integrating those traits into your life will take intention, support, patience, and practice.

The Scenic Route Tending the Sacred Garden activity is used as a way to provide ongoing nurturing and care so that continuing growth and personal development maintain momentum. We all have to learn how to cope with adversity and to refuse the temptation to entertain negativity. Choosing good care and personal maintenance is far better than having to fix something that has fallen into disrepair. If the Sacred Self is actively tended and nurtured, the "weeds" that begin to grow back can be easily pulled. If the Sacred Self is neglected, the weeds (dysfunctional unconscious distortions) will surface once again. Your perceptual distortions have had active mental pathways for years, perhaps most of your whole life. *It takes time and attention to extinguish the old pathways and to forge new ones.* If you allow yourself to go on autopilot, those former dysfunctional pathways will try to re-establish. You get to choose functioning at higher levels over being at the mercy of a multitude of limiting patterns, but you have to *stay awake* and proactive to do it. The Sacred Garden is a symbolic place for you to go to stay awake and to allow your higher consciousness to continue to make positive headway in your life.

Grow, bloom, shine, and discover.

Photograph 199547
by morguefile.com
user: Lisa Solonynko

Direct Route Activity #8
Planting the Seed of the Sacred Self

Environment Setting: Chamber of Light

Complementary Scenic Route Activities
SR 8 A: Masterpiece Theater
SR 8 B: Tending the Sacred Garden

Purpose: Planting of the Seed of the Sacred Self ushers in the official anchoring of the Sacred Self patterns within ones system. Those patterns serve as a continual guide to cultivate, remember, grow, and bloom the qualities of the Sacred Self in life.

Usage Suggestions: The Planting of the Seed of the Sacred Self activity is a ceremony, not a maintenance protocol. You only have to do it once. You can do it again, if you ever feel the need to, but Tending the Sacred Garden is intended as the maintenance activity. You could always request a "Seed of the Sacred Self Refresher Attunement" as part of an Expansion Attunement session if you would like.

Activity Props: You may use pictures of your favorite flowers, big blossoms, fresh flowers, or do this activity in a blooming garden. You may also wish to have favorite pictures of yourself around as a visual of your best self.

Summary: The Planting the Seed of the Sacred Self is the activity to celebrate the anchoring of the Sacred Self patterns into your heart, protected and nurtured by the ember of the Eternal Flame of God's Grace and Love. The old self is dissolved in the Eternal Flames of God's Grace and Love and reformed with the All Element Mud. The Seed of the Sacred Self is then planted in the heart as a way to imagine the anchoring of the Sacred Self within.

Helpers: All of your Divine Advocates attend the Planting of the Seed of the Sacred Self.

New Concepts: Seed of the Sacred Self, Dissolution, Reconsecration, Sacred Self Refresher Attunement.

Intentions Supporting Activity

- Intentions added from anywhere else in the book that are relevant to this work.
- All Assistance, as appropriate, for any matter that needs attention.
- Preparation of the system to receive anchoring of the Sacred Self patterns and energies.
- Dissolution of distortion, illusion, and limitations, as appropriate.
- Support to refuse temptations or distortions that suppresses the expression of the Sacred Self.
- Sacred Self seen as the version of the self in its highest and purest form, the template of the "self" that God created and intended without distortion of any kind.
- Support to bring physical wellness in alignment with the Sacred Body.
- Support to bring emotional and mental wellness in alignment with the Sacred Heart and Mind.
- Perfected integrity of the system to maintain the foundation for the Sacred Self.
- Anchoring and grounding of the Sacred Self patterns within the system of self.
- Graceful and gentle reconditioning and rectifying of distorted patterns to Sacred Self patterns.
- All guidance and support necessary to succeed anchoring and expressing the Sacred Self in life.
- All guidance and support to make choices and decisions that cultivate the Sacred Self in life, promoting spiritual growth and evolution, and the experience of the goodness of life.
- Support to perceive oneself as an instrument of God's Grace and Love, and as a blessing to the world with humility and grace.
- Support for the Sacred Self to express and manifest as needed during events of great potential and consequence in order to activate free will as an instrument of Divine Will.
- Support for the Sacred Self patterns of one person to call for and entrain the Sacred Self patterns of others, such as a positive domino effect.

- The Sacred Self as an instrument of God's Grace and Love flowing into the world as appropriate and in Divine Alignment.
- *Seed of the Sacred Self*: seen as the full anchoring of the template of the Sacred Self, as God intended, within the Whole Self. The Seed of the Sacred Self grows, takes root, and is seen to blossom at this level of being through graceful personal evolution.
- *Dissolution*: command used by Divine Advocate to initiate the melting away and dissolving of the "former self", and any remaining distortions, such that the Journeyer can experience and imagine being pure spirit.
- *Reconsecration*: command used by Divine Advocate to initiate the reformation and rebuilding of the structure of the self, as a pure and holy vessel of the Sacred Self, such that the Seed of the Sacred Self is planted within "fertile ground" capable of allowing it to take root and blossom.
- *Sacred Self Refresher Attunement*: an Expansion Attunement used as maintenance to revitalize and energize the Seed of the Sacred Self within.
- Listed intentions reaffirmed as part of the Cooperative Contract already signed over.
- Engagement of this activity, if a Cooperative Contract has not yet been signed, an affirmation of acceptance of these intentions, corrected in perfection, and brought within Divine Will.

Action Statement:

"I request to initiate the Planting of the Seed of the Sacred Self, now please."

Step-by-Step Activity Instructions:

1. Enter *Angelscape* at the Lotus Pool. Complete the spouting Water Breath Cleanse, sip your Lotus Nectar Elixir, and put on your Work Wrap to prepare for your journey. When you feel ready, you may continue.
2. A helper escorts you to the Chamber of Light. Light a candle for the Planting of the Seed of the Sacred Self within. Your main Divine Advocate emerges from the Eternal Flame of God's Grace

and Love, holding your Sacred Self file, and hands you the Sacred Self Elixir to drink to prepare your system for the work.

3. The rest of your Divine Advocates and spiritual helpers emerge from the Eternal Flames and form a large circle around the fire. Your main Divine Advocate takes your hand and smiles. You are led directly into the heart of the Eternal Flames of God's Grace and Love. Your main Divine Advocate stands just outside, but near enough to keep you calm and steady. You are reminded to keep breathing and to have faith and trust in the process.
4. Your main Divine Advocate calls for *"Dissolution"*. The sensation feels like the loosening of the sense of self as being separate from the flames until you feel unified with the flames. It is as if your physical body has melted away and what is left is pure spirit and consciousness.
5. Next, your main Divine Advocate calls for *"Reconsecration"*. The ground under the Eternal Flames begins to rise in a funnel of All Element Mud, the physical building blocks of all creation. Your physical body begins to reform and mold itself to be the vessel of your spirit. You are like a clay version of yourself, awaiting new life.
6. The Divine Advocate takes your Sacred Self file and places it inside the Eternal Flame. It transforms into a glowing golden orb the size of an apple. It is the original divine blueprint of you in Sacred Self format. Your Divine Advocate places this seed into an ember of the Eternal Flames of God's Grace and Love and then within your heart. The ember protects this seed from all distortion. Your Divine Advocate calls for *"the Planting of the Seed of the Sacred Self"*.
7. You feel the seed as it is planted within your heart, encased within the ember of God's Grace and Love. Your body and spirit merge together to form the person you were born to be. Your body looks as if normal now, but radiant and glowing from within. You are shown the flower of your soul blossoming with brilliant petals of light. You can feel the roots move down into the earth. The Seed of your Sacred Self is planted in fertile ground.
8. Your Divine Advocate reaches for your hand again, and leads you out of the central flames to the gathered crowd of your helpers. It is a joyous event. They celebrate with you and offer you love and support. Your Divine Advocate says a blessing to conclude the

ceremony. You light a candle for your Sacred Self to bloom and grow with ease and grace.

9. When you are finished, you may continue with the Scenic Route activities, or your main Divine Advocate escorts you to the TLC Bath where you will coat yourself in the soothing energies, sip your Graceful Integration Elixir, and then wrap yourself in the Resiliency Comfort Wrap. Do not drive, operate heavy machinery, or do any activities that are dangerous, or that require you to be fully attentive, until you feel fully shifted back to a normal waking state. Take some time to journal or take notes before your memory of the experience fades.

Continuing Thoughts

Remember that manifesting your Sacred Self in the world is a process and a journey, not an event. Every morning when you wake up, you have a new opportunity to express the very best of yourself into the world. You are asked to be mindful in your actions, thoughts, deeds, and motivations. Often you will succeed in holding yourself to the higher standards of behavior and conduct of your Sacred Self. That is the goal, but you will not always reach that goal. We will sometimes stumble, doubt, fear, and roll around in the usual muck. No one expects you to be a perfect person. That is unreasonable and absurd. The expectation is for you to continually strive to be the best person you can be, to continue to reach for higher functioning, and to continue to reflect upon your journey, your inner motivation, and even your mistakes.

Mistakes happen to be excellent teachers, even if the bill is expensive. You have to be willing to stay awake at your own wheel and to be mindful of the small and big steps you take. Evolution is the goal. Do your best. When you can do better, do better. When you fall, get back up again and use your tools and what you know how to do to create a plan of action to get back on track.

My father used to say, “If it is too hard, you aren’t doing it right.” Do not take yourself too seriously. We are, after all, more like wobbly grinning toddlers just learning to use the potty instead of “making” in our pants. Accidents will happen, no need to complain about it or make it worse by having a tantrum of self-loathing. Just clean it up and keep moving forward. It’s a part of the adventure of life. Sometimes the only sane response is hysterical laughter, sometimes it is a bar of chocolate, a nap, and a few days staring at the wall. Whatever. Do your best. That’s all.

Scenic Route Activity #8 A
Masterpiece Theater

Environment Setting: Garden of the Little Ones, Stage of Life Theater or outdoor amphitheater

Purpose: The Masterpiece Theater activity is a way for you to get more acquainted with the voice, qualities, and attributes of your Sacred Self so that you can learn to express more of it in life.

Usage Suggestions: You can use this as a continuing way to cultivate and manifest your Sacred Self in life. Use it as often as you feel it will be helpful, when you are reflecting on choices, or when you are actively putting positive energy into the Highest Outcome of a situation (manifestation).

Activity Props: You may use pictures of yourself that you find most beautiful, lists of Sacred Self qualities from the Sacred Self Portrait activity, and the lists of talents, dreams and skills you made during the Wishing Well activity.

Summary: The Masterpiece Theater is an activity that leads you through times in your life when you *did* allow your Sacred Self to shine through. You are asked to remember what strategies you used to push beyond the temptation to suppress it. You are then walked through current challenges so that you can express your Sacred Self within them as practice. This is another option to use in the Stage of Life Theater to help create the strategies and plan of action to empower your Sacred Self be the leading actor in your life.

Helpers: Your Sacred Self, your Stage of Life Crew and Guide Teams, and any other Divine Advocates you wish to include.

New Concepts: Sacred Self Resiliency Wrap.

Intentions Supporting Activity

- Intentions added from anywhere else in the book that are relevant to this work.
- All Assistance, as appropriate, for any matter that needs attention.

- Connection to the guidance and wisdom of the Sacred Self within.
- Support to attend to the voice of the Sacred Self over distortions.
- Support to use evolving insight, mindfulness, and choice to express the Sacred Self as often as possible.
- Support to find joy and freedom in manifesting and expressing the Sacred Self.
- Support to love the self as a work in progress, and as a journey underway, with flexibility, adaptability, and self-compassion.
- Remembrance of instances in life when the Sacred Self did express, and what traits and qualities were accessed.
- Increasing feelings of empowerment, courage, and strength to accomplish what you feel you are called to accomplish.
- Support for the increasing feelings of self worth, purpose, competency, productivity, and to see the self as a blessing to the world.
- *Sacred Self Resiliency Wrap*: used to enhance system integrity and strength to triumph over challenges that require a level of functioning that is not yet mastered (aka: Grace covering the spread).
- Listed intentions reaffirmed as part of the Cooperative Contract already signed over.
- Engagement of this activity, if a Cooperative Contract has not yet been signed, an affirmation of acceptance of these intentions, corrected in perfection, and brought within Divine Will.

Action Statement:
"I request to initiate Masterpiece Theater, now please."

Note: *Skip to step 2 if you are coming immediately from the previous activity.*

Step-by-Step Activity Instructions:

1. Enter *Angelscape* at the Lotus Pool. Complete the spouting Water Breath Cleanse, sip your Lotus Nectar Elixir, and put on your Work

Wrap to prepare for your journey. When you feel ready, you may continue.

2. A helper escorts you to the Garden of the Little Ones. You may meet up with a symbolic version of your own Sacred Self, Little Ones who hold memories of your hopes and dreams, as well as any of your Divine Advocates, Stage of Life helpers, or other helpers.
3. The mood is playful and light. Imagine inhaling the sweet fragrance of the flowers growing in the garden. Several of the flowers remind you of the symbolic flower of your Sacred Self, growing and blooming within your heart. A helper hands you a Sacred Self Elixir, which was gathered from the nectar of those flowers. You sip the nectar and feel it enliven the Sacred Self within you. Your heart feels aglow and buoyant.
4. You and your entourage walk to the Stage of Life. You are told to sit down in the audience and imagine breathing into your heart until you feel a strong presence of your Sacred Self within your system. As you breathe, you become more and more radiant. A sense of peace and joy settles over you and you may experience several moments of bliss. Your heart feels full and complete. This is the sensation of your Sacred Self expressing within your awareness.
5. Your Stage of Life director asks you to remember a time in your life when you felt this kind of inner peace and spiritual presence within you before. Select an instance that your Sacred Self shined in your life. Move on to the stage with other re-enactors so you can replay it in your imagination. Your director will ask you what you were feeling, how you expressed your Sacred Self qualities, and what strategies you used to push past any temptation to suppress that presence. Replay as many instances and memories of your Sacred Self expressing in life as you wish before moving on.
6. Next, the director asks you to select a current challenge to play out. You can select from situations that you fear or some personal challenge that is pushing your growth edges. Play out how you would *normally* behave if you were not centered within the energies of your Sacred Self. "Tag, Refuse, and Rescript" the scene. Rip up and toss the old script and tag(s) into the fireplace.
7. The director instructs you to breathe into your heart until it warms and the blossom of your Sacred Self is bright and active. Imagine growing the presence of your Sacred Self within you until it fills your whole body. You are asked to say, *"I am my Sacred Self."* The

director hands up a beautiful robe for you to wear. It is the Sacred Self Resiliency Wrap and it will help you to bring your Sacred Self to the forefront when you are having difficulty. Put the Sacred Self Resiliency Wrap around you and allow yourself to be supported and strengthened.

8. Now imagine replaying the same challenge or event. Listen to your inner guidance to move fluidly and gracefully through the scene, allowing your Sacred Self to shine and express itself. You sign off on the new scene and tag that simply says, "I am my Sacred Self." All future revised scripts can be titled "I am my Sacred Self" from now on.
9. You may practice with any other current challenges that you wish to empower with the presence of your Sacred Self. Chat with the director about any insights, strategies, and potential applications where you can safely shine your Sacred Self in actual situations. Discuss what you will do to center yourself within your heart when involved in a situation that challenges you in real time.
10. Your director has a surprise for you. Your Sacred Self Portrait is carried into the theater and onto the Stage of Life with much fanfare. It is perhaps more detailed than last you saw it, or perhaps it has modified a bit as you have begun to define and modify your thoughts about your Sacred Self qualities. You are asked where you would like to hang it on the Stage of Life. It is placed there as inspiration for you to express your Sacred Self and to explore more and more aspects of yourself as you grow and evolve.
11. When you are finished, you may continue with the next Scenic Route activity, or your main Divine Advocate escorts you to the TLC Bath where you will coat yourself in the soothing energies, sip your Graceful Integration Elixir, and then wrap yourself in the Resiliency Comfort Wrap. Do not drive, operate heavy machinery, or do any activities that are dangerous, or that require you to be fully attentive, until you feel fully shifted back to a normal waking state. Take some time to journal or take notes before your memory of the experience fades.

Continuing Thoughts

You have been asked to think about your Sacred Self qualities, attributes, and natural talents and skills throughout the course of the *Angelscape* journey. This is a good time to go through your old notes. What were your hopes and dreams as a child? What did you see yourself doing that utilized your Sacred Self qualities? You can use those wishes or dreams to run through updated scenes, inspired by your own childhood innocence and fortified by a lifetime of experience and maturity.

You will find that it gets easier and easier to run through the scenes and rescript them to express your Sacred Self. The easier it becomes here, the easier it will be in real life when you are called to action. If you have to face something that makes you fearful, or that tempts you into falling into distorted or limiting patterns, breathe into your heart and fill your body with the presence of your Sacred Self. The more you allow your Sacred Self to shine, the quicker you will stop feeling like you are *acting*, and more like you are simply growing and evolving into a higher level of relating to yourself and the world around you.

Growth happens in steps, sometimes with bursts of rapid movement. It is important for you to create strategies for maintaining momentum that is both gentle and productive. When you hit a ceiling in your growth, this can often be cause for some frustration, but just as it is important to love yourself "warts and all", you must also honor the process of your own blossoming. Everything happens in perfect time. You, at this level, do not have the wisdom to force the timing of your own breakthroughs. Let them unfold under the oversight of Sacred Self and Divine Wisdom. Use the insight of your own inner guidance to help you find your way.

You are absolutely permitted to "fake it until you make it". You have to establish the new patterns of behaving by exposing yourself to them as often as possible. Once the new pathways are formed, they will become spontaneous and rooted in your true authenticity. Unlearning a lifetime of dysfunctional patterns is a process, but you have to consistently "Tag, Refuse, Rescript" them to finally and fully replace them with something better. You get to choose. You get to decide. Decide well.

"Far away in the sunshine are my highest aspirations. I may not reach them, but I can look up and see their beauty, believe in them, and try to follow where they lead."

Louisa May Alcott

Scenic Route Activity #8 B
Tending the Sacred Garden

Environment Setting: Garden of the Little Ones, personal Sacred Garden

Purpose: This activity provides the tools and protocols useful for the cultivation and development of the Sacred Self. Tending the garden is a tool for you to be mindful of your growth and development, to nurture it, remove the weeds that grow, and to center yourself in the beauty of your inner sacredness.

Usage Suggestions: This is a skills building and teaching activity. It provides you with tools and a working platform to continue to tend and nurture your Sacred Self. I would recommend tending your Sacred Garden as often as you would tend an actual flower garden (that you like and want to keep alive).

Activity Props: You can tend an actual garden, plant, or other landscaping project to help you visualize this activity.

Summary: The Tending the Sacred Garden activity leads you through a process of creating and landscaping an area in the gardens that is your own personal and private space. Your Sacred Garden will symbolize your inner space and the mindful tending that you need to do to grow and bloom your Sacred Self. Your Divine Advocates will assist you to add all of the elements you need and to work with you to weed and water your garden. Several tools will be introduced to you to help you keep your Sacred Garden growing and beautiful.

Helpers: Any of your Divine Advocates or helpers.

New Concepts: Sacred Garden, Golden Watering Can, Golden Rods, "Optimize, Stabilize, Amplify, Seal", Positive Pathway Attunement.

Intentions Supporting Activity:

- Intentions added from anywhere else in the book that are relevant to this work.
- All Assistance, as appropriate, for any matter that needs attention.

- Nurturing the Sacred Self to bloom and grow through the cultivation of positive aspects of your human potential.
- Removal and cleansing of distortions or dysfunctional patterns of behavior as they emerge.
- Support to dissolve the roots of dysfunction and distortion within the system.
- Support to maintain compassionate self-awareness and mindfulness.
- Support for the cultivation of a proactive and effective routine of self-care and maintenance.
- Internal alarms and sense of strong urgency to maintain most beneficial schedule of self-tending, especially when being tempted to engage dysfunctional unconscious patterns.
- Resilience and support to refuse the influence of others who are viewing you through distortions, or who are unable to acknowledge your positive growth.
- Graceful growth and expansion that maintains stability, groundedness, self-acceptance and a healthy sense of self-worth.
- Support for you to be the best person you can be at your level of personal development.
- Support for you to feel momentum to move forward without needing to move forward too fast for optimal growth and evolution.
- Support to stabilize the self and system during growth spurts and times of rapid expansion.
- *The Sacred Garden*: used as a symbolic activity to cultivate the positive qualities of the Sacred Self and "Tag, Refuse, and Rescript" the distortions as they emerge.
- *Golden Watering Can*: used as a delivery system to move the Sacred Self Elixir energies to the symbolic blooms of the Sacred Self, to enliven and strengthen the Sacred Self to express in life.
- *Golden Rods*: used as follow up support to extinguish and dissolve the roots and origins of distortions as they emerge, and also as fertilizer for the Sacred Self.
- *Positive Pathway Attunement*: an Expansion Attunement protocol to highlight, empower, and strengthen newly

rescripted positive pathways and to weaken, dismantle, and extinguish negative pathways of distortion.

- *"Optimize, Stabilize, Amplify, Seal"*: intention command used to request that a healing process be optimized to the Journeyer, the various elements stabilized as a coherent unit, then amplified to the optimal intensity for maximum benefit, then sealed in perfection such that the integrity of the process is sustained over time.
- Listed intentions reaffirmed as part of the Cooperative Contract already signed over.
- Engagement of this activity, if a Cooperative Contract has not yet been signed, an affirmation of acceptance of these intentions, corrected in perfection, and brought within Divine Will.

Action Statement:
"I request to Tend the Sacred Garden, now please."

Note: *Skip to step 2 if you are coming immediately from the previous activity.*

Step-by-Step Activity Instructions:

1. Enter *Angelscape* at the Lotus Pool. Complete the spouting Water Breath Cleanse, sip your Lotus Nectar Elixir, and put on your Work Wrap to prepare for your journey. When you feel ready, you may continue.
2. A helper escorts you to the Garden of the Little Ones. You may meet up with your main Divine Advocate and any other helpers as you wish. You are escorted through the main garden area to another area of the garden that is more secluded. You are asked to select and create your Sacred Garden, where you will symbolically tend to your own blossoming potential.
3. Your helpers assist you in any way you feel is appropriate to set up your sacred garden. Select where you will place your flowerbed and whatever other plants you want. You may place a comfortable meditation bench, perhaps a birdbath, a well, an outdoor fire pit, grotto, a table, a reclining chair for sunning yourself, and so on. This space is your private back yard and you can make it as multi-purpose as you wish so that it is a place that you enjoy and use often. You may add your own private Lotus Pool if you wish. This

space can be modified and expanded upon as you grow and develop.

4. Your Divine Advocate brings you to the flowerbed where you see flowers that remind you of the blooming Sacred Self within your heart. You are asked to meditate on the flowers, which represent the many qualities and attributes of your Sacred Self. Meditate on the various qualities that the flowers represent to you. As you consider these qualities, you are to acknowledge yourself for having those qualities, such as love, faith, kindness, compassion, wisdom, competence, and so on. As you meditate on those sacred qualities, imagine breathing in through your heart to fill yourself up with the vibrations and patterns of that quality.
5. As you meditate on your sacred qualities, and nurture their expression within your system, be mindful of any negative backtalk that is not accepting these qualities. The negative backtalk are the weeds of self-doubt and limitation. You may be tempted to listen to them, but it is your duty and responsibility to refuse them as they emerge. See them as weeds that you pull. As you pull them, you are instructed to say, *"I refuse this and all distortions like it."*
6. Imagine pulling all the rest of the weeds until you have a pile. When you are finished, ask your Divine Advocate to burn the pile of weeds with the Eternal Flame of God's Grace and Love. You may repeat, *"I refuse these distortions"* as the pile is set on fire. Turn your attention back to the flowerbed, full of beauty, and imagine breathing through your heart until the presence of your Sacred Self is bright and strong within you. When you feel your inner sacredness and beauty fill you up, you are instructed to say, *"I am my Sacred Self."*
7. Your Divine Advocate hands you a golden watering can that is filled with the Sacred Self Elixir. You may take a sip and then water the garden, especially where the weeds have grown. Drink down whatever is left over in the watering can once you have finished watering the whole garden.
8. Next, your Divine Advocate hands you small golden rods, the size of pencils. The golden rods are to be inserted where the weeds began to grow. They tag and target the roots of distortion and self-doubt until they are finally dissolved. You may use as many of them as you wish. They represent the entire process of tagging, refusing, and then repatterning to your Sacred Self.

9. When you are finished with your work, your Divine Advocate asks you to wash up after the dirty work of pulling weeds. It is now your Divine Advocates turn to tend your Sacred Garden with as many other helpers as you would like. You do not have to tend your Sacred Garden alone. Your helpers turn their attention to your garden while you clean up.
10. When you are finished, your main Divine Advocate escorts you to the TLC Bath where you will coat yourself in the soothing energies, sip your Graceful Integration Elixir, and then wrap yourself in the Resiliency Comfort Wrap. Do not drive, operate heavy machinery, or do any activities that are dangerous, or that require you to be fully attentive, until you feel fully shifted back to a normal waking state. Take some time to journal or take notes before your memory of the experience fades.

Continuing Thoughts

The Sacred Garden itself is a conceptual tool that you can use to help you stay on track with your growth and development. It gives you the chance to take an abstract process and transform it into a more tangible one. Becoming a better person is essentially the process of dumping negative qualities for positive ones. Tending the Sacred Garden is another way to “Tag, Refuse, Rescript”.

Tending the Sacred Garden is also another way to initiate a healing session for yourself, such as passive sleep healing sessions and the active Team Self-Healing sessions. You can be flexible in the way you see your Sacred Garden since it is a metaphor for your personal system. You can play with the imagery and the tools in whatever way works best for you. Please see the Golden Rod Team Self-Healing description, which allows you to visualize your physical self as the Sacred Garden.

The Stage of Life can be used as a follow up activity if you notice that there are certain distortions that create complications and challenges in the way you interact with others. It is appropriate for you to take those dramas, fueled by the distortion, to the Stage of Life to work through it and rescript the outcome to be in alignment with the Sacred Selves of all involved. In addition, you can ask for a “Positive Path Empowerment” Expansion Attunement, after weeding, to entrain your system to create strong pathways for the positive patterns to establish and thrive and the negative ones to extinguish.

Golden Rod Team Self-Healing Session

You can use this technique as an active healing session that you can do in cooperation with your Healing Team. You can select an issue, or several issues, that you need to work on dissolving at the core. These will be issues that are more entrenched and distortions that have had a lot of "play time" in the circuits of your energy system. You will use your physical body as the "garden" in this exercise. Your Healing Team will tell you *where* in your body you have the energy pathways of distortion. They will indicate the spots by a spontaneous twitch, an itch, a pressure, or a little jab.

They will get your attention to the area on your body that needs to have a Golden Rod tapped into it. When you get the prompt where on your body you need to imagine tapping in the Golden Rod, you will imagine tapping it in *while reciting the positive affirmation*. You can use your actual hands to physically tap on your body when you can reach the spot. Where you cannot reach the spot, you will imagine your Healing Team using a little hammer to tap the Golden Rod into the area that has been revealed. When you have gone through all your issues and performed the tap/rescript as often as it was indicated, you will ask your Healing Team to initiate the Positive Pathway Attunement to activate the positive pathways and gracefully dissolve the distorted ones.

- Lie down, get comfortable, and connect with God and your Healing Team. Request a *Golden Rod Team Self-Healing Session*.
- Pick an issue, or list of issues, to work with during the session. You will be dealing with one issue at a time, but you can run down a list of many in the single session for time management.
- For the issue you are going to work with, formulate a positive, present-tense affirmation to use as the rescripted perception. If you are sick, for example, you could use the affirmation of, "My body is healthy and vibrant." You could also use, "I am healthy and vibrant." The affirmation should counteract the distortion you seek to dissolve.
- Indicate to your Healing Team that you are ready and waiting for their prompts as far as which area on your body needs the Golden Rods. When you feel it, use your fingers and imagine tapping in a Golden Rod while reciting the positive affirmation. If you cannot physically reach the spot, you may imagine your Healing Team tapping it in for you with a little golden hammer.

- Continue until you no longer feel any pings or pangs going on in your body. When you are finished with one issue, you can begin on another and repeat the process. Do as many as you feel you can, but try to keep the session under an hour long.
- When all the Golden Rods for all the issues have been properly tapped and rescripted, request for your Healing Team to initiate the Positive Pathway Empowerment. Imagine one of your Divine Advocates putting his/her Sword of Light down into your head and body and then spinning it like a top to initiate the positive path activations. You may feel a rush of warmth or some other energetic shift.
- Once your positive pathways have been empowered, ask to *"Optimize, Stabilize, Amplify, and Seal"* the pathways in perfection under God's oversight and authority.
- Close the session with the TLC Bath, Graceful Integration Elixir, and the Resiliency Comfort Wrap. Do whatever else you feel prompted to do, like take a shower, dance, sing, shake your body around, walk in the sunshine, journal, and so on.

More Continuing Thoughts

This Golden Rod session may be a very good way to imagine disrupting the circuitry of the pathways of distortion through the energy system of your body. You may have to do many sessions, sometimes working on the same issues. The idea is to continue to degrade the pathways and circuits of the distortions wherever they are found. One session may pave the way for the next session to be even more productive and more deeply entrenched pathways to be fleshed out and finally dissolved. You have to keep feeding your system the rescripted perception, the new positive affirmation, and start getting the positive perception as much "play time" on the pathways of your system as possible. It may be a long journey, but keep moving forward. Persistence is the key to success.

Summary and Wrap Up

Complementary Activities

- Research about your "flower".
- Buy fresh flowers to put in your home.
- Grow a plant.
- Water the plants you have.

- Practice integrating your Sacred Self into situations that require it.
- Paint a picture of your Sacred Garden.
- Decorate your home with artwork that reminds you of your Sacred Garden.

Project Ideas

Obviously, creating a real Sacred Garden for you to use as a personal meditation spot would be a fabulous idea if you like gardening. You can use the time that you are tending your real garden to imagine tending your inner Sacred Garden. Those of you who do not have a green thumb, however, may want to skip this and just start with one single houseplant. You do not want to engage in an activity that you are likely to fail, creating guilt or shame. Create a garden if it makes you happy. If you are not good growing things, you can create a rock garden or a meditation garden that does not require a lot of green thumbing.

Reflection Questions

1. Describe how you were feeling before and after the activities.
2. What were the most vivid details of your imagery during the activities?
3. Describe your helpers, the tools, and their assistance.
4. What surprised you the most about your experiences?
5. What was your favorite activity in Section 8?
6. What was your least favorite activity in Section 8?
7. Can you integrate your new skills into your more familiar practices?
8. Were there any details that seemed highlighted to you that you might want to think about?
9. Do you feel inspired to do any research in any other related area? If so, what is it?
10. What did the flower of your soul look like?
11. How do you intend to cultivate your Sacred Self qualities in life?
12. What will be the easiest quality to cultivate?
13. What quality will take time to cultivate?
14. How many times do you remember expressing some of your Sacred Self qualities in life?
15. What Sacred Self qualities would like to shine more often?

16. What sensation do you get, if any, when you say, *"I am my Sacred Self?"*
17. How did your Sacred Self Portrait evolve, if at all, since the last time you saw it?
18. Have you recently expressed your Sacred Self in a situation where you surprised and amazed yourself or others? How was it different from usual?
19. What Sacred Self qualities did you affirm in the Sacred Garden activity?
20. What weeds did you have to pull and what distortion did they stand for?
21. Were you able to use the Stage of Life to work through any recurring distortions?
22. How does it feel when you fill yourself up with the positive energy of your Sacred Self?

Focus Group Feedback

Sharon

Planting the Seed of the Sacred Self

This was a beautiful experience. I notice that the activities that I feel are most important to me, I usually run into some kind of internal interference that I have to push through to get where I want to go. But that's okay, because at least now I'm aware of what's going on, can address it, move past it, and go forward. So, it's all good.

I enter the Chamber of Light where one of my angels is standing waiting for me. He always gives me a sense of protection and peace. I light my candle and move down toward the Eternal Flame. I'm nervously excited about this exercise and my angel puts his beautiful gold wing around me in silent reassurance. Jesus emerges from the Eternal Flame accompanied by the Blessed Mother. She hands me a thick green drink that tastes a lot like very strong medicine. The rest of my team appears.

Jesus takes my hand and guides me lovingly into the Eternal Flame. I take a couple deep breaths to try to settle myself a bit. Then the "Dissolution" starts. It was pretty amazing. I felt like I was a part of the flames flickering, dancing, and twirling. It was lovely and very freeing. Jesus calls for the "Reconsecration" to begin and the earth rises up from the flame and creates an "earthen vessel" waiting to be awakened to a new awareness and life. Then Jesus places the seed with my heart. The "mud" melts off and I am glowing a magnificent white and gold light. A large, glimmering, pure white rose with dozens and dozens of petals appears surrounded by plumeria flowers. The roots go down into the ground and stabilize me. For just a moment, I can smell the rose and plumeria. How marvelous. Jesus reaches in to help me out of the Flames.

My team surrounds me with love and reassurance. I know this is a very special day, although I get the feeling that I don't realize just how special it really is, not yet anyway. I thank Jesus, Blessed Mother, and my team and leave the Chamber. I thank God for this very special gift.

Tending the Sacred Garden

Ironically, I had already created this garden a while back as a part of my healing garden. I had been guided to create a garden of peace and solitude that was just for me, away from the main path. It has been a place to talk one-on-one with my main guides, to "weed" out any problems or issues. I had always referred to it as my Resurrection Garden because, for one, it really did remind me of an Easter Garden, and secondly, it was a place of renewal, peace and solace. So I guess I was right in naming it such because my personal sacred garden was, in essence, a garden of "resurrection", rebirth and awakening of my true higher self.

My Resurrection Garden is surrounded or enclosed by tall "berms" of earth, rocks, foliage and flowers. The entrance to the garden is a beautiful archway carved out of stone. On top, draping over the edges of the berm and opening are beautiful and fragrant spring flowers; tulips, daffodils, hyacinths, lilies, bluebells, honeysuckle, lilacs and flowering trees, all amazingly beautiful, lush and green. Sitting in front of the archway is my noble friend, Aslan, the lion. He is the guardian and protector of my sacred garden. As you walk across the stone entrance, you pass directly into and through a waterfall that cascades into a lovely pond. A small wooden bridge leads you into the garden over the pond. A stone pathway guides you to the middle where there is a swing with green cushions and pillows. The inside is magnificent. Around the perimeter are flowers of every kind and color along with flowering trees and shrubs, all glorious. There are songbirds singing, bees humming, butterflies gliding and other forest animals resting amid the foliage and shade. It is simply perfect.

Blessed Mother guides me over to one of the flowerbeds, which is filled with white daisies, blue violets, lavender, cosmos and coneflowers of all colors. There is a beautiful statue of an angel standing in the middle. Mother Mary takes my hands and helps me to start pulling weeds that are strangling my beautiful flowers. She gently helps me pull each one and place them in a basket. There is a small fire pit close by. As the basket fills, one of my other guides takes it and throws the weeds into the fire. They begin to burn, sizzle, pop and then "poof", the weeds turn into a shower of glittering ash that settles down over my garden. The glittering ash turns into small delicate flowers as they reach the ground. We continue to weed. The next time the weeds are tossed into the fire, the ash turns into butterflies. It's an extraordinary sight and we all are filled with awe at the wonders of God's love for us. That He can transform our weeds into the best of who we are- -"flowers and butterflies".

After I am finished weeding I "water" the garden and myself. Mary hands me the golden rods and I place many in all the holes that were left from the weeds. I go over to the waterfall and wash off after working so hard. I let the beautiful and gentle waterfall cleanse me. Mother Mary and my other guide wrap me up. This is an amazing place to recharge and remember our "roots" and heritage, to "resurrect" the memory of our Sacred Selves.

Laura

Planting the Seed of the Sacred Self

I entered the Chamber of Light, and when I went to light the candle, it looked more like a very large candle quartz point than a candle I could light. I touched the point, and it felt like an activation of some kind. Archangel Michael came before me, and I asked before I consciously knew what to say, "Am I ready for this?" His reply was spontaneous, "You certainly are." The Sacred Self Elixir had the taste and consistency of warm coffee liquor, one of my personal favorites.

As I was led to the heart of the Eternal Flames, still only aware of Archangel Michael with me, the flames became purple. I was aware of the "last vestiges of old self" (as I heard) melting away during the "Dissolution". It left me with that sensation of liquid light that I have had before, where my personal boarders melt into the liquid so the sensation of where I begin and end is lost in the light sensation.

The next section, with the "Reconsecration" with All Element Mud, was very difficult for me. I felt like to be reformed with this substance felt hard, rigid, dense, and heavy. It seemed that this might be similar to how we feel going from a spiritual form into the newborn physical form. It's a "downer" feeling, like having to wear an outfit your mother is making you wear, but it is uncomfortable, scratchy and stiff. However, as soon as the golden orb is planted, it came with the immediate effect of the clay cracking off, like coming out of an eggshell. I was back to feeling light-filled and brightly lit. The gardenia flower was superimposed over the mental picture of me in this state and the smell of them was everywhere.

Afterward, I felt like I'd been through a very difficult process. I heard, "this is how you feel when you come home." Coming home, as in, after a death process and return to the spirit side of life. I was relieved, tired and yet satisfied with what took place.

Masterpiece Theater

The Stage of Life was formed as soon as I closed my eyes. It was set in the family room of the house I grew up in, with the Christmas tree in its usual spot. The lighting was dim except for the Christmas lights. I used to play for days with some angel ornaments we had on the tree, making up stories and playing out little scenarios with them. I'd get totally lost in that world--feeling "funny" (which I know now to be an altered state)- - the rest of the room would fall away. All that existed was the tree, the lights and these little angels.

When the director asked me what I felt, I said, "like I was in sacred time, not my time." I thought it was pretty amazing that when I got in that zone I was never interrupted, never heard a sound except what I was doing/feeling/narrating the little stories and adventures I'd "dreamed up."

When I went to say, "I am my sacred self," I was corrected. I heard, "Not quite yet. You are *still becoming* your Sacred Self." I talked with the director about some situations that were still troubling me and whether the way I was handling them (interactions with problematic people) was holding me back from the progress I was hoping to make, or if I was upholding my own values, moral obligations, things like that--and should hold my ground. His advice was to continue healing scenarios, candle lighting, and so on, and to be sure to include myself in these activities. I thanked him for the insight.

The Sacred Self portrait came out and was placed at the side of the stage on a gold easel. It now looks more like an aura photograph than a simple portrait: the background had a lot of luminous color behind me. I was almost self-conscious to look at it, and never did feel like I could look right at it. That was a funny feeling. I had absolutely no clue where to hang it. I just said, "Wherever would be best." I lit candles for whatever was giving me such a hard time with this portrait. I know I need to ask my advocates more about this in meditation.

Lourdes

Planting the Seed of the Sacred Self

I loved this exercise. It was so calming and soothing. I went up to *Angelscape* and found myself enveloped in a warm pink cape. I was able to watch the sunrise over the ocean and it was beautiful. Archangel Michael greeted me and asked me if I was ready. I said yes and entered the cave. I lit a candle for someone who needed it and then prepared to light the candle for the work. My candle had an icy pink flame and it was bigger than it had been for a while.

Out of the Eternal Flames came Archangel's Michael and Gabriel, who was holding my file. Someone gave me the Sacred Self Elixir, something strawberry, a cross between a smoothie and milkshake. Then I watched as the rest of my guides came out, including some animals and my grandparents. They all formed the circle as I went in. Archangel Michael called for the dissolution. That was wonderful! I felt as if I was free and my light was bright and big. I kept wanting to bounce around since it felt great. I didn't want my physical form back, but eventually, I gave in to it.

When Archangel Michael called for the "reconsecration", I could still feel myself as "light". As soon as the eternal seed was placed inside of me, I felt a glow and a sense of peace that I had not felt for a while. It was so calming and soothing. It felt gentle and warming. I felt as if I had energy roots going to the ground from my feet and even extending through my hands. It was an incredible sensation. When I came out of the flame, everyone congratulated me and it felt so comforting. I eventually came back down. This was one of the best feeling exercises I have done and it was perfect!

Masterpiece Theater

This is another exercise I found myself reluctant to do. I didn't want to do the theater setting (reminded me of work), so I placed it in an informal setting in the Garden of Little Ones. When I entered the garden, my Little Ones were having a field day around the garden. There was laughing, jumping, running, and even hiding in the flowers playing Hide 'n Seek. I was amazed at the beautiful topiaries made from all the flowers. There were even tables made from the plants and flowers so that the kids wouldn't hurt themselves if they ran into them. I enjoy smelling the roses, so I stayed a while inhaling their scent.

My energy drink was made of pink, red, and violet flowers and it was lovely and warm. For some reason, I had felt worn out and cold during the day and the drink helped me warm up. Instead of going on stage, we found a clearing in the garden (before the stage) and sat down on the grass. As I breathed in pink, I felt a familiar sense of calm come down over me. When the director asked me to recall a time when my Sacred Self made itself known, I realized that it came out in all the unexpected acts of kindness I have done for others, and most of all when I do my energy work to help others. There is a feeling of warmth, love, joy and peace that is hard to describe. There is a sense of being one with the universe.

The hard part of this exercise was when the director asked me to select a current challenge where my Sacred Self could express itself. This was easiest to do with work-related matters, but I could not do it with my home life. I froze up completely. Archangel Michael came up behind me and put his hands on me to warm me up, physically and psychically. I was fine until then, but at that point, I stopped functioning. I could "Tag, Refuse, and Rescript" with scenes from work, but the home scenes I couldn't get started on.

Before being moved, the director did show me the portrait, but more importantly gave me a pocket snapshot to take with me. My portrait portrayed me with more of a glow than before and that was really nice. I was then taken to a warm, cozy room and was placed in front of a fire and given a warm drink and blanket. I could remain there and rest as long as I wanted. I stayed there for a bit, until I was warm enough to move and get back to my regular life. Why I "froze" when it came time to work on my home life is something I need to reflect upon.

Tending the Sacred Garden

This was a wonderfully relaxing exercise. I found a new home. I went to *Angelscape* with my Sacred Self and Little One. My Sacred Self said she could see me glow a little more today, which was wonderful. I felt a little different this morning. My Little One couldn't wait to go play. As we reached *Angelscape*, my child went to play in the garden with the other children. Archangel Michael, Archangel Gabriel, and my Sacred Self took me to a secret door that was set in the rock wall of the garden. As I entered, I knew I was in the most serene place I have ever visited.

Across from me was another rock wall, but in the right hand corner was this beautiful waterfall. The waterfall extended to the left side of the wall. The falling water formed a stream that went from one wall to the next. The perpendicular wall on the left was covered with roses. Underneath them, were zinnias, begonia, and evening primrose, to name a few. Behind me, there was a huge tree in the corner. The rose wall continued underneath to the corner where the tree was. Next to the tree in the middle of the wall was a birdbath. Next to the birdbath was the secret entrance. Perpendicular to the secret entrance was an arched natural stone doorway that led to a labyrinth and a reflexology path. I was in absolute heaven just looking at all of this.

Back in the main garden room there was a center circle of crystals with enough space for me to rest on my back. There were lots of beautiful bright colored silk cushions. The wall that had the arch doorway had a small fountain built into the wall where I could go for my "soul fertilizer" drinks. My first spot to enjoy was the rose wall. That was amazing. Every colored rose imaginable grew on that wall in sections from light to dark. They started with white and ended with a deep dark purple. I have never seen so many beautiful roses in one spot. The fragrance was unbelievable.

I sat down in front of the wall with Archangel's Michael and Gabriel. All I could sense was a beautiful scent and a luminescence that I have never experienced before. They told me that these sensations were being cultivated inside of me. I was to breathe in the fragrance and let it fill my bloodstream and energy body. It felt wonderful. After doing this for a while, I could weed if I wanted too. I was given beautiful golden tools that took out the weeds gently. I placed them on a tray where they were going to be transmuted and recycled. Then the archangels put in the fertilizer sticks and the roses took on a brighter glow. I was able to get a drink of the water and it was amazing. I was given a beautiful pitcher to water the plants and they loved it. I washed up and had the energy drink. I was given a blanket that I could use to rest on in the middle of my crystal circle. It was so peaceful. I'm going to be here quite often in the future!

"In the hopes of reaching the moon, men fail to see the flowers that blossom at their feet."

Albert Schweitzer

Photograph 26700
by morguefile.com
user: bobby

Section 9
When Many Are Gathered

Activities Introduction

This is my favorite part of the book. This is the section where we get to empower the perspective that we are not helpless observers in a world gone mad--we get to imagine that it matters for us to show up and add our good wishes to the unfolding destiny of our world. The activities in this section foster the concept that, together, we are a powerful synergy of collective free will. This section also seeks to provide conceptual protocols, tools, and continuing opportunities to activate this synergy of collective free will in elegant and purposeful ways.

There are many of us who believe (or hope) that our intentions matter and that they *do* influence the unfolding possibilities of our shared reality. In my opinion, it is time that we start working this theory through whatever practical applications we can imagine. It is time to dream big and think good things are possible despite all reports to the contrary on the evening news. Plus, I'd rather be a happy delusional optimist than a pessimistic realist any day of the week. Wouldn't you? If we are wrong about our intentions mattering, we *still* have cultivated feelings of hope, resiliency, optimism, competency in coping with challenge, and a stronger sense of purpose in life. *Those things matter*, even if we are wrong about our intentions mattering. I'd say that it is a win-win situation regardless, and that we should *go for it* without apology. This section is written in the spirit of the theory being true--that the synergy of our collective free will *does* matter to advocate for the Highest Outcomes to unfold in the world.

We imagine creating the structure of our collective free will in the activity, Weaving the Tapestry of Light. Imagine that each person who anchors his/her Sacred Self within becomes a *Point of Light* on the surface of the planet, each acting as conduits of God's Grace and Love to flow outward. The Points of Light can be connected and woven together, through God as the central foundation, to form a *Tapestry of Healing Light* that encircles the globe. The Tapestry of Healing Light is seen as a way to organize and synergize our intentions to distribute God's Grace and Love outward into the world. We can imagine that the structure of it knits a powerful unified force of compassionate global action.

The Tapestry of Light is a beautiful working model to encourage us to shine our Sacred Selves into the world with new hope and optimism. We can imagine that the collective "brightening" of our shared environment can empower others in the world to gently evolve in a way that does not violate their free will. This is called *Holding Space* because it creates a lighter place through the agency of our presence, not by forcing change. It is our right to *shine* if that is what we want to do. It is also our right to organize as a community, such as the concept of a Tapestry of Healing Light, to maximize the potential impact and influence of God's Grace and Love on our world and environments. *Angelscape* can be considered a "spiritual meeting place" for a congregation of Sacred Selves around the world because it functions as a church or temple *within*.

The Opt In Hourly Global Meditation activity is something that I hope everyone who reads this book will engage as often as possible. After the first time you do this activity, it should only take you five seconds to refresh these intentions at whatever "top of the hour" you select. The idea is that enough people around the world will opt in with global prayers at any given top of the hour to constitute "more than one gathered" on a rolling and continual basis. Those who participate actively are doing so within a structure of those who have also agreed to be there passively, through the Tapestry of Light. Overall, it is not a bad investment in time just in case we are right about the whole "our prayers and intentions matter" theory. It is an excellent way for us to put our "money where our mouths are" and to keep the conduits of unlimited positive potential open for business 24/7.

Lighting Master Advocacy Candles is a protocol that you can integrate into the way you do global advocacy prayer work, if you are so inclined. Lighting any candle in *Angelscape* is the same as making a request for the Highest Outcome within Divine Will to unfold for any particular matter. Master Advocacy Candles are essentially a large listing of specific issues, situations, or populations of continuing and consistent need that we can all light at least once. Instead of creating many candles, the *flame* just gets larger every time the Master Candle is lit. It is as if a growing bonfire of flowing assistance is created to advocate for the intended subjects. The more times a Master Advocacy Candle is lit, the merrier, but if you do not care for the technique, you can just go through the list one time. If everyone hits the list one time, that is still one huge bonfire per area of need. You can always select a small handful of your favorites to re-light when the mood strikes you.

The Tree of Life Meditation is an alternate protocol that you can use for the Opt In Global Meditation activities when you have a little bit more time to dedicate to your efforts. It does not necessarily have to take more than five minutes, but it can still be a powerful way to connect in with prayerful intentions. The meditation is essentially identical to the Healing Hearts and Hands Activation, except that the "sacred circuit" is already established. You can simply walk outside, hold your arms up to the Heavens while standing solidly footed. Imagine that your arms are branches that reach high up into the sky, connecting with God. Imagine your feet are like giant roots that go deep into the earth. You can ask for the flow of God's Grace and Love to "activate" and then allow the energies to run while you pray for the Highest Outcome to unfold within Divine Will on earth.

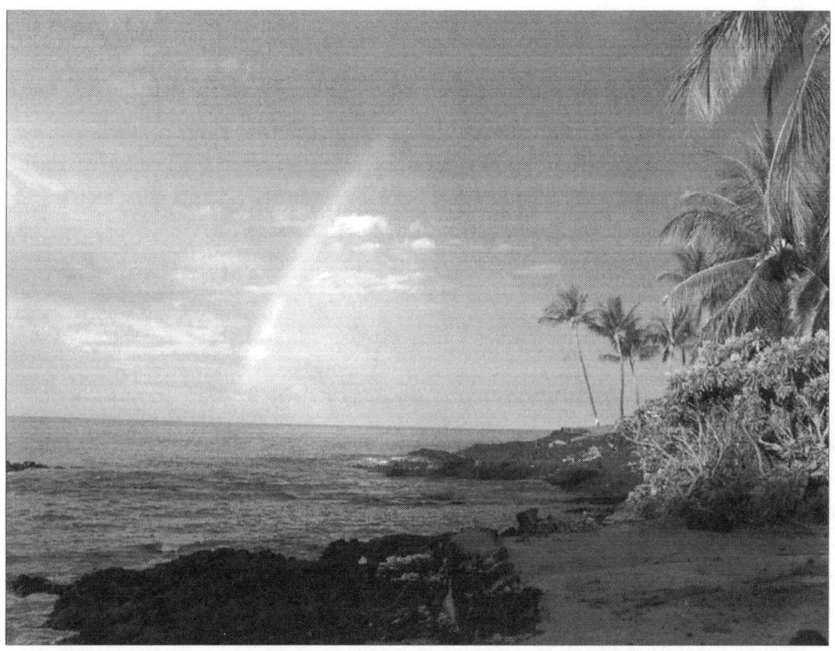

You will be imagining a beach scene filled with people. This photo may help you to envision the rainbow that is described in the activity.

Photograph 147082
by morguefile.com
user: mitchlee83

Direct Route Activity #9
Weaving the Tapestry of Healing Light

Environment Setting: *Angelscape* Beach

Complementary Scenic Route Activities
SR 9 A: Opt In Hourly Global Meditation
SR 9 B: Master Candle Lighting

Purpose: Weaving the Tapestry of Healing Light (aka: Tapestry of Light) is a process by which all those who have anchored the Sacred Self within may work together, unified in spirit, to influence the Highest Possible Outcomes in life through the syncrgy of collective free will in alignment under Divine Will.

Usage Suggestions: Weaving the Tapestry of Light is another ceremonial activity that allows for a rite of passage from one state of being to another. You do not have to imagine weaving the tapestry again, but you can if you want to. It can be a powerful moment to feel as if you are being plugged into larger systems of providing care and assistance, not just receiving it.

Activity Props: You can do this meditation at the ocean, use photos of the ocean, photos of the earth, a globe, or the multi-cultural pictures of people holding hands in peace.

Summary: The *Angelscape* beach is used in this activity because a large outdoor space is required to visualize such a large gathering of people. People will gather, bathe and cleanse, wrap, and then the Divine Advocates will arrange everyone in a particular design on the beach. The Eternal Embers within everyone's hearts will act as the connection point between members. The Breath of God will come in from the ocean and will blow energetic heart lines that weave the large crowd together in a delicate lacy pattern. The Tapestry of Light will act as a unifying connective structure for all of those who wish to advocate for the healing and wellbeing of the world. It is a system where people of good heart can pray and have faith that they are doing so "as a group". The heart bond, forged by God, allows us to empower the Highest Possible Outcome as an organized body of compassionate action.

Helpers: Any or all of your Divine Advocates may be present at this activity.

New Concepts: Tapestry of Light, Point of Light, Pillar of Light, Holding Space, "All Involved and All Affected", Tapestry of Light Synergy.

Intentions Supporting Activity

- Intentions added from anywhere else in the book that are relevant to this work.
- All Assistance, as appropriate, for any matter that needs attention.
- Membership of Tapestry of Light dependant upon acceptance, appropriateness, and approval under Divine Will, with automatic upgrading and modification as required.
- Establishment of Sacred Self as Point of Light in Tapestry of Light.
- Appropriate weaving of Sacred Self into Tapestry of Light.
- Tapestry of Light as platform or tool for Divine Will to manifest at this level as authentic assistance for the highest good of all.
- All work initiated through the Tapestry of Light, or any individual member, to be corrected in perfection and brought within Divine Will before application.
- Tapestry of Light and all members under full oversight, protection, and authority of God/Divine Will.
- Immediate disengagement and rectification from drama of any kind, from any direction, influencing any aspect or individual within the Tapestry of Light.
- All work initiated through the Tapestry of Light to be exponential, synergistic, and successful, with enhanced strength and potency when needed.
- Sacred Self as active and/or passive conduit and channel of Healing Light and God's Grace and Love, as appropriate.
- Optimal distribution of resources to areas of need with optimal distribution of work load through Tapestry of Light to maximize efficiency, comfort, and stability.

- Sacred Self to Hold Space in Tapestry of Light for advocacy of any kind, initiated by any member, as appropriate within Divine Will.
- Sacred Self to receive or activate support and resources from Tapestry of Light, as appropriate, within Divine Will.
- Synergy of growth, development, and healing within Tapestry of Light.
- Positive teamwork, cooperation, humility, and compassion within Tapestry of Light.
- Support for members of Tapestry of Light to organize and assemble in *Angelscape* as well as in real time, for peer support and special projects, as directed.
- *Tapestry of Light (aka: Tapestry of Healing Light)*: energetic and conceptual construct used to unify the synergy of collective free will in alignment with Divine Will. It is used as a way to imagine the mobilization of God's Grace and Love, directed by volunteers who have agreed to be conduits for healing love to flow to this level of being. It allows us to imagine empowering the Highest Outcome for the path of the world.
- *Point of Light:* concept that anyone who has anchored his/her Sacred Self within becomes a Point of Light on the face of the planet, such as a conduit of God's Grace and Love to flow outward. Points of Light are woven together to form the Tapestry of Light.
- *Pillar of Light:* idea or concept that each person is connected directly to God, visualized as a Pillar of Light, and through the direct connection, can be in service as a conduit of God's Grace and Love to flow into this level of being.
- *Holding Space:* term for passive assistance, such that the Journeyer is not actively engaged in advocacy work, but has agreed to *support* active work being done by adding strength and quantity to the overall structure involved in organizing and activating the synergy of collective free will in alignment with Divine Will.
- *Tapestry of Light Synergy*: a prayer request to activate the potency of the full Tapestry of Light for any individual situation, such that all members Hold Space for any other prayer requests, as long as the requests are appropriate and

within Divine Will. It is the synergy of collective free will, such that group potency is requested and activated for individual projects, as appropriate.

- *"All Involved and All Affected"*: prayer request for All Assistance to be provided to all directly involved in any situation and all who are consequently affected by it, whether they are sympathetic or objectionable recipients, such that all beings involved are provided with healing light.
- Listed intentions reaffirmed as part of the Cooperative Contract already signed over.
- Engagement of this activity, if a Cooperative Contract has not yet been signed, an affirmation of acceptance of these intentions, corrected in perfection, and brought within Divine Will.

Action Statement:
"I request to initiate Weaving the Tapestry of Light, now please."

Step-by-Step Activity Instructions:

1. Enter *Angelscape* at the Lotus Pool. Complete the spouting Water Breath Cleanse, sip your Lotus Nectar Elixir, and put on your Work Wrap to prepare for your journey. When you feel ready, you may continue.
2. A helper escorts you to the *Angelscape* beach. A large gong is sounded three times, summoning the Sacred Self aspects of all of those who have signed over a Cooperative Contract and have committed to expressing their Sacred Selves in life and in advocacy of shared larger systems. Within moments, imagine a huge gathering of bright smiling people fills in the beach as far as the eyes can see.
3. Imagine that one of the Divine Advocates climbs onto a lifeguard stand with a megaphone and announces that you are all invited to be included in the Tapestry of Light that will span the planet. This is a position of deep honor and service and every member of the crowd cheers, some with tears of joy streaming down their cheeks.
4. The Divine Advocate invites the crowd to jump into the ocean to initiate the water breath cleanse to prepare for the weaving process. Everyone on the beach happily splashes into the water to begin the cleansing water breaths. Soon, everyone is laughing and spraying

spouts of water higher and higher. A gentle sun shower begins to fall from the heavens. A beautiful rainbow arches over the horizon.

5. The Divine Advocate instructs the crowd to come back to the beach and to dry up and wrap themselves in a Sacred Self Resiliency Wrap. The Divine Advocates then situate everyone in interlocking geometric patterns up and down the beach. Rays of sunshine connect to each patterned grouping like giant pillars of light.
6. Everyone is instructed to allow the presence of their Sacred Selves to grow and bloom in their hearts. The members of the crowd center themselves within their hearts and begin to breathe deeply until each person is surrounded in a glowing orb of light. The orbs of light begin to touch and overlap.
7. The Divine Advocate says, *"May the Tapestry of Light be woven now. Amen."* The Breath of God, as a sweet ocean breeze, blows in under the rainbow and moves through the crowd. The imbedded embers of the Eternal Flames are enkindled and fanned within each individual by the growing wind. Thick threads of fire begin to stream out from the hearts of those in the crowd, like ribbons of fire dancing in the air, weaving and connecting one heart to another. The wind softly subsides when the Tapestry of Light is fully woven. It looks like an intricate lacy quilt of light covering the entire beach.
8. The Divine Advocate then says, *"May the Tapestry of Light serve as a blessing to the world through God. Amen."* The crowd responds in unison, *"Amen."* The spaces between the members in the Tapestry of Light are glowing and bright. It is through this overlap that the spaces in between may be gently illuminated.
9. You may remain as long as you wish to pray or center yourself in the sensation of being a part of a larger system. When you are finished, you may continue with the Scenic Route activities, or your main Divine Advocate escorts you to the TLC Bath where you will coat yourself in the soothing energies, sip your Graceful Integration Elixir, and then wrap yourself in the Resiliency Comfort Wrap. Do not drive, operate heavy machinery, or do any activities that are dangerous, or that require you to be fully attentive, until you feel fully shifted back to a normal waking state. Take some time to journal or take notes before your memory of the experience fades.

Continuing Thoughts:

You can request to access the *synergy* of the Tapestry of Light to empower your personal requests and work. For example, if you are doing the Team Self-Healing session for yourself, you can request to initiate the synergy of the group while you work. If you are doing anything that requires clarified intention and spiritual support, you can ask for the weight of the group to be added to the outcome, *as if everyone in the group is in active prayer with you.* Everyone in the group has agreed on the front end to weigh in as an organized front for whomever in the group requests it, if it is within Divine Will. Proper allocation of resources is a part of the intentions setting up the system. If you ask for something unnecessary or inappropriate, it just will not run.

Some general examples of the proper use of the group synergy is to throw extra resources into serious matters, situations of urgency, to empower the movement of healing light to prayer lists, and so on. You can be creative with it since the authority and oversight of the process is placed in Divine Hands. If you stick to "Highest Outcome" intentions for any situation, you do not have to worry that you are asking for something that is ultimately inappropriate or harmful. The Highest Outcome means that you are asking for the highest possible outcome available within Divine Will with Grace and Love. Since it is safe to say that the Divine Wisdom trumps our own, it is always a good choice for assembling a basic prayer request or intention. Trust is a part of faith.

Action Statement:

"I request to initiate the Tapestry of Light Synergy on behalf of the Highest Outcome to unfold for ________(whatever it is). Amen."

Practice Ideas for Advocacy Work

Practice initiating the group synergy of the Tapestry of Light with others who belong to it, such as an on-line group or with friends who are engaging this book too. What experiences do you have when you put your intentions into something with other people who are also plugged in? How does this inspire you to engage in advocacy work?

Practice "Lighting Up the Stands". Depending on how popular this book may become, any time you are in a large crowd, there is likely going to be one or two people who have opted into the Tapestry of Light, just like you. Whenever you are in a large crowd, you can request to connect to all other Tapestry of Light members, known to you or not, and to imagine flowing healing light into the whole crowd.

Practice Blanket Coverage. In every situation, there are those with whom you identify and those with whom you do not. It is important for you to allow healing light to flow to All Involved and All Affected in every situation for which you advocate. You cannot deny healing light to the very people it would most assist just because you do not like them. Practice watching the news and praying for the Highest Outcome to unfold for *"All Involved and All Affected"*, even if the person involved is a criminal who has done bad things. It is no great effort to pray only for those we love or like. Since the criminals are usually shown in headshots, you can imagine a candle superimposed in the middle of their faces, using the bridge of their nose as the stem with the flame burning in their minds. There is an ancient Chinese proverb that states, "Do not curse the darkness, light a candle instead." Indeed!

Action Statement:

"I request to light a candle for All Involved and All Affected by this situation. Amen."

"I ask for All Assistance to be provided to All Involved and All Affected by this situation. Amen."

Scenic Route Activity #9 A
Opt In Hourly Global Meditation

Environment Setting: Chamber of Light

Purpose: The Opt In Hourly Global Meditation activity is to support an organized system of prayer on behalf of the Highest Outcome to unfold for the world.

Usage Suggestions: This activity is an educational one that shows how to join into a global meditation. The intention is that every single "top of the hour" is an opportunity to Opt In to pray for the Highest Outcome to unfold on earth. You can join in every top of the hour that you are aware of and interested in joining in. Someone, somewhere, will be joining you.

Activity Props: You can use a globe, map of the world, or a fabric panel map of the world (Earth Quilt, see Project Ideas section) as a focal point to imagine the brightening of the planet or the Tapestry of Light grid lines.

Summary: I use the Chamber of Light as the setting for this work because the Chamber is the closest to a church or temple within. The process is essentially imagining the planet floating in the Eternal Flames of God's Grace and Love (not catching fire, mind you, but centrally located) with grid lines of light symbolizing the Tapestry of Light system. We use the imagery of the planet to intend for the overall light to expand and grow and to overlap the light in all the darker spaces. For urgent work, specific focus can be given to a location, event, or to individuals who hold great consequence in their hands (world leaders, summits, elections, and so on). You can integrate the use of lighting candles or just visualizing the enlightening and evolution of the planet. You may also use the Tree of Life Meditation technique, which is explained in the Continuing Thoughts section.

Helpers: Any of your Divine Advocates can assist here.

New Concepts: Earth Hologram, Tree of Life Meditation.

Intentions Supporting Activity:

- Intentions added from anywhere else in the book that are relevant to this work.
- All Assistance, as appropriate, for any matter that needs attention.
- Platform for hourly global prayer and meditation events to support Highest Outcome to unfold on earth with synergy of collective free will in alignment with Divine Will.
- Tapestry of Light members to activate optimal flow of God's Grace and Love into relevant systems.
- All members of Tapestry of Light agree to passively support meditation event through the structure of the system, with full potency, even when not actively meditating/participating.
- Quick Opt In methods to be fully functional, potent, and efficient, and to include cleansing of all participants before work, even if cleansing water breaths are not visualized.
- Clear promptings for available Tapestry of Light members to actively participate in global meditation each hour, such that optimal active numbers are attained.
- Clear promptings for Tapestry of Light members to attend hourly or spontaneously emergent prayer opportunities during times of great potential, consequence, or urgency.
- All general and specific prayer intention through Tapestry of Light corrected in perfection for the Highest Outcome within Divine Will to unfold with Grace and Love.
- Support for all global shifts, growth, or changes to be as graceful, gentle, and compassionate as possible in appropriate proportion to optimal rate of manifestation.
- Support for Tapestry of Light members to feel as if they are making a useful contribution, such that they are self-motivated to participate in perpetuity.
- Support for the idea of hourly positive prayer for the planet to be effectively shared throughout faith based communities, such as positive domino effect.
- Support for the renewal of hope, optimism, joy, and positive expectations to blossom in the collective systems of humanity.
- Support for the sustainable positive evolution of humanity within Divine Will.

- Support for humanity to harmoniously rebalance with God and All Creation.
- Support to inspire individuals to engage personal projects of global advocacy, as appropriate.
- Support to refuse and rescript absurd, negative, or catastrophic global possibilities.
- *Earth Hologram*: imagined and used as a focal point for global meditation, the Tapestry of Light, and the process of enlightening the planet with God's Grace and Love.
- *Tree of Life Meditation*: protocol for global prayer meditation in which one visualizes him/herself as a large tree with arms outstretched to the Heavens and feet firmly rooted to the ground, such as in the Healing Hearts and Hands Activation, to create a sacred circuit and active conduit of God's Grace and Love to open and flow into the earth.
- Listed intentions reaffirmed as part of the Cooperative Contract already signed over.
- Engagement of this activity, if a Cooperative Contract has not yet been signed, an affirmation of acceptance of these intentions, corrected in perfection, and brought within Divine Will.

Action Statement:
"I request to Opt In to the Global Meditation, now please."

Note: *Skip to step 2 if you are coming immediately from the previous activity.*

Step-by-Step Activity Instructions:

1. Enter *Angelscape* at the Lotus Pool. Complete the spouting Water Breath Cleanse, sip your Lotus Nectar Elixir, and put on your Work Wrap to prepare for your journey. When you feel ready, you may continue. (Optional if you are doing this meditation as a quick Opt In, instead of a full visualization.)
2. A helper escorts you to the Chamber of Light to stand in front of the Eternal Flame of God's Grace and Love. A gong is sounded three times, calling all members of the Tapestry of Light who make up the optimal active attendees for this particular event. Members

file into the Chamber of Light and quickly take their place in a large circle around the central flames.

3. A large holographic image of the earth appears in the Eternal Flames of God's Grace and Love. The Tapestry of Light shows up on the image of the earth like glowing grid lines, similar to longitude and latitude lines. Some parts of the earth are bright and some parts look muddy and darker.
4. A gong is sounded again, indicating it is time to focus intention. The members breathe deeply three times, enkindling the ember of the Eternal Flame and the presence of their Sacred Selves within their hearts. The circle of attending members emits a glowing orb of light around themselves, which overlap and connect the group to each other and the Eternal Flames of God's Grace and Love.
5. The Divine Advocates and the active Tapestry of Light members recite this simple prayer while imagining the earth growing brighter, *"We request for the Highest Outcome within Divine Will to unfold on earth with Grace and Love. Amen."* The image of the earth slowly glows with divine healing light until it is bright and star-like. The image is held for a moment and then the glowing appearance of the earth fades back to just a bit brighter than before the event.
6. Another gong is sounded indicating the work is done for this session. Many members leave immediately, some stay to light candles, to work on special projects, to focus light to particular geographical areas, or to pray in whatever way they feel prompted.
7. When you are finished, you may continue with the next Scenic Route activity, or your main Divine Advocate escorts you to the TLC Bath where you will coat yourself in the soothing energies, sip your Graceful Integration Elixir, and then wrap yourself in the Resiliency Comfort Wrap. Do not drive, operate heavy machinery, or do any activities that are dangerous, or that require you to be fully attentive, until you feel fully shifted back to a normal waking state. Take some time to journal or take notes before your memory of the experience fades.

Continuing Thoughts

Those of you who are prompted to do a short prayerful global meditation on a consistent basis can do so on the hour, whatever hour, day, month, or year it happens to dawn on you to do it. You can know, that regardless of how often you remember to do it, that probably someone, somewhere in the world, is joining you in spirit to Hold Space for the Highest Outcome to unfold on earth. You do not have to wait for a large prayer event to be scheduled to feel like you are doing something spiritually proactive in your world. *Every hour* there is an agreed upon global prayer event. Make it a point to join in as often as possible; at least one time a day, if you can. If you cannot, that is okay too. There is no guilt involved with this process, only *opportunity*. Your own guidance will tap you when it is time for you to join in. The idea of it will just pop into your head, right on time, and when it does, join in!

This activity is meant to empower you as a global citizen of compassionate action. Some people will choose to live their life as a living prayer, as possible. Others will only remember to plug in when things seem urgent. The Tapestry of Light is symbolic of both the structure and the platform for activating our free will in alignment with Divine Will to influence our environment and outcomes in the highest possible way.

When you notice the top of any hour, like 1:59, or any time that seems special, just Opt In by intending for the Highest Outcome to unfold on earth. You can use an action statement of some kind, instead of visualizing your meditation. You can use a quick visual instead of the full scene described in this activity. When you have more time, or feel prompted to engage it with more enthusiasm, do so. Otherwise, the quick Opt Ins are set up to be graceful, non-intrusive, and easy.

Action Statement:
"I request to Opt In to the Global Meditation, now please."

"Opting In to Global Meditation"

"We ask for the Highest Outcome within Divine Will to unfold on earth."

Quick Visual Ideas:

- Imagine the earth glowing with a golden or bright light.
- Imagine a candle superimposed over an image of the earth.
- Imagine a bright flower blossoming within the earth.

Tree of Life Meditation

The Tree of Life Meditation is an alternate protocol that you can use for the Opt In Global Meditation activities when you have a little bit more time to dedicate to your efforts. It does not necessarily have to take more than five minutes, but it can still be a powerful way to connect in with prayerful intentions. The meditation is essentially identical to the Healing Hearts and Hands Activation, except that the "sacred circuit" is already established. You can simply walk outside, hold your arms up to the Heavens while standing solidly footed. Imagine that your arms are branches that reach high up into the sky, connecting with God. Imagine your feet are like giant roots that go deep into the earth. You can ask for the flow of God's Grace and Love to "activate" and then allow the energies to run while you pray for the Highest Outcome to unfold within Divine Will on earth.

When Urgent Situations Arise

Some folks will only actively show up to do advocacy work when urgent matters are afoot and unfolding. Please pay attention to urgent situations, small or large, that you feel drawn to attend. Keep in mind that sometimes you will not have conscious knowledge that something is urgent, but you may feel undeniably prompted to pray (perhaps very intently) in a way that feels urgent. You can ask for the Highest Outcome for that particular emergent situation, as appropriate, or just plug in using the Tree of Life Meditation and intend for God's Grace and Love to flow wherever it is most needed. Examples of urgent situations can include hearing news of a missing child, a critical vote in the senate, a hostage situation, when you pass an automobile accident, and so on. An urgent situation is any situation when "poo" is hitting the fan *at that moment.* It can also be the care and assistance required in the aftermath of some type of significant urgent or critical event.

Advocacy assignments are somewhat personal; you will be prompted and guided to attend to the events to which you are best matched. There are a lot of us, so you can pick your battles and not feel obligated to hose down every single situation that comes up. Opting In to help is no more involved than one moment of your attention and intention. The sentence below takes less than ten seconds to articulate. You can also use the quick visuals for urgent situations. If you feel like doing more, take it to the Chamber of Light and use a full guided meditation to do your advocacy work or go outside and do the Tree of Life Meditation.

You matter too, but p*lease do not ignore those moments when you are tapped on the shoulder.* If you are being tapped, you are being tapped for a good reason, whatever it is. Again, sometimes you will feel the urgency *before* you are aware of the event. Sometimes you may *never know* what the event was about or why you were tapped for advocacy work. I find it is better to just go with it, do the work, and then release the need to explain it any further. It can be weird enough, feeling that sense of urgency, there is no reason to go screaming down the mountain if you do not have to. We are on a "need to know" basis. If you do not need to know, just do your thing and keep walking. Honest, it is better that way.

Action Statement for Urgent Situations:

"I ask for the Highest Outcome to unfold within Divine Will for All Involved and All affected in this situation (whatever it is). Amen."

It is our right to shine and to pool our light together as a potent influence of compassion in a sea of unfolding possibilities.

Photograph 80192
by morguefile.com
user: hamstersphere

Scenic Route Activity #9 B
Lighting Master Advocacy Candles

Environment Setting: Chamber of Light

Purpose: Master Advocacy Candles are lit as conceptual prayer aids to ask for the Highest Outcome for categories, groupings, issues, or subjects that have common and consistent need.

Usage Suggestions: This is an educational activity that shows you how to light Master Advocacy Candles. You can light them once, and hereafter, light them when you are prompted to light them. If you feel like you want to linger in a global meditation, but havc no personal advocacy projects, you can always light the Master Advocacy Candles again.

Activity Props: You can light actual candles, such as tea lights, or real church candles if you are in church.

Summary: I have organized a list of Master Advocacy Candles that detail specific subgroups that are in common need of healing light. The Master Candles that are listed are general subcategories. It is not an exhaustive list. Every time you light a new candle with a new topic, it has the potential of becoming a Master Advocacy Candle if other people light one for the same subject. This technique is a way of maximizing a collective of healing wishes, as well as joining in with others who are also praying for the same subject that may not necessarily be volunteers in the Tapestry of Light agreement. You will go into the Chamber of Light and simply light a bunch of candles whose subjects are already defined.

Helpers: Any of your Divine Advocates can assist here, Candle Runners can be employed to run your candles to the appropriate places in the perimeter so that you can just sit with your basket of candles and roll down the list.

New Concepts: Master Advocacy Candles, Candle Runners.

Intentions Supporting Activity

- Intentions added from anywhere else in the book that are relevant to this work.

- All Assistance, as appropriate, for any matter that needs attention.
- Master Candles, and activated group synergy, under full authority, management, and oversight of Divine Will/God.
- Master Advocacy Candles to provide focused flow and healing light to intended subjects as a prayer for All Assistance and Highest Outcome within Divine Will to unfold for subject.
- Master Advocacy Candles to be synergized through Tapestry of Light, or any other collective of prayer support.
- All individual prayers provided on behalf of others who are not aware of the collective synergy, to be added to the synergy of potential assistance as within Divine Will.
- A candle to be lit on behalf of the Highest Outcome of every individual who lights a candle or prays for an advocacy issue of any kind.
- New subjects of Master Advocacy Candles to be dynamic and evolving with the needs of humanity or emergent situations, as appropriate, under oversight of Divine Will.
- Any member of Tapestry of Light can call for or define a new candle, which may become a Master Advocacy Candle within the authority and oversight of Divine Will.
- Guidance and prompting to urge the lighting of any Master Advocacy Candles such that an optimal amount of lightings occurs for the Highest Outcome to manifest.
- Master Advocacy Candle lighting as a way for Tapestry of Light members to assist others to activate free will intentions within group synergy who are not yet members of tapestry.
- A Master Advocacy Candle to be lit any time a specific individual from the subgroup is prayed for, such as, the specific person acts as a proxy for the others in subgroup.
- *Master Advocacy Candles*: types of advocacy candles that represent a pre-defined group, subgroup, condition, blessing, or need. The Master Advocacy Candles are empowered with more flow of healing energy each time they are lit. They may be re-lit by the same person and lit by multitudes of others sending healing light to the same subject of the candle.
- *Candle Runners:* background helpers that take your lit candles and place them where they belong in the Chamber of

Light, such that you can light many candles without the trouble of visualizing the placement.
- Listed intentions reaffirmed as part of the Cooperative Contract already signed over.
- Engagement of this activity, if a Cooperative Contract has not yet been signed, an affirmation of acceptance of these intentions, corrected in perfection, and brought within Divine Will.

Action Statement:

"I request to light the Master Advocacy Candles, now please."

Note: *Skip to step 3 if you are coming immediately from the previous activity.*

Step-by-Step Activity Instructions:

1. Enter *Angelscape* at the Lotus Pool. Complete the spouting Water Breath Cleanse, sip your Lotus Nectar Elixir, and put on your Work Wrap to prepare for your journey. When you feel ready, you may continue.
2. A helper escorts you into the Chamber of Light to stand in front of the Eternal Flame of God's Grace and Love. Center yourself within your Sacred Self and enliven the embers of the Eternal Flame within you by taking several deep breaths.
3. A spiritual helper approaches you carrying a large basket of candles. This is your Candle Runner(s) and you will be able to hand off the lit Master Advocacy Candles to this helper so that you can continue down the list. Your helper will place the candle where it needs to be in the perimeter of the chamber.
4. The basket contains many candles that are inscribed with the subjects below. Pick up each candle and light it with the Eternal Flame of God's Grace and Love, pass it on to the Candle Runner, then go on to the next one in the basket. They are placed in categories for organization purposes.

Subject Candles

My Family	All Families
My Children	All Children
My Little Ones	All Little Ones
My Community	All Communities

Humanity
All Plants
Earth
All Animals
All Sentient Life
All Creation

Condition Candles

All Those in Darkness
All Those in Grief
All Those Lost
All Who Seek the Light
All Those Near Death
All Those in Poverty
All Those Affected by War
All Those in Danger
All in Service to God/Divine Will
All Those Who Suffer
All Those Oppressed
All Who Have Fallen
All Those Who are Sick
All Those Who Have Died
All Those in Positions of Power
All Those Affected by Violence
All Events of Great Consequence
All of Good Heart
All Those Who Need Divine Intervention

Blessing Candles

Love
Mercy
Grace
Beauty
Truth
Strength
Healing
Innocence
Harmony
Prosperity
Miracles
Light
Compassion
Forgiveness
Absolution
Redemption
Endurance
Balance
Purity
Equality
Faith
Atonement

Gratitude Candles

My Loved Ones
All Helpers of Any Kind
God's Grace and Love
God
All Spiritual Guidance
All My Blessings

Personal Master Advocacy Candles

My Sacred Self
Protection of the Self
All Healing of the Self
Self Forgiveness
Overcoming of Obstacles
All Aspects of my Whole Self
Purification of the Self
Wholeness of the Self
Authentic Perception of Self Worth
Overcoming of Weakness

Integrity on All Levels
Walking the Path of Light
Forgiveness from Others
Those I Consider My Enemy
Awareness of Authentic Truth
Right Alignment with Power
Ability to Surrender
Trust and Faith

Growth on All Levels
Release from Illusion of Any Kind
Forgiveness for Others and God
Those I Consider My Loved Ones
Graceful Dissolution of Distortion
Grace When It is Needed Most
Being in the Hands of God
Restoration of Innocence

To Feel God's Grace and Love as Real
Choice Points and Critical Decisions
Balance in Relationships and Affiliations
Contribution and Purpose of the Self
To All I Have Trespassed Against
To All Who Have Trespassed Against Me

5. Make note of which candles you lit seemed to have the biggest response. This may give you feedback as to a special project, a service path, or an area of advocacy to which you are most aligned. When you are finished, your main Divine Advocate escorts you to the TLC Bath where you will coat yourself in the soothing energies, sip your Graceful Integration Elixir, and then wrap yourself in the Resiliency Comfort Wrap. Do not drive, operate heavy machinery, or do any activities that are dangerous, or that require you to be fully attentive, until you feel fully shifted back to a normal waking state. Take some time to journal or take notes before your memory of the experience fades.

Continuing Thoughts

Can you think of any more candles you would like to define and light? Define them and light them. Pay attention to repetitive themes or subjects that appear to have a bigger response when you light them. The biggest responses may be areas that you should focus more attention, or which may help you define your special advocacy projects, or areas for personal growth and development. Keep a listing of the new candles you define and the ones that seem special to you for whatever reason.

Summary and Wrap Up

Complementary Activities

- Join a local meditation group.

- Start a local meditation group.
- Start a local Tapestry of Light group.
- Watch the news for opportunities for advocacy work.
- Pay attention to prompts to Opt In.
- Pay attention to prompts to light candles.

Project Ideas

You can purchase a fabric panel of a map of the world and sew the longitude and latitude lines with golden or metallic colored thread. You can use your intuition to sew in stone beads or whatever focal pieces you like. You can place your hands on the "Earth Quilt" to let your Divine Advocates work on it, such as with Team Self-Healing, except it would be Team *Earth* Healing. You can spend time focusing healing light in areas of deprivation, turmoil, war, famine, or suffering of any kind. You can spray holy water, flower essences, or other vibrational preparations directly onto the Earth Quilt. You can smudge it with cleansing herbs. You can use the Earth Quilt as a group meditation focal point, letting everyone pray in their own way, doing whatever they feel prompted to do. It is a fantastic tangible prop for Global Meditation work of any kind.

Reflection Questions

1. Describe how you were feeling before and after the activities.
2. What were the most vivid details of your imagery during the activities?
3. Describe your helpers, the tools, and their assistance.
4. What surprised you the most about your experiences?
5. What was your favorite activity in Section 9?
6. What was your least favorite activity in Section 9?
7. Can you integrate your new skills into your more familiar practices?
8. Were there any details that seemed highlighted to you that you might want to think about?
9. Do you feel inspired to do any research in any other related area? If so, what is it?
10. How did your inclusion to the Tapestry of Light affect how you viewed your own ability to be effective as an advocate?
11. What specific global advocacy projects would you be passionate to engage?

12. What areas of the image of the earth were brightest and darkest to you? Why do you think that is?
13. Were you guided to do any more intensive work, and if so, what was the nature of it?
14. How did it feel to participate in the Global Meditation event?
15. What special projects would you like to work on when you do the Global Meditation work?
16. Did this process feel like time well spent? How quick can you Opt In and finish your intention?
17. Have you noticed automatically looking up at the clock at the fifty-ninth minute of the hour, as if prompted to join into the global meditation? Any other times seem to continually grab your attention?
18. What candles did you light that you really enjoyed, or which seemed special?
19. What candles were more difficult to light, or which seemed resistant?
20. If there were candles that were harder to light, why do you think that is?

"An age is called Dark, not because the light fails to shine, but because people refuse to see it."

James Michener

Focus Group Feedback

Sharon

Weaving the Tapestry of Light

This activity was unbelievably amazing and I'm going to have a hard time describing any of it and doing it justice. I am led to *Angelscape* Beach. It is a perfectly gorgeous day. The gong is sounded and more people then the eye can see have gathered. On one side of the lifeguard stand are the people that have assembled. On the other side are all of the Divine Advocates, of every imaginable kind, and people from the spirit world. It's unbelievable how many people are there. Archangel Michael climbs the stand and announces that we have been invited into the Tapestry of Light. The crowd is crazy with excitement as we stand locked arm in arm in unity. There is a low murmuring pulsing through the crowd, a true excitement of coming together with like-minded people. I feel so honored and happy to be a part of this assembly.

We all jump into the water to prepare ourselves for this special process. Even with so many people in the water, it doesn't feel cramped, just happy, fun and exhilarating. The rainbow appears and we are all in awe of its splendor and size. It's amazingly large, almost like you can reach up and touch it. We are then arranged into interlocking circles, something like the Olympic Rings, but every circle on the beach intersects and interlocks one to the other and each person is arm in arm with the person next to him. Large cylinders of light shine down and enfold each circle. Each person starts to glow like pearls of light as they allow there Sacred Selves to shine. As the breeze blows and moves over the crowd, it looks like the most beautiful piece of lace, shimmering, glistening, translucent prisms of threads. It is beyond description, beyond comprehension; total connectedness, total belonging, total peace within your heart.

I begin to pray, "I thank you Father for allowing me to be a thread in this beautiful Tapestry. I thank you for the rainbow within my heart, the colors gleaming and spinning the fabric of your love to cover the world with compassion and hope. I thank you dear Father for your light that shines so bright as to bring us home safely to you. I thank you for the triumph of your mission, the greatness of your love for all humankind. In the glorious name of our Beloved Lord, we praise your magnificence now and always. Amen."

Opt In Hourly Global Meditation

When I first read this activity, I got very, very excited. *This* is what we are all about. *This* is what we are here to do, to come together as a collective whole. *I love it.* I will add this to my daily morning prayers and will put a copy of the Action Statement on my refrigerator as a reminder through out the day to stop and pray for the world community. Super, super, super. Love it, love it, love it.

Lighting the Master Advocacy Candles

This was a very peaceful, loving activity, beautiful on so many levels. I walk into the Chamber of Light and down to the Eternal Flame. I sit "Indian" style on the ground. My beloved golden retriever, Roxie, runs up and sits beside me. Two lovely young girls, perhaps in their early teens, come forward with my baskets of candles. Before I start to light them I thank God for the opportunity to be a part of His divine spark and light. I light each candle with compassion, intent and gratitude. I feel honored and humbled to do this for my family, friends and all those in need. I light each and every candle listed plus others. What a great way to tend to and service those in need (including myself). Beautiful and simply perfect.

Laura

Weaving the Tapestry of Light

The pattern I was shown is one that I've seen in meditations since last year. It was comprised of triangles. Beginning with tiny ones just involving three people, then three in a city-sized area, then larger to be sort of state sized, then country sized. The colors were brilliant purple, green, gold and blue--with pink woven in as well. The threads glowed beautifully as the heart energies were activated--like a quilt with metallic thread in the weave.

It felt wonderful to be a part of this group energy. I stayed in it for a short time as I also heard a narration speaking about "riding a wave of co-created energy", which was "lifting all souls to allow them access to new levels of awareness".

For the action statement, I first used planet earth, and the globe was illuminated with the visual of the network of triangles. I then did the exercise for smaller group situations, and each time the triangles fit the situation exactly, all with the same color areas as the first tapestry. I felt, but did not hear anything explaining this, that these colors were the frequency I tapped into regularly. It was very comfortable, peaceful, healing to me visually.

Lourdes

Weaving the Tapestry of Light

This was the perfect morning wake up exercise! I was looking forward to this exercise all week and now I know why. I went to *Angelscape* and it was so nice to see a lot of people there. I loved the ocean cleansing and my wrap had a lot of pink in it. It seems to be my color for the month. It was easy to feel the energy growing, and then when we all connected, I felt a shiver go through my body. It was calming, soothing and even joyful. It looked like a 3-D nylon net of all different colors. It was so serene and yet energetic. After doing the exercise, I went and lit more candles. What a great way to start the day!

Opt In Hourly Global Meditation

This exercise was another perfect one for me. I loved being able to do something to help, not only people, but also the earth. I went to *Angelscape* and did a cleaning by the ocean. I didn't go in since I was cold, but the water's energy was able to get to me. I went to the cave, lit some candles and then found a beautiful purple silk cushion to sit on. Other people soon came and they had all multi colored cushions to sit on. As we started deep breathing, I could feel the heat come up through my body (love this!). We focused on the earth and it was beautiful to see the grid. I sent prayers and light to where ever it was needed most. I know I'll be doing this one often. Like all the exercises this week, this was comfortable, like an old familiar blanket. These were the easiest exercises for me to do and it felt great to be able to help others that I can't always help physically.

Lighting the Master Advocacy Candles

I absolutely loved this exercise. I was very at "home" with it. I went up to *Angelscape* very happily. It was still dark outside, and although there was no moon, the land was luminescent. I went into the cavern and centered myself. I could feel the flame warming me up, I was soon tingling, and there was heat running through me. There was a young angel coming forth to help me. She looked about ten or eleven and was very happy. She made me happy just looking at her. Then she requested another angel to help when I told her that I was lighting a lot.

When I lit the light for my family, the flame was all rainbow colored. It was very colorful and the colors merged into one another happily. For my husband's job location, I had to light four for each corner and a very big one in the center. The two angels needed to carry the big one that was for the center of the store. This one burnt a lot and there was a lot of smoke initially with this one.

For a friend who has had a hard life, the candle was pink and big. For the planet earth, the candle flame was immense. For the kid's in my daughter's school there seemed to be a lot of flame for that one. I plan to keep the list of candles handy to keep lighting them. It felt as if I helped bring some light into the world. There was a deep sense of satisfaction in being able to help others in this way. Ever since beginning the candle exercises, I seem to be lighting more candles physically and going to the cavern to light more candles each time. This was a wonderful exercise!

When even a little light shines on the pathways we share, everyone can travel a little easier.

Photograph 167054
by morguefile.com
user: somadjinn

Section 10
Stretching for Home

Activities Introduction

Section 10 marks the end of the formatted *Angelscape* program. If you have made it this far, you have completed all of the activities and have done an *incredible* amount of work. You may have unloaded baggage that was difficult to release. You may have faced things that were scary, unknown, and sometimes painful. You have stood up to be counted as an active and responsible co-writer of your life. You have learned many different ways to continue facing your challenges, to keep yourself clear and on track, and to advocate for others. This was a lot of work to accomplish and to get this far *is* something to be celebrated.

The Commencement Ceremony is deeply touching to most who visualize it. You receive your own Sword of Light, such as the Divine Advocates use. It is an honor you can visualize being bestowed upon you for all your hard work and your commitment to express your Sacred Self and to be in Divine Alignment. You are encouraged to work with your Sword of Light as a conceptual tool to empower and intensify your focus and intent. If you have special projects or are a healing practitioner, you may find that the Sword of Light is very helpful to your work.

The Path of Light Gifting Ceremony is designed to provide you with conceptual tools to use as you take each new step forward in your life. The Path of Light is defined as the path you choose that keeps you in alignment with Divine Will while upholding the Highest Possible Outcomes for yourself and the world. The Path of Light is the highlighted path, the best path, the most appropriate path for you within Divine Will at any stage of your personal development. All of life is a series of learning experiences that are punctuated with events of consequence. The Path of Light gifts are used to symbolize the support you can receive from the spiritual level to guide your way and help you exercise soul wisdom in your choices.

The last exercise of the book introduces you the *Angelscape* Elixir Café. There is a menu of new energy drinks that you can use to support you whenever you feel you need the "boost". The tasting party teaches you how to make your own vibrational elixir drinks from now on. This is a lovely lighthearted way to end your journey through the *Angelscape* program, but the journey itself does not end. The last section of the book is a summary of how you can integrate many of the activities that are good for continuing care and maintenance into your Dream Room. The Dream Room is designed as a main way for you to continue visiting *Angelscape* for support and to have a dedicated workspace. So, do not be sad, while your formatted program may be over, your connection to *Angelscape* and the support you have found there will roll on and evolve with you.

Taking the scenic route means that you appreciate where you are and where you are going. You are to be congratulated for your hard work.

Photograph 117416
by morguefile.com
user: Richard_b

Direct Route Activity #10
Commencement Ceremony

Environment Setting: Chamber of Light

Complementary Scenic Route Activities
SR 10 A: Path of Light Gifting Ceremony
SR 10 B: Elixir Tasting Party

Purpose: The Commencement Ceremony acknowledges the accomplishment and hard work of the Journeyer. It ushers in the conclusion of the *Angelscape* journey and the continuation of the journey through life.

Usage Suggestions: This is a ceremony and rite of passage; you do not have to do it again. You may, from time to time, request an upgrade to your Sword of Light if you are engaged in special healing projects. You need only to place your Sword of Light into the Eternal Flames and request to be gifted with whatever additional energies are appropriate. You will receive what you need. You can do steps 5 and 6 to reaffirm Sword of Light activation if you want to do that, you could just simply ask for it to be fully activated and grounded.

Activity Props: You can use pictures of a knighting ceremony, graduation, or any other ceremony acknowledging a large accomplishment. If you have pictures of your high school or college graduation, it may help to bring back an emotional memory of having successfully completed something.

Summary: The Commencement Ceremony is a graduation from the formatted journey and the activities that you have completed. It acknowledges and honors you for your deep commitment to your own healing process, as well as a deep commitment to the betterment of the world. The imagery is set up like a knighting ceremony where you receive your own Sword of Light, which is meant to symbolize empowerment through God's Grace and Love. You can use your Sword of Light as a conceptual tool of healing, hope, renewal, and focused intention within Divine Will.

Helpers: All of your Divine Advocates attend the Commencement Ceremony.

New Concepts: Personal Sword of Light.

Intentions Supporting Activity

- Intentions added from anywhere else in the book that are relevant to this work.
- All Assistance, as appropriate, for any matter that needs attention.
- Acknowledgement, validation, and respect for the accomplishment of all of the tasks, healing assignments, and advocacy work within this book.
- Gifting of Sword of Light of God's Grace and Love as a tool and instrument of empowerment within Divine Will.
- Sword of Light under thc authority, oversight, and protection of God/Divine Will.
- All healing work in progress, or still integrating, to run to completion and sealed in perfection under authority and oversight of Divine Will.
- Support for the Journeyer to feel satisfaction, a sense of closure, a sense of hope, optimism, and service for his/her continued journey.
- Support for the Journeyer to remain connected to the *Angelscape* environment, tools, Divine Advocates, and assistance, as needed or desired.
- Support for the Journeyer to feel renewed faith and empowered service within Divine Will.
- *Personal Sword of Light*: energetic and conceptual tool of activated and empowered compassionate action through God/Divine Will. It is a tool of focus and directed flow of God's Grace and Love, to be used as prompted.
- Listed intentions reaffirmed as part of the Cooperative Contract already signed over.
- Engagement of this activity, if a Cooperative Contract has not yet been signed, an affirmation of acceptance of these intentions, corrected in perfection, and brought within Divine Will.

Action Statement:

"I request to initiate the Commencement Ceremony, now please."

Step-by-Step Activity Instructions:

1. Enter *Angelscape* at the Lotus Pool. Complete the spouting Water Breath Cleanse, sip your Lotus Nectar Elixir, and put on your Work Wrap to prepare for your journey. When you feel ready, you may continue.
2. A helper escorts you into the Chamber of Light. Light a candle for your Commencement Ceremony. The Chamber of Light is adorned with many bright and fragrant flowers. All of your Divine Advocates are present, as well as any passed over Loved Ones who have been invited to show their support to you. Everyone is smiling broadly with expressions of love and acceptance.
3. You are asked to approach the Eternal Flame of God's Grace and Love by your main Divine Advocate. You are directed to kneel and offer a prayer of your own heart to express your feelings about the journey you have taken, gratitude for God and all your helpers, and to reaffirm your commitment to express your Sacred Self in the world. When you are finished with your prayer, the crowd in the chamber joins you in saying, *"Amen."*
4. Imagine that your main Divine Advocate calls for your Sword of Light to be forged in the Eternal Flames of God's Grace and Love. The Eternal Flames crackle and grow brighter. Your Divine Advocate reaches into the flames and retrieves a beautiful Sword of Light. You are knighted with that Sword of Light as your Divine Advocate offers a blessing to you from God.
5. You are asked to rise and to hold out your hands. Your Sword of Light is handed to you, hilt first. You are instructed to hold the Sword of Light out in front of you. Your Divine Advocate pulls out his/her own Sword of Light and touches the tip of his/hers to the tip of yours and says, *"I request that this Sword of Light now be activated and empowered as a tool of God's Grace and Love, Amen."* Imagine a bolt of light moving through your Divine Advocates Sword of Light to your own; your entire body may feel electric.
6. Next, you are instructed to bang the tip of your Sword of Light on the floor of the Chamber of Light three times to symbolize it being grounded to the physical level. When you have completed that, you may put the Sword of Light away wherever it feels like it belongs on your body.
7. You may remain as long as you wish to pray or meditate on your accomplishments. When you are finished, you may continue with

the Scenic Route activities, or your main Divine Advocate escorts you to the TLC Bath where you will coat yourself in the soothing energies, sip your Graceful Integration Elixir, and then wrap yourself in the Resiliency Comfort Wrap. Do not drive, operate heavy machinery, or do any activities that are dangerous, or that require you to be fully attentive, until you feel fully shifted back to a normal waking state. Take some time to journal or take notes before your memory of the experience fades.

Continuing Thoughts

The Sword of Light is a powerful symbol of compassionate action. It is not a weapon, but a tool of concise, laser-like *focus*. Connect with your Guidance Team and request information about how to use it for self-healing, directing prayer, grounding energies, creating vibrational elixirs, sacred space, during advocacy work, or in your healing practice. It is an especially good conceptual tool to use for scanning the energy field to check for areas of congestion or misalignment. Scan yourself with your Sword of Light. It can double as a suction device if you require congestion to be removed or burned away. You may use it during the Opt In Global Meditation opportunities, such as you did when removing congestion from your body, upon the holographic image of the earth. You may also use it to direct a strong beam of healing light to a specific area of the planet in need.

"The future belongs to those who believe in the beauty of their dreams."

Elenor Roosevelt.

Picture 69739
by morguefile.com
user: dee

Scenic Route #10 A
Path of Light Gifting Ceremony

Environment Setting: *Angelscape* Beach, Sacred Garden, or as desired

Purpose: The Path of Light Gifting Ceremony gives your Divine Advocates a chance to provide you with gifts and tools for your continuing journey to support your Path of Light in life.

Usage Suggestions: This is a ceremony and does not need to be done again. You can request additional specialty tools or gifts for your Path of Light if you feel you need updates. You can ask for Pearls of Wisdom any time you need more of them.

Activity Props: You may use pictures of a party or celebration, a special pair of shoes, and pearls or large sphere. You might like to use a picture of the Ruby Slippers in the Wizard of Oz, but do not let the idea of "ruby" limit the properties of your own shoes.

Summary: There are two gifts that everyone receives: the Path of Light Shoes and the Pearls of Wisdom. The Path of Light Shoes are attuned to your Path of Light and designed to give you feedback when you have to make choices and need assistance. The Pearls of Wisdom are given to you as a way to help you look at all of life as a stage of learning, and that all events, whether they challenge or delight you, can be turned into Pearls of Wisdom that bring you to higher levels of functioning. Other personal gifts may be presented to you by your Divine Advocates that relate directly to your specific Path of Light, your special talents, skills, or abilities, which presumably, you can/should eventually be using as you unfold your enlightened human potential. It is possible that you are given gifts that you cannot open or which you cannot identify. Gifts like that are generally those that you are not ready to receive yet. Just keep them in a safe place until you are prompted to attend to them again.

Helpers: All or most of your Divine Advocates show up either to give you a hug or to give you a special gift.

New Concepts: Path of Light Shoes, Pearls of Wisdom, Path of Light.

Intentions Supporting Activity

- Intentions added from anywhere else in the book that are relevant to this work.
- All Assistance, as appropriate, for any matter that needs attention.
- Acknowledgement and validation for commitment to follow Path of Light to the best of your ability and level of personal development.
- Support for you to discern your Path of Light and to behave and make choices in alignment with the Highest Outcome within Divine Will.
- Support to be prompted and inspired by the wisdom of the Sacred Self in practical and actionable ways.
- Distribution and receiving of appropriate tools and gifts to support the unfolding Path of Light and other blessings of life, as appropriate within Divine Will.
- Support for happy coincidence, synchronicity, and positive opportunities that provide feedback and a sense of things being "meant to be" when in Divine Alignment.
- Enhanced momentum, motivation, vitality, passion, and persistence to Path of Light, such that pursuing Path of Light is self-sustainable and fulfills deep sense of personal purpose.
- Support to trust and have faith that you are progressing on your Path of Light in Divine Timing (aka: Trust the Process).
- *Path of Light Shoes*: used as a way to keep the Journeyer on his/her Path of Light with grace, ease, support, and warning and rectifications when non-beneficial paths are taken.
- *Pearls of Wisdom*: used to focus and empower the process of learning through life lessons with wisdom, grace, and ease, and to enhance the flow of inner wisdom from spiritual sources, such as from your Guide Team and Divine Advocates, as well as soul wisdom from your Sacred Self.
- *Path of Light*: term defined as the path you choose that keeps you in alignment with Divine Will while upholding the Highest Possible Outcomes for yourself and the world. The Path of Light is the highlighted path, the best path, the most appropriate path for you within Divine Will at any stage of your personal development.

- Listed intentions reaffirmed as part of the Cooperative Contract already signed over.
- Engagement of this activity, if a Cooperative Contract has not yet been signed, an affirmation of acceptance of these intentions, corrected in perfection, and brought within Divine Will.

Action Statement:
"I request to initiate the Path of Light Gifting Ceremony, now please."

Note: *Skip to step 2 if you are coming immediately from the previous activity.*

Step-by-Step Activity Instructions:

1. Enter *Angelscape* at the Lotus Pool. Complete the spouting Water Breath Cleanse, sip your Lotus Nectar Elixir, and put on your Work Wrap to prepare for your journey. When you feel ready, you may continue.
2. A helper escorts you to your selected destination within *Angelscape* (you can choose where your party is held). There is an outdoor covered reception area, like a large gazebo, that is outlined in banquet tables loaded with treasures of celebration. There is a seat of honor in the center of the festive atmosphere. Your Divine Advocate takes your hand and walks you to your seat.
3. Imagine that your main Divine Advocates, and all of the other helpers, have come for your celebration. Their faces are full of joy and love for you. One of your Divine Advocates approaches you with a silver tray. Upon the tray is the most wonderful pair of shoes you could imagine. These shoes are gifts to you to help you walk your Path of Light with Grace and Love. They are placed on your feet. Your Divine Advocates says, *"Activate Path of Light Shoes, now please."* You can feel them energize and become a part of your system.
4. Imagine another Divine Advocate approaches you with a silver tray. Upon this tray is a large white pearl the size of a grapefruit and a necklace or pouch of pearls. These are Pearls of Wisdom to help support you to be open and receptive to your own higher wisdom and Divine Wisdom.
5. Now that you have received the two general gifts given to everyone, it is time for your Divine Advocates to give you a hug,

or to give you other tools and gifts as are unique and specific to you. Be sure to write down these gifts, or describe them as best you can, if you do not know what they are. You may find that you have gifts of gratitude to give to your Divine Advocates. If so, you may exchange your gifts to them when they give their gifts to you.

6. Congratulations. When you are finished, you may continue with the next Scenic Route activity, or your main Divine Advocate escorts you to the TLC Bath where you will coat yourself in the soothing energies, sip your Graceful Integration Elixir, and then wrap yourself in the Resiliency Comfort Wrap. Do not drive, operate heavy machinery, or do any activities that are dangerous, or that require you to be fully attentive, until you feel fully shifted back to a normal waking state. Take some time to journal or take notes before your memory of the experience fades.

Continuing Thoughts

The Path of Light Shoes are conceptual tools to help you make good decisions according to your path in life. It is your responsibility to create a "language" of feedback to help you to decide and choose well. For example, you may request for your feet to hum or feel energetic when you are on the right track, or for images of the Path of Light Shoes to flash in your minds eye when you consider the best choice out of a list of possible choices. Perhaps you will ask for your shoes to change colors, like a mood ring, when you are approaching paths or choices that are definitely okay, not okay, or somewhere in between. The system you use is your decision. Use a system that works easily for you and that is not overly complicated. You can use imagery of walking upon a path that is glowing, or is a rainbow, moving one-step at a time.

The Pearls of Wisdom are additional tools, like the Path of Light Shoes, that are designed to provide you support for increased wisdom when you ask for it. Wisdom is different from knowledge. Wisdom helps you to chart a reasonable course using previous understanding, but it also allows the outcome to unfold without expectation. Wisdom allows you to move forward with a plan of action, but also lets you upgrade your understanding when new and spontaneous information or experiences unfold for you. Wisdom is a form of competent problem solving which results in higher levels of functioning that is aligned with your Path of Light.

You can use the conceptual tools in whatever way seems right to you. The grapefruit-sized pearl, for example, can be used like a crystal ball to gaze into, or a paperweight on your Dream Room desk. The smaller pearls, such as the necklace or pouch, can be used by you as needed. You can imagine putting one in a drink to make an elixir or you can pop it into your mouth like a dissolving candy, or candy necklace. You can also wear the necklace or put it in your pocket for support. You can receive more Pearls of Wisdom at any time by asking for your challenges to help you to evolve.

Sweet Pearls of Wisdom can be visualized strung together on a necklace or loose in a pouch.

Picture 128972
by morguefile.com
user: chelle

Scenic Route Activity #10 B
Elixir Tasting Party

Environment Setting: *Angelscape* Elixir Café

Purpose: The Elixir Tasting Party is used to introduce you to the menu of elixir drinks that you can use for continuing care and to show you how to make your own elixir energy drinks using a glass of water.

Usage Suggestion: The elixir drinks are meant to provide you with booster support for specific goals, or to help you move yourself gracefully through various growth, healing, and learning processes. You should use them often as part of your daily routine if you enjoy this particular energy working technique. If you do not know which elixir to request, the *Angel Surprise* is designed to be a "catch all" mutable elixir for whatever you might need at the time you ask for it.

Activity Props: This activity *requires* you to use props. Please see the instructions below to get the directions.

Summary: The Elixir Tasting Party will introduce you to the various choices in support that you can access through the energy drink method. You will go to the café and sit at the counter. The Angelic Barista, which may be one of your favorite Divine Advocates in costume, will serve you several samples on the menu. You will get the opportunity to observe the effects while having a good time. The elixir energy drinks are essentially a delivery system for a chunk of goal oriented energetic support. The Elixir Café is designed to be a casual and fun place that has social overtones. You may enjoy having a real gathering of your friends to do the tasting party. You can use the tasting assessment sheet provided to document what your elixirs were like and how they affected you.

Empowering Water for Tasting Party

- You will need a pitcher full of pure filtered water and a smaller glass. A wine glass, shot glass or champagne flute will work nicely for this. Clear glass is the best medium for making elixirs, but ceramic is fine too if you prefer to use a coffee mug. Water from your tap is fine if it tastes good to you, if not, get spring water, not distilled water (which is better only if you are trying to preserve an elixir).

- For each new elixir to taste, you will pour a small amount of water into your glass and use the glass as the vessel to empower each drink before you taste it. You do not want to create the elixir in the pitcher unless you want the whole pitcher to be empowered with that “flavor” of vibrational download. That *is* handy when you want a whole pitcher of the same empowered elixir energy drink, but you will taste ten different kinds for this activity.
- Hold the glass with both of your hands *and imagine the barista pouring the elixir energy drink into your actual glass*. Repeat the action statement for each new drink. If you feel a sensation in your hands, wait until it feels like the energies have run to completion. You may see that the water looks a little smoky between your hands. You should not have to wait more than a minute or two to complete any download empowerment. If all else fails, just hold the glass for two minutes. The “Optimize, Stabilize, Amplify, and Seal” statement included in the Action Statement is part of an efficient protocol to create vibrational elixirs that maintain integrity.
- When the empowerment is completed, you have to use your imagination and full senses. Imagine what the elixir looks like, tastes like, if it is warm or cold, and so on. It will likely remind you of some actual drink of some kind. You may close your eyes and hold your glass, while imagining you are in the *Angelscape* Elixir Café. When you are ready, you may sip the elixir drink. Pay attention to what is going on in your body and where and how you experience the energies. Use the tasting assessment sheet to describe your experience. If you are doing this activity with others, it might be more fun to wait until everyone has written down their private reactions before the group members swap experiences. However, if you can imagine your whole group sitting at the counter and interacting with the barista together, your experiences of what the elixir looks and tastes like will likely be similar, which is also fine.

Helpers: The Angelic Barista (perhaps one of your Divine Advocates in costume), café staff, and whoever else you would like to imagine having a good time with you.

New Concepts: The elixir drinks on the menu, described below, Angelic Barista.

Intentions Supporting Activity/Elixirs

- Intentions added from anywhere else in the book that are relevant to this work.
- All Assistance, as appropriate, for any matter that needs attention.
- *Angelscape* Elixir Café to provide a sense of a social and casual space within *Angelscape* and to provide goal oriented energetic support through the menu of elixirs.
- Support to create actual vibrational elixirs in liquid medium as a real time anchor for the elixirs.
- Support for a sense of fun and playful exploration with the different energy downloads available through the elixir energy drink technique.
- *Golden Bubbles Elixir*: supports a burst of golden light into the energy system that can push your vibrational state to a higher place, empower pathways of Light through your system, or to give you a jolt of joyful energies.
- *Epiphany Elixir:* supports perspective expansion, sometimes cosmic expansion, clarity, and the capacity for us to "think bigger" or to "think out of the box" so that we can make spontaneous leaps in understanding.
- *Core Balance Elixir:* assists to keep your energy system stabilized during rapid changes, challenging circumstances, or for any instance when you are thrown off center.
- *Eternal Fire Ball Elixir*: supports bringing a primal underground stream of raw vitality and fire within the body. It can help to burn off what does not belong within your system and fan the flames of your imbedded embers for potency, motivation, and a passion for life.
- *Sacred Body Elixir:* supports moving your body into alignment with the Sacred Self body, such that perfected physical health and wellness can be manifested and the obstacles to wellness are removed with Grace and Love; including enhanced

understanding and learning of appropriate soul lessons taught by illness so that they can be released.

- *Angel Surprise Elixir*: a changeable elixir, it gives your Divine Advocates a chance to assemble an energetic download for you that is "just what you need" at the time.
- *Breakthrough Elixir*: supports you with assistance to shatter whatever "glass ceilings", stubborn perceptual distortions, habits, or other obstacles that limit your growth/healing.
- *Sacred Wisdom Elixir*: support to help uncover and connect with relevant Sacred Self and soul wisdom that may be used to make good decisions, or to assist you to cultivate natural talent or skills that you need for your Path of Light.
- *Authentic View Elixir*: supports the ability to see or assess something with authenticity, without emotional reactivity, to lessen bias as possible, and to correct perceptual distortions that create rose-colored glasses or poo-smeared glasses.
- *Perky Mind Elixir:* supports regrounding after doing expansive energy work. It is also used to help you bring your focus and attention to whatever task you have to accomplish. It has a mental clarity and focus quality that is useful in real world situations to bring a supported productivity to what you have to accomplish.
- *Angelic Barista*: the spiritual helper that mixes and makes the energy drinks and assists you to create vibrational elixirs of your own, or to empower and zoom up any drink.
- Listed intentions reaffirmed as part of the Cooperative Contract already signed over.
- Engagement of this activity, if a Cooperative Contract has not yet been signed, an affirmation of acceptance of these intentions, corrected in perfection, and brought within Divine Will.

Action Statement:

"I request to empower my water with the __________ elixir, now please. Optimize, Stabilize, Amplify. and Seal."

Note: *Skip to step 2 if you are coming immediately from the previous activity.*

Step-by-Step Activity Instructions:

1. Enter *Angelscape* at the Lotus Pool. Complete the spouting Water Breath Cleanse, sip your Lotus Nectar Elixir, and put on your Work Wrap to prepare for your journey. When you feel ready, you may continue.
2. A helper escorts you to the *Angelscape* Elixir Café. The café is decorated for a party. Many of your helpers and advocates are already there having a good time, waiting for your arrival.
3. Your Divine Advocate brings you up to the counter of the café. You take a seat and look around. An Angelic Barista, a specialist in elixir making, comes up and puts a napkin and glass of water down on the counter in front of you with a big warm smile.
4. You put your hands around the glass (in actual time too) and say, *"I request to empower my water with the [Golden Bubbles Elixir], now please. Optimize, Stabilize, Amplify, and Seal."* The barista begins pouring different fluids into your glass, transforming it into the Golden Bubbles Elixir. S/he may give you a nod and a smile when it is ready.
5. Before you drink, make note of what the water has transformed into in your imagination. Jot down your findings on your assessment sheet. Take a single sip of the elixir and hold it in your mouth for a moment before swallowing. Make note of your impressions and sensations. Finish the rest of your elixir and then jot down whatever additional impressions you have. When you are completed documenting your reactions, ask for your pallet to be cleared so you can move on to the next elixir.
6. Repeat the tasting process for each of the ten elixirs listed above. Remember to use the Action Statement for each new elixir and to cleanse your "energy" palate between tastings.
7. You may linger in the café for fun if you want. When you are finished, your main Divine Advocate escorts you to the TLC Bath where you will coat yourself in the soothing energies, sip your Graceful Integration Elixir, and then wrap yourself in the Resiliency Comfort Wrap. Do not drive, operate heavy machinery,

or do any activities that are dangerous, or that require you to be fully attentive, until you feel fully shifted back to a normal waking state. Take some time to journal or take notes before your memory of the experience fades.

Continuing Thoughts

Vibrational elixirs are fun because they link a real world activity with an energetic reality. They are my favorite tools because I can squirt a little of this or that into my water, such as flower essence, medicinal tincture, gem elixir, or homeopathic remedies, and then zoom up my drink into a personalized and potent elixir energy drink. Those of you who respond well to the tasting party will likely really enjoy this method of energetic support and will want to use it often.

If your Golden Bubbles Elixir tasted like ginger ale to you, you may use ginger ale as the elixir medium next time you want to use it. The same is true for the rest of your elixirs. If they reminded you of a real time drink, you can use that kind of a drink in the future when you want to download those energies to empower your real drink. The Angel Surprise will probably change every time you ask for it because you are asking to receive whatever it is that you need in your highest good at that moment in time. If you do not know what elixir is best to support your needs, just ask for the Angel Surprise.

You may find yourself drawn to different pre-made liquid vibrational or medicinal products. There are many different kinds on the market. I am particularly fond of flower essences, which you can find in any healthy foods grocery store.

You *can* make your own (*and I encourage that!*), you do not need any special skills or abilities to do it, but if you prefer to have the elixirs in handy and pre-made dropper bottles, please visit: http://www.thegardencrew.com.

The owner of The Garden Crew and I have created a full line of vibrational elixirs that correspond to the ones described in this book. Each blend has been lovingly created using flower essences and gem elixirs that best match the intended goals of the blend. In addition to the inclusion of flower essences and gem elixirs, I utilized all the principles of responsible Cooperative Spiritual Energy Work to create and stabilize each blend. You can also visit my website at http://www.awakeinangelscape.com for more details.

Elixir Energy Drink Tasting Party Assessment Sheet

Golden Bubbles
Appearance:____
____
Smell: ____
Taste:____
Energy
Sensations:____
Impressions:____
____
____
____

Epiphany
Appearance:____
____
Smell:____
Taste:____
Energy
Sensations:____
Impressions:____
____
____
____

Core Balance
Appearance:____
____
Smell:____
Taste:____
Sensations:____
____
Impressions:____
____
____
____

Eternal Fire
Appearance:____
____
Smell:____
Taste:____

Energy Sensations:____
____
Impressions:____
____
____
____

Sacred Body
Appearance:____
____
Smell:____
Taste:____
Energy Sensations:____
____
Impressions:____
____
____
____

Angel Surprise
Appearance:____
____
Smell:____
Taste:____
Energy Sensations:____
____
Impressions:____
____
____
____

Breakthrough
Appearance:____
____
Smell:____
Taste:____
Energy Sensations:____
____

Impressions:______________________________________

Sacred Wisdom

Appearance:______________________________________

Smell:______________________________________

Taste:______________________________________

Energy
Sensations:______________________________________

Impressions:______________________________________

Authentic View

Appearance:______________________________________

Smell:______________________________________

Taste:______________________________________

Energy
Sensations:______________________________________

Impressions:______________________________________

Perky Mind

Appearance:______________________________________

Smell:______________________________________

Taste:______________________________________

Energy
Sensations:______________________________________

Impressions:______________________________________

Notes:

This picture reminded me of the Golden Bubbles elixir.

Photograph 218878
by morguefile.com
user: omdur

Summary and Wrap Up

Complementary Activities

- Go shoe shopping for a pair of shoes that remind you of your Path of Light shoes.
- Decorate a pair of slippers or socks.
- Have a party with vibrational energy drinks.
- Treat yourself to a "spa day" to acknowledge your hard work.
- Go to lunch with a good friend.

Project Ideas

Make a special vibrational elixir blend for yourself by asking the *Angelscape* Barista to create an Angel Surprise Elixir that will support you through the *next month*. Use a dropper bottle, properly sanitized (I soak mine in a bleach/water solution to kill germs, then rinse.), and fill it with forty percent brandy *or* fifty percent apple cider vinegar, for preservation. Fill the rest of the bottle with distilled water and add a half pinch of sea salt. Hold your dropper bottle, as you did for the tasting party, and allow the *Angelscape* Barista to pour the proper energetic and vibrational components into your dropper bottle. Use the Action Statement to properly seal the elixir and bring it to optimal potency. You can place several drops directly under your tongue, as you are prompted (as a daily routine or when you need them), or you may drop several drops into a larger glass of water and then imagine *stirring* it with your Sword of Light while repeating the Action Statement.

Action Statement:

"I request to empower my water with the Angel Surprise, now please. Optimize, Stabilize, Amplify, and Seal."

Reflection Questions

1. Describe how you were feeling before and after the activities.
2. What were the most vivid details of your imagery during the activities?
3. Describe your helpers, the tools, and their assistance.
4. What surprised you the most about your experiences?
5. What was your favorite activity in Section 10?
6. What was your least favorite activity in Section 10?

7. Can you integrate your new skills into your more familiar practices?
8. Were there any details that seemed highlighted to you that you might want to think about?
9. Do you feel inspired to do any research in any other related area? If so, what is it?
10. What does your Sword of Light look like? Are there any gemstones on the hilt, if so, what kinds?
11. What was the blessing that your Divine Advocate said on your behalf when you were knighted with your new Sword of Light?
12. How did the activation from your Divine Advocate feel?
13. Do you feel empowered by this activity and this gift?
14. What did your Path of Light Shoes look like?
15. What method of communication will you be using to determine yes/no feedback on your Path of Light?
16. Did you have any physical sensations when you accepted and received your shoes, if so, what were they?
17. Describe your Pearls of Wisdom and how they made you feel.
18. What other gifts or tools did you receive from your Divine Advocates?
19. What gifts or tools were a mystery to you?
20. What do you think your Path of Light is, or will be, as you move forward?
21. What changes or steps do you have to make in your actual life to begin walking your Path of Light with Grace?
22. If you could do anything, be anything, or have any job (volunteer or for pay), and money was no object, what would you be doing?
23. Imagine yourself totally fulfilled, satisfied, and at peace with your life. What does it look like? What are you doing?
24. What decisions do you need to make, and actions that you need to take to move one-step closer to what your life looks like totally fulfilled and at peace?
25. What was your Angel Surprise? What did it taste like?
26. What do you think it was designed to support?
27. What did your elixirs look like? Feel like? Taste like?
28. When do you think you will use the elixirs in the future?

Focus Group Feedback

Sharon

Commencement Ceremony

This is by far the hardest activity to even begin to describe. No words can even come close. It was an intense and beautiful experience. I certainly didn't want it to end. Beyond *wow*!

I enter the Chamber of Light. It is beautiful and luminescent. Draping around its perimeter is garland made of magnificent white roses, gardenias, freesia and greenery. In front of each statue of the Divine Advocates are lovely bouquets of the same white flowers. I am wearing a long, flowing, white dress with gold embellishments and have a wreath of flowers in my hair. Everyone there is dressed in white and gold. One of my main angels greets me, takes my hand, and leads me down to the Eternal Flame. I light my candle of glimmering gold. Jesus, Blessed Mary, and my entire guide teams are waiting for me. The chamber is full and so is my heart. I see my dad, grandparents and many others. I cannot be any happier or more grateful.

I kneel down and say my prayer of gratitude, "Oh dear loving and merciful God, whom all creation bows down before in adoration and praise, I thank thee for the blessings of this day, for the gifts of healing, awareness, forgiveness, mercy, compassion, goodness, loyalty and love. For all the abundant blessings that shower down upon me like rain. You are all merciful. Shine your light brightly upon my path that I may always do your will. Guard and guide me. Help me to be courageous in the face of uncertainty and fear, compassionate and merciful in the face of hate. Let me be your light in the mist of the darkness, a window for your glory to shine radiantly out into the world. I ask only to love and service you Lord, completely and fully all the days of my life. I am here Lord; use me to do your will. Amen."

Jesus brings forth my Sword of Light and taps each shoulder three times. Once again, I cannot explain my feelings at this time. It is awesome and powerful. I am beyond humbled at this experience, beyond grateful, beyond any words. I hold out my hands and am handed the most beautiful sword I've ever seen. Inscribed down the center of the blade are the words "Beautiful is the Work of God". Circling around several times at the very bottom of the blade just above the handle is a beautiful "vine" made of gold. Attached to the "vine" is a ruby ladybug, a sapphire butterfly, flowers made out of citrine, pink quartz and clear quartz, with leaves of emeralds. Everything is so delicate and perfect, extraordinary…indescribable.

When the sword was activated and empowered, it was very moving. I am not a very tactile person but I felt the energy and weight of that sword as sure as if I was holding it. I was so grateful so humbled, so in awe of the whole process. I finished with tapping the sword three times on the ground. I stood for a very long time just holding it and marveling at the beauty and power of it. It vibrated in my hand and was alive with God's eternal love. After some time, I place my sword in a sheath on my back. I stayed for a long time afterward, thanking and hugging everyone that had come. I didn't want to leave. Unbelievable…indescribable…extraordinary…beyond words.

Path of Light Gifting Ceremony

My reception is set up in a beautiful meadow surrounded by a rainbow of flowers, flowering bushes and trees. It's splendid and fragrant. I am met by Jesus, Blessed Mother, along with my whole Garden Healing Team; so many have come to celebrate this special time with me. The tables look lovely with linen tablecloths, decorated with garland of white and pink flowers and large bouquets of flowers with candles on top. Jesus hands me a pair of flat red silk shoes with elaborate black embroidery and sequins. They are simply extraordinary and, me being me, ask Jesus how am I suppose to "work" (walk my path of life) in such beautiful and delicate shoes. He smiles and says that I need beautiful shoes to walk the path of beauty. They will help me not to take "life" or myself so seriously and to enjoy the journey. To rejoice in the giving, learning and loving, and to skip and dance down the path, rejoice, and be glad in it.

I am then handed a bag full of rather large pearls. They are each different pastel color; the softest pink, purple, blue, pale yellow and vanilla, like Easter colors, just incredible. My Native American Guides walk over to hand me a "satchel" made out of buckskin that has an eagle and hawk feather, along with some beads and shells tied around the bottom of the shoulder strap. They say that everything I need is contained within the bag and to remember this when I doubt myself. I give each of my team a small heart-shaped pink quartz to signify that they are always within my heart and how much I love and appreciate them all. I stay for quite a while eating delicious cookies and celebrating this wonderful day. Glory be to God!

Laura

Commencement Ceremony

The candle I lit was huge, gold in color, and on an elaborate candle stand. It had three wicks, which was the first time I'd seen this before in the candles I've lit. My prayer was, "Dear God: Continue to support me as I strive to perfect my soul in service to mankind. And so it is. Amen." The "amen" came on a swell of energy from unseen (out of ring of light, but I could feel their presence) support figures.

Archangel Michael emerged with a violet sword. When touching my shoulders with it, he said, "As an advocate for Father/Mother God, you are an instrument of that peace." When I took the sword (feeling like I was not really up to having it...it's very humbling to be in such a company/subject of such invocations), there was a rush of energy that began in my hands and shot all though me until it rooted itself in the floor--even before the banging three times.

I put it in a sheath that I was wearing on my left hip with some sort of belt or tie at the waist to hold it there. It was like the feeling of being "in uniform" to have it there. I can't explain that one. I left the exercise hoping a little nervously that I could live up to the designation.

Path of Light Gifting Ceremony

The sense as soon as I began this exercise was a preparation to leave *Angelscape* and "go out into the world" to do my work. There was a graduation party feeling, much like when I graduated from school--like back somewhere in the car, all your stuff is packed and ready to go!

I was given a staff, as in a shepherd's staff, with the narration that understanding of natural law would be my Divine Guidance. The symbol for synchronicity on the road was a golden key--as if it would be the key to show I was steady on the path. Episodes of synchronicity were going to be like mile markers on a highway.

Everything kept moving toward the entrance/exit of our *Angelscape* mini-world. I felt a mixture of not wanting to go and yet wanting to celebrate the time arriving when I could/was ready to go. The shoes I couldn't see, but when I put them on--or stepped into them--I felt a wave of energy go straight from my heel to my heart chakra. It was lovely.

On the tray was a small purse, red, which had a long shoulder strap. I put it over my head and across my body so it fell at my left hip and rested on my right shoulder. Inside were pearls, and I knew without hearing that at appropriate times I could reach in and receive an insight, or pearl, to assist with any given situation. I was really "fortified" with it being with me, as if I was ready for anything. I heard it was "wisdom to take in".

I also was given a rather big book, but no explanation, no understanding what it was for or what I should do with it. I just accepted the fact that it was for future use. I don't even know what happened to it after I was handed the thing! It sort of escaped into some future scenario when it would be time to access it.

Then came the sense that it was time to "get going". I felt like I'd been through "finishing school", but I could come back at any time for tune ups, rest, schooling, "graduate courses"--like the welcome mat would always be out for me. That eased the sense of leaving "home" that was making me a bit apprehensive! Again, at this point, I physically fell asleep.

Lourdes

Commencement Ceremony

This exercise was a joyous occasion. As I got to *Angelscape*, I realized that the path to the cavern was lined with the kids and they were throwing flower petals. They were waiting for me to walk down so that they could throw the petals! I was very excited and happy to skip down the path and feel the petals on my skin. It was fun and emotional at the same time.

When I got to the cave, there were all different colored roses in vases along with flower arrangements all around the cave. Of course, all the candles I have been lighting were there too. Archangel Michael is my main advocate, and after the prayer, he pulled out the most beautiful sword. The hilt was made of pink rhodocrosite, and the shaft was a pink gold beam of light. It was absolutely breathtaking. He said I was to use it often, especially with my healing work. When he touched his sword to mine, there was a vibration. It was soft and low, but still powerful. After the entire ceremony was done, I thanked everyone and went to sleep. I seemed to need lots of rest after this one.

Path of Light Gifting

This exercise was very warm and loving. My celebration took place on the beach. Archangel Michael greeted my Sacred Self and me. We walked over to an outdoor tent decorated with white and pink roses. What was unusual for me about this is that you could smell the roses with the ocean scent and I never thought of combining those two. At this celebration, I met up with Mary, Jesus, Mother Theresa, St. Therese, and a few other of my guides. All were extremely happy for me. Archangel Michael proposed a toast with the golden bubble elixir, and as we drank it down, bubbles flowed from all of us. This was an *Angelscape* tent so the bubbles went from us to the kids to play with.

I then was to receive my shoes. My shoes were white ballet slippers that had a mother of pearl tint. They were to help keep me on my path and keep me protected in a mother of pearl light. The Pearls of Wisdom were so appropriate, because I have been saying the Serenity Prayer for the past two weeks. They were 8mm pearls and had an amazing finish. I have never seen pearls with such luster. The last gift was a small treasure box and in it was a large ruby. This ruby is to help rejuvenate my heart whenever it is worn down. I have a tendency to give too much of my heart and this is to help me whenever I feel drained.

After this, we had the most amazing cake. It was a yellow cake with the lightest white frosting I have ever had. It was creamy, but light and melted in your mouth. It wasn't too sweet, but very satisfying. It was a great way to start the day! I left soon afterwards.

"If you have built castles in the air, your work has not been lost; that is where they should be. Now put some foundations under them."

Henry David Thoreau

Take whatever helpful tools you have gathered in Angelscape and apply them to the real world.

Photograph 209262
by morguefile.com
user: clarita

Part 3: Summary & Wrap Up

I
Continuing Care in Your Dream Room

At the beginning of the book, you were instructed to create imagery for the environments used in *Angelscape.* One of those environments to construct was your very own Dream Room. The Dream Room was described as a special personal place for you, a place within *Angelscape* that you could call your own and create in whatever way you could possibly imagine. Since you have set up your *Angelscape* environments, we have not visited or discussed the Dream Room. Some of you may have visited it from time to time, and some of you have probably not given it another thought until now. Now that your formatted journey through *Angelscape* is completed (congratulations!), it is time to fully introduce you to the special functions of the Dream Room.

Your Dream Room is designed to be your "place" in *Angelscape.* Functions from many of the activities are built into the design and function of the room. This is a space of personalized care, simplicity, and refuge. Instead of having to run all over *Angelscape* in elaborate meditative processes, as was necessary for the activities, you can stay in your room and access almost everything you need to keep yourself maintained and supported. You can always go back to the more elaborate settings and re-do whatever activities you feel you should, or visit other *Angelscape* environments, as you see fit. Your Dream Room, however, can easily replace a lot of the "running around". After all of the work you did in the formatted journey, you likely feel quite happy to just "veg out" in your own room for a while.

Summary of Dream Room Features and Functions

When you created your room, you were asked to include the features in the following list. Please review their purposes and processes for your continuing care.

- A bed with blankets: The bed is the station for your Maintenance Healing Sleep and your blankets stand in for any of the energy wraps used in *Angelscape.*

- Nightstand: You can request for a glass of water (energy elixir) or a book (guidance) to be placed next to your bed. You can also use it to hold any of your other gifts and tools you want near you as you sleep.
- Desk with a computer: You can use this to imagine writing to your Guide Team, writing out your thoughts, or accessing the *Angelscape* Library (while you sleep).
- Window with a view: Your view is to help you meditate and reflect upon beauty and all things sacred. This should also come with a balcony, if your Dream Room is an apartment.
- Bathroom with a tub, shower, sink, and medicine cabinet: The bathtub is a stand in for all healing baths, the sink faucet is an elixir dispenser, and the medicine cabinet has whatever healing supplements your Healing Team leaves for you.
- Closet: The closet holds all of your *Angelscape* gifts, tools, and accessories that you do not have out on display. You also can request a full "wardrobe" of clothing that function as energy wraps to help you for whatever issue you have for your day.
- Globe of the earth: This will stand in as the holographic image of the earth used during Global Meditations. You can imagine that it has the Tapestry of Light grid lines on it and all of the other functions that the main one has in the Chamber of Light.
- Prayer shelf of candles: This is a stand in for an informal candle lighting prayer function.
- Fireplace: The fireplace is a stand in for the Eternal Flame of God's Grace and Love.
- Small wishing fountain: This is a stand in for the Wishing Well in the Garden of the Little Ones.
- Potted flower plant: This is a stand in for your Sacred Garden. If it looks dry or haggard, it is time to water and tend. It is like an alarm clock to keep you on schedule.
- Your Sacred Self Portrait: Add this to your room and place it where you want in order to remind you to anchor your Sacred Self as often as possible.
- Gifts that you received along your journey: Since this is your personal space, this is where your "stuff" belongs. You can display them, put them in a drawer, or put them in the closet.

Close your eyes and imagine your Dream Room to refresh yourself with the features. You may make modifications and updates to your room whenever you wish. If you created a collage or drew any pictures, please refer to them as needed and update them as needed. If you feel like you want to scrap your Dream Room and start all over again, you can do that too. This is your room. You do exactly what you want with it. You can even move your Sacred Garden to your balcony or backyard if you wish. Begin seeing your Dream Room as a personalized extension of *Angelscape* itself. What would you like to add to your room that is not mentioned? What were your favorite features of *Angelscape* that you would like to adapt to your Dream Room? Have fun with it. You have earned the right to enjoy something simple and fun.

Dream Room at Bedtime

The Dream Room is intended to be visited at night before you go to bed, such that you can imagine sleeping in your Dream Room as you are sleeping in your real room. The time before you fall asleep can be dedicated to your "me time" in *Angelscape*. You can visit your Dream Room as a meditative activity without it being linked to your bedtime, but there are benefits to having a whole night of rest to allow the work you initiate to run to completion. It is also very practical to schedule your care and upkeep into an activity you know you will do once a day: sleep! If you fall asleep so fast that you doubt you can do the work, just sit up in your bed while you do your upkeep work, and then fall over and sleep when you move into your bed in the Dream Room. For me, this is the best time to work; it helps me fall asleep and provides an entire night of rest to allow everything to settle in. You can consider it your bedtime prayer routine.

Suggested 6-step Bedtime Maintenance Routine

1. **Enter *Angelscape***

   You do not have to take a bath in the Lotus Pool because you will be cleansing within your own room. If you cannot imagine walking from the transition platform, where the Lotus Pool and TLC Baths are located, then just imagine being brought directly to the front door of your Dream Room.

   Action Statement: *"I request to enter* Angelscape *and to go to my Dream Room, now please."*

Imagery: Walk into the front door of your Dream Room and proceed directly to your bathroom.

2. **Maintenance Cleansing**
   The bathtub in your Dream Room bathroom is a stand in for every single healing bath station in *Angelscape*. You can access the Lotus Pool, TLC Bath, All Element Mud Bath, or the Mineral Bath any time you wish. All of the corresponding tools are available for you as well, the suction hoses, Angelic Scrubbing Bubbles, and so on. You do not need helpers for this anymore; you have graduated to a higher level of self-reliance.

   Action Statement: *"I request to initiate Maintenance Cleansing, now please."*

   Imagery: Get undressed and prepare your tub or shower. You can do this fast or slow, depending on how sleepy you are. If you are taking a shower, you can imagine sucking the water down through your head and out your feet, instead of the other way around. If you had a stressful day, spend more time doing the water breath cleanse. If you feel clear, you can get in and get out quickly. Use whatever tools you need to use and soak longer when you feel you need it. Call upon the other healing bath features (mud, mineral, TLC) when you feel you should.

3. **Maintenance Wrap**
   Anything you wrap around yourself in your Dream Room stands in for any of the energetic wraps used in your *Angelscape* activities. You can ask for a specific wrap, if you know what you want, or allow your towel, pajamas, and blankets, to be whatever energy wrap is perfect for you at the time. When you do not know what to ask for, simply call it the Maintenance Wrap.

   Action Statement: *"I request to receive a Maintenance Wrap, now please."*

   Imagery: Wrap your towel around you and dry off. You can imagine it melting into your body, once you are dry, or you can hang it back up where it belongs. Your pajamas are also Maintenance Wraps.

4. **Maintenance Elixir Drink**
   All water from your faucets, drinks, or medicines in the medicine cabinet are considered symbolic of energy drink elixirs. You can ask for a specific elixir, if you know which one you want, or ask for a Maintenance Elixir.

Action Statement: *"I request to receive the Maintenance Elixir, now please. Optimize, Stabilize, Amplify, Seal."*

Imagery: When you are in dried off and in your pajamas, you go to your bathroom sink, pour yourself a glass of water, and ask to receive one of the drinks on the menu. You can always ask for the "Angel Surprise", "Sacred Self", or "Sacred Body" Elixirs. You can look in your medicine cabinet to see if your Healing Team left you any specialized supplements to take. If you want to imagine your Angelic Barista pouring your elixir, you can imagine him/her briefly showing up on your bathroom mirror to pour over your drink.

5. **Maintenance Bedtime Prayer**

Before you go to bed, you have the opportunity to empower positive affirmations/re-scripts, request guidance and support, or to initiate healing sessions. You also have the opportunity to light some candles, make some wishes, or pray for the Highest Outcome on earth one last time before zonking out. You should construct a bedtime prayer of your own so that it is personalized to your needs. I will just reference a general prayer that you can use until you can construct your own. The *Lord's Prayer* or some other personal favorite would be just fine here too. It should be whatever is meaningful to you.

Action Statement/General Prayer: *"I ask for the Highest Outcome within Divine Will to unfold for myself, my family, and the entire planet, with Grace and Love. I ask to receive whatever I need in order to anchor and express my Sacred Self in the world. Thank you God, for all my blessings and for allowing me to be a blessing in return. Amen."*

Imagery: What you do here will depend on what you *feel* like doing. You might just want to head right into your Dream Bed, say a quick prayer, and then go to sleep. You can stop at the Prayer Candle Shelf and light a few candles. You can send healing light to the planet by meditating at your globe. You can make a wish in your little fountain. You can stand in front of your Sacred Self Portrait and ask to receive soul wisdom for a particular matter on your mind. Whatever you want to do is fine. Your nighttime routine may be whatever length you want. I am slow to fall asleep, so I can get all sorts of work done at this time. Some of you may need to do it more quickly.

6. **Maintenance Healing Sleep**
   Sleep is good. Get plenty of it, especially if you are doing a lot of healing work. In your Dream Room, your bed should be the most comfortable place you can possibly imagine. The blankets, pillows, and sheets should all be simply *divine*. When I imagine settling into my bed, I cannot help sighing in relief. It makes my real bed feel so much more comfortable when I imagine that I am in my Dream Bed. Before you fall asleep is when you should spend a little time reaffirming your positive re-scripts or initiate whatever healing session you feel is appropriate. You can ask your Healing Team to work on you while you sleep to empower the positive re-scripts and to do whatever healing work you need. You can also request to initiate a Team Self-Treatment (Hands or Golden Rod) if you want, and ask your Healing Team to just finish the session after you fall asleep.

   Action Statement:
   "I request to initiate the Maintenance Healing Sleep, now please"

   Imagery: Sit on your bed, make your requests for whatever work you want, and then slide in between your sheets and get comfortable. If you are doing a Team Self-Treatment, you can start anytime. Do not worry if you fall asleep. Your Healing Team will complete the work once you are out. Empower and affirm the positive re-scripts that you want to "sink in" during the night.

One of the accessories you can imagine in your room is a globe. This is a tool to help you pray for the earth.

Photograph 214490
by morguefile.com
user: Grafixar

II
Angelscape Problem Solving

Personal growth is all about triumphing over personal problems and challenges until higher levels of functioning are achieved. The tools and processes you have learned in *Angelscape* can become part of the way you solve and address emergent needs and challenges, if you care to use them. You can use the following basic problem-solving models to help you find your unique rhythm and flow. The steps that are described may not be an exhaustive listing. You are encouraged to tweak it and modify it to find your own unique and useful template for solving personal challenges with wisdom and grace.

No two people will solve the same problem the same exact way, but we can all benefit from using problem-solving models of some kind because they provide a road map *to begin* tackling whatever is in front of us. The common work flow is to move from the simple to the complex, the singular to the plural, the familiar to the innovative, and from within to without. Start with what you know (or think you know) and then allow your understanding and perspective to be expanded. Problem solving is often a process of taking an educated guess, using insight, and then just going at the problem through a trial and error method.

Growth is often achieved through events of personal challenge and crisis. Something will simply happen to knock you off balance and toss you into a direct confrontation with some kind of personal issue, event, or situation. The challenge can be personal, involving no one else, or it can be interpersonal, involving one or more people. It can be urgent, needing immediate attention, or emergent, which allows you some time to breathe before having to take decisive action.

Suggested 8-step Problem Solving Model

1. **Affirm Guardian Angel Shield and Connection to Guidance**
   Your immediate reaction to any challenge event should be to affirm your Guardian Angel Shield and to empower your connection with your inner guidance; God, and your Divine Advocate Teams.
2. **Assess Urgency and Decision Window, Ask for Assistance**
   Before you begin dealing with your challenge, you have to assess whether it is something you must address immediately, or if you have time to work the problem more thoroughly. Obviously,

having time to consider your options and your choices is preferable to having to make snap decisions. If you have an emergent, not an urgent or critical challenge, you can think about your tools, take time to stabilize yourself, work through possible scenarios, and make sure your own perceptual distortions and bias are minimized. Avoid making decisions that *can* be put off until you are stabilized and have had time to reflect.

3. **Stabilize within Your Sacred Self**
   You cannot begin to act until you are functioning with as much stability and balance as possible. Sometimes you do not have the luxury of taking a "time out" to re-group, so you have to ask your Divine Advocates to provide you with "perfected integrity". This means that they are covering the spread for you if you are confronted with a situation that is beyond your current level of functioning. Use the heart breathing technique to empower your Sacred Self to enliven and grow in presence. Empower your Sacred Self to express as strongly as possible within the current situation. Get centered. You have to fight to keep *aware* and "behind the wheel" so that unconscious dysfunctional patterns do not emerge during emotional reactivity. Always, *always* ask yourself "What are my tools?"

   What are your tools? TLC Bath, Resiliency Comfort Wrap, Sacred Self Resiliency Wrap, Core Integrity Elixir, Sacred Self Elixir, Heart Breathing, and so on.

4. **Assess the Challenge and It's Relationship to You**
   You have access to many tools and protocols. Before you begin to use them actively on your situation, you have to make some assessments as to the nature of your challenge. If it is a challenge that is like something else you have dealt with successfully before, you immediately have a place to begin working the problem. If you have dealt with it before, but *not* successfully, you know what *not* to do. Do not repeat things that you know are not helpful.

   Questions to Ask Yourself

   1. What is the closest match to a challenge I have dealt with before?
   2. How did I deal with similar challenges?
   3. Is there a common theme or pattern between this challenge and others?
   4. Did the strategies I used before work or not?
   5. Do I need assistance for this problem?

6. What about this bothers me the most?
7. How does this make me feel?
8. When have I felt like this before?
9. What are my possible distortions related to this issue?
10. What are my biases?
11. What are the inconsistencies in the story, situation, or information?
12. What is the original event of the distortion?
13. What kind of growth is necessary for me to triumph over this challenge?
14. How do my perceptions have to change in order to express my Sacred Self here?
15. Is the challenge something that needs me to "Tag, Refuse, Replace"?
16. Does it involve other people and *their* issues or bias?
17. Is this actually *my* challenge, or is this challenge about someone else?
18. What is the drama here?
19. What role(s) in the drama am I being tempted to play out?
20. How do I remove myself from the drama and express my Sacred Self?
21. How do I empower the others to express their Sacred Selves?
22. Are there advocacy care and assistance issues I should address first?

What are your tools? Stage of Life, Authentic View Elixir, Relationship Rebalancing (if interpersonal), Family Care and Assistance (if family), consulting with your Guide Team, "Tag, Refuse, Replace", Serenity Prayer, and so on.

5. **Empower the Highest Outcome before Acting**
   No matter what you do, or ultimately decide to do, you want to throw as much energy and intention into the matter resolving in the best possible way for all involved. You want to ask for and receive as much intervention as possible and to establish a strong flow of healing light through yourself to address the solution. Sometimes, if the situation involves others who are functioning from within significant distortions, the only solution is the remove yourself completely from the situation. *You cannot fix what is not yours that*

is broken. Everyone has to do his or her own work. You cannot rescue anyone without involving yourself in continuing challenge and drama.

It is not your job or responsibility to fix anyone else's problems for them, but you *can* ask for and empower the Highest Outcome for all. Once you do that, sometimes the only thing left to do is hand the situation back to God and release it from your heart. Everyone gets to choose his or her own path to one that is in alignment or not. That is the nature of free will. You only get to choose *your* path. It is your responsibility to stay on your Path of Light in the best way that you can, and to function as faithfully as you can in expressing your very best self in the world with as much integrity as you have. When you can do better, do better.

What are your tools? Lighting Candles, Tapestry of Light Synergy, Prayer, Path of Light Shoes, Pearls of Wisdom, Soul Wisdom Elixir, Stage of Life, Masterpiece Theater, and so on.

6. **Address Personal Healing and Care**
   It may take time to work through your personal relationship to the challenge. Refinements in understanding are often made when you begin to scratch the surface. Your goal is to discover the personal patterns that have a relationship to the challenge so that you can shift those patterns. You also need to continue vigilant cleansing and comfort so that you can keep your balance while you move forward.

   What are my tools? Double Dip, Healing Sessions, "Tag, Refuse, Replace", Tending the Sacred Garden, and so on.

7. **Assess the Consequence of Possible Solutions**
   Your goal, when confronted with challenge, is to respond with a choice or action that keeps you on your Path of Light. Ask your Guides to help you work through your possible responses so that you can evaluate, with support, the pitfalls and consequences of your range of possible choices. What choice would lead you in the right direction? What consequences might unfold for you and others? What path seems highlighted to you?

   What are my tools? Stage of Life, Rescripting the Event, Consulting with your Guides, and so on.

8. **Follow the Path of Light One-Step-at-a-Time**
   Ultimately, problem solving culminates in a choice that should lead over your obstacle and place you back on the Path of Light. Take one-step-at-a-time when you have properly worked the problem. If

you confront continuing issues, assume that you have a cluster of related issues and that you are being brought through releasing them a single layer at a time. So long as you are moving forward with genuine reflection, caution, and care--proceed forward gently and be open to continuing assistance. You may have to place your faith and trust in the process to proceed. Do not bog yourself down with considering many steps down the line; consider only the *next step*. We often cannot see more than a few steps ahead on the Path of Light. Work what is in front of you. You will likely not be able to see the big picture until you tend to the individual chunks.

Continuing Thoughts on Problem Solving

If you follow a problem-solving model, you always have a place to begin moving forward when you are confronted with a challenge. Personal growth is often a direct result of being confronted with, and triumphing over, some kind of personal challenge. It may not be fun, but it is *effective*. Do not just stand there like a deer caught in headlights when you run into obstacles on your path. Work the problem like it is a personal mystery to unravel. Work the pieces by themselves, and then work the pieces together. Use your resources wisely. Always remember your tools. *Act*. If your solution does not work, make note of it for the next time. Try something different. Every problem and challenge is an opportunity for you to express your Sacred Self in life. It is an opportunity for you to bring yourself to higher levels of functioning. Have a plan. Work your plan. Re-work your plan. Work it until it works. It is not just about that problem, it is about the process.

III
Creating Innovative Healing Sessions

Innovation is an organic process that starts with the familiar and works the pieces in different patterns, orders, and progressions--then adding less familiar pieces, subtracting, testing, and refining the work until it is as potent, effective, and simple as possible. Creating innovative healing sessions is a little like creating a quilt of many different modalities and practices. The construction begins by mixing and matching familiar modalities that you think may be complementary or synergistic. This is often a trial and error process or "playtime" with your tools and protocols. You basically see and assess what works well together by considering if the modifications improve or dilute the intended effects. Sometimes, you come up with a nifty addition, but it remains essentially the same protocol. Sometimes you combine and modify modalities and come up with the inspiration for something that is unique and new. Sometimes you decide that the original protocol is still the most efficient and simple. If you enjoy problem solving and creative development, you will enjoy experimenting and exploring the many ways you can be a mixologist and innovator.

The Golden Rod Team Self-Treatment on page 242 is an excellent example of creative method mixology. I started doing Sacred Garden weeding by imagining that the Golden Rods were being placed into my body, as if my body was a garden. This reminded me of the Emotional Freedom Technique (see the link in the resource section where you can download a free manual on line), where there is tapping on the body in certain areas to disrupt a negative thought and empower a positive one. So, I connected in with my Healing Team and requested for them to put the Golden Rods wherever they needed to go to correspond with the meridian system (energy circulatory system within the body, part of Chinese Medicine). I felt pings and pangs in various areas of my body (not the typical EFT areas), and visualized tapping in a Golden Rod while stating my positive rescript affirmation. In the areas that I could not reach, I requested that my Healing Team tap in the Golden Rods. EFT has a particular pattern and way to affirm that I did not use, instead I allowed my Healing Team to tell me where in my body I should focus and tap in the Golden Rods. At the end of the session, I imagined my Healing Team using the Expanded Attunement function to activate all the positive pathways and break up the negative ones. I felt a wonderful rush of energy when I did this. There was a strong energetic reaction, which is essentially how I assess the "bang" of a protocol.

I liked the application of these various elements so much that I added it to the book as an optional healing session idea. It combines the following ideas: hands on healing, passive healing, active healing, Golden Rod "fertilization and weed management", meridian tapping (aka Emotional Freedom Technique), positive affirmation and "Tag, Refuse, Rescript" (which some would consider self-hypnosis), and Empowerment Attunements. It could also include energy elixirs, wraps, healing baths, and so on, if you wanted to add them before, during, or after the session. This is a good example of a "kitchen sink" innovation. You start by using familiar techniques, but you keep working them, with your spiritual assistance and guidance, until you come up with something that is uniquely efficient.

This also suggests that the more exposure you have to various healing modalities, practices, and ideas, the more creatively you can mix, match, combine, and be inspired to create something that is innovative and new. Take many workshops and read many books. It all adds to the possible raw material you have to be inspired by when you sit down to do your work. Then you just have to apply the process of trial and error, refining and observing, adding and subtracting, and so on. Some people enjoy this kind of process; other people would prefer to follow a protocol that is tried and tested already. If you want to innovate, you can certainly do that.

Step-by-Step Innovative Healing Session Creation Process

1. **Consider the Issue.**
    - What issue do you want to work on?
    - Identify familiar solutions, tools, and protocols.
    - Which familiar solutions might complement or synergize each other?
2. **Mix, match, add, subtract, and run through possible combinations.**
    - Was the result better, worse, or about the same?
    - Were you inspired to add something else, or did some other solution, concept, or tool come to mind?
    - Is there something new to try, something less familiar?
    - How would it best combine with the more familiar protocols?

- Is the result better, worse, or about the same?

3. **Add a cooperative spiritual assistance element.**

   What can your Healing Team do on your behalf within the context of your session? Ask, try, combine, mix, *listen*.

4. **Ask, try, combine, mix, *listen.***
   - Was the result better, worse, or about the same?
   - If the result was better, is there anything that can make it even more potent? How do you usually increase the potency of something? ("Optimize, Stabilize, Amplify, Seal" is a biggy--so is the simple command to "activate".)
   - If the result was better, is there anything that can make the process more simple?

5. **Share, explore, refine.**
   - If you find a process that is better, more potent, and simple, does this process also work for other people?
   - Can it be placed into a standardized format? (That is how this book was developed.)
   - What is the feedback from other people? Did they have suggestions for refinement, improvement, or expansion? Ask many people. The more, the better. Many heads are better than one.

6. **Mix, match, add, subtract, and run through the possible improvements and refinements.**

7. **Create a working protocol, subject to updating and improvement as your understanding improves.**

   And so on. Eventually, you settle on a process that makes the most sense, integrates the best elements, and is streamlined to be as simple as possible. Then viola (aka: wha-la!), you have just innovated a healing session (or whatever else you were trying to do).

IV
Creating Your Own Cooperative Contracts

The use of free will in alignment with Divine Will is a huge part of why I think this work is potent and helpful. I think it is important for us to be clear about what we want to accomplish and to define our goals up front so that there is a clear plan of action. Cooperative Spiritual Energy Work combines our best effort to be aware and mindful of what we need with the greater wisdom and resources of a spiritual reality. It is not difficult to create your own Cooperative Contracts in order to request assistance for unique work. Like any other skill, using the process will help you to find your own personal interactive style and your own unique modifications. You may or may not have any desire to invent your own wheel. The Cooperative Contract and intentions in this book are thorough, but everything can always be improved by specificity. If you are interested in *how* this kind of work is developed, this will get you started. Have fun with it, but please, always be responsible and place yourself in Divine Hands in all work that you do.

The Three Main Structural Elements to a Cooperative Contract

1. **Goal:** You must define your challenge and then create a goal action that you want to cultivate. Be as clear as possible and do not multi-task. It is best to state one issue and goal at a time when you begin developing your own work. You have seen examples of purpose and goal statements throughout the book. You can use them as your guide until you find your own style. You should also have a working title for the specific work.
2. **Supporting Intentions:** You will not always know every single intention that you need to add, but be as complete as you can. I think it matters that we show up with some awareness of our problem and what it takes to solve it. The intention listing is something like a homework assignment that shows that we understand *something*. Always consult former intentions in case there are relevant ideas from other similar lists. You can use the lists of intentions found throughout the book to inspire you to create your own. Never waste a good intention, recycle and reuse it where relevant.
3. **Divine Will Alignment Statement:** This is the important part. I highly recommend that you use the one that I use or something in

your words with the same elements. The goal of this section is to fully give permission for God to edit your requests to be within Divine Will and to include other intentions that would benefit the stated or related goals. You also want the work to unfold gracefully, not through crisis.

Statement Used in Book: *"I request for, and give unlimited permission to God (Highest Divine Power or Consciousness), to initiate and complete, at His discretion, any and all activities related to the fulfillment of the goals and intentions described in the Cooperative Contract and all corresponding* Angelscape *environments and activities. I further request and give permission for God to correct, improve, or include any other intentions that have not been listed, but which are favorable to meet all of the stated or related goals. I ask that this work be blessed and eternally applied as directed by God. I ask that it unfold for All of Me, in the most appropriate way, across all relevant dimensions or aspects of my Whole Self. I ask that all work manifests in perfection with Grace, Ease, Mercy, Compassion, and Love. Amen and Thank You."*

The Three Procedural Elements of a Cooperative Contract

1. **Sign it Over:** Every contract must be signed in order to be valid. You can write your Cooperative Contract on paper and actually sign it, and then imagine the paper as a scroll that you place in the Eternal Flame of God's Grace and Love.
2. **Action Statement:** You should have a short working title to call the work you are addressing with the Cooperative Contract. The Action Statement calls for the energy work supplied by your Divine Advocates through God to initiate. You use that working title to call for the scope of the resources every time you wish to use that support. Because the title becomes a representative for a specific chunk of work, you put it in capitals. I use Action Statements throughout the book and through follow up suggestions because it is an effective way to initiate a clear start of active work. You may use the Action Statements used throughout the book as inspiration for the ones you create.
3. **Imagine the Work:** Place yourself in *Angelscape* in the most appropriate setting and ask for the work to initiate through the Action Statement. You may have an idea of what kind of guided meditation to create for yourself, or you may want to just kick back

and observe what unfolds. At the end of your work, you can always add the "Optimize, Stabilize, Amplify, and Seal" Action Statement to add another layer of integrity and cooperative interaction to the process. I also recommend that you use the TLC Bath or the customary integration support strategies to support the work being received. Use your familiar tools and protocols, adapt them as needed, or create totally new tools, protocols, or activities.

Go Forth and Prosper

Okay, we're done. This is just about the sum total of everything I have that is worth sharing about Cooperative Spiritual Energy Work. This way of doing things is not the only way, not by a long shot, but I hope that it has been a worthwhile investment in your time and energy. It is my hope and intention that you leave this work feeling empowered, optimistic, and *well equipped*. It is my belief that once people have good tools and a solid platform for functioning--that they have everything they need to move forward with independence. I think all people really need is a cosmic hardware store that does a few demonstrations on the weekend. That is how I view this book. I hope that it has provided useful tools and helpful suggestions that you can take and make your own.

The goals of this book were spelled out on page 11 in the Cooperative Contract before we started the journey. There will be times when you meet these goals. There will be times when you do not. Love yourself anyway, and do your best to love others anyway. I think that at the end of the day, we are all just doing the best we can. The revolution is in the *evolution*. We can do anything if we *believe*. Thank you for letting me be a part of your personal journey. It has been a deep and sacred honor.

Amen. *(It seemed more appropriate than "the end".)*

Suggested Reading and Resources

Books
God, Faith, and Health by Jeff Leven, Ph.D.
Guided Imagery for Self-Healing by Martin L. Rossman
Healing Words by Larry Dossey, M.D.
Love, Medicine, and Miracles by Bernie S. Siegel, M.D.
The Relaxation & Stress Reduction Workbook by Martha Davis, Ph.D., Elizabeth Robbins Eshelman, M.S.W., and Matthew McKay, Ph.D.
Spiritual Emergency by Stanislav Graf
Staying Well With Guided Imagery by Belleruth Naperstek

Websites (no affiliation with *Awake in Angelscape*)
http://www.mercola.com/forms/eftcourse1.htm
http://www.curezone.com/

Public Domain and Royalty Free Image Resources
http://burningwell.org
http://morguefile.com
http://pdphoto.org
http://www.publicdomainpictures.net

You can also visit me at my website. I'll do my best to provide additional resources, links, and information about book signings, workshops, events, and anything else that is relevant. You can visit *The Garden Crew* website for *Angelscape* elixir supplies.

http://www.awakeinangelscape.com
http://www.thegardencrew.com

Reviews

"If anyone is trying to find a way to clear out their mind, find more focus, or become more in touch with their inner selves, then they have come to the right place with the exercises in the Awake in Angelscape. *In a loving and comforting environment, you can explore your true self without fear and leave away with more insight than before. You become more grounded and in-tune with your inner guidance. Doing the meditations in the book has made me, not only more intuitive, but more compassionate than before. The changes in my life are too numerous to name and I couldn't have accomplished them without this book. I highly recommended this book to anyone hoping to improve their lives on many different levels."*

Lourdes
Focus Group Member

"I think that the activities used in Awake in Angelscape *are perfect for beginners and experts alike. You need bring nothing other then a desire to heal, grow and transform into a higher, healthier, and happier you. I believe that each of us contains an individual spark of God with our own path of light to walk, and that we come pre-packaged with everything we need to walk that path. Sometimes we just need a little* something *to wake us up so we can get moving. For me, the activities were like a "cup of coffee" that helped me rub open my eyes and shake off the sleep. I highly recommend that you let the work in* Awake in Angelscape *and your "imagination" help bring you to a place of peace, self-love, acceptance and healing."*

Sharon
Focus Group Member

"I found Awake in Angelscape *to be an amazing journey into discovering different dimensions of myself. I think it would be a wonderful opportunity for anyone to heal, discover and develop a better relationship with themselves and their Spirits. People may find themselves growing in ways they may not have imagined they could"*

Lori
Focus Group Member

"Most men are not interested in doing a lot if introspection. However, I found that in reading Awake in Angelscape, *I became naturally introspective in spite of myself. I found the entire experience to be uplifting and I would highly recommend it to all people, male or female. It is an easy process to do and is a self-paced and independent approach to finding your spiritual self. It does not require lots of time or lots of effort to do the simple guided imagery activities. If you so choose, there are many suggestions for props or other ways to enhance the experience to make visualization even easier. I hope that you will gain as much from the experience as I feel I did."*

Patrick
Focus Group Member

Stacie Coller has a BA in psychology, is a trainer, writer, artist, Reiki Master, and certified hypnotherapist. She is internationally known through her on-line business, learning groups, and has facilitated workshops within the US; including the Center for Human Consciousness Studies at UNLV. She lives a peaceful life on a mountain near Asheville, NC, with her husband and teenaged daughter.

Photograph by Stacie Emerson Ruppe, copyright 2008

For Wholesale Inquiries or to schedule a book signing with the author, please contact:

PO Box 851556
Westland, MI 48185

www.lspdigital.com
admin@lspdigital.com

Made in the USA